LIVING TOGETHER AND
CHRISTIAN ETHICS

Living Together and Christian Ethics is the first positive, in-depth study of cohabitation outside marriage from a mainstream Christian theological perspective. The book retrieves the traditions of betrothal from the Bible and church history, and shows how these can transform Christian attitudes to living together before marriage. A crucial distinction is made between prenuptial cohabitation where marriage is intended, and non-nuptial cohabitation where it is avoided. Since betrothal was widely understood as a real beginning of marriage, the book argues for a complete pastoral, theological and liturgical renewal that reclaims the riches of forgotten Christian marital traditions and redeploys them in conveying the good news of the faith to women and men who are not yet married. The book takes issue with theologians who marginalize marriage, and suggests that the recognition of marital values can act as a helpful bridge between Christian teaching and people who are not formally married.

ADRIAN THATCHER is Professor of Applied Theology at the Centre for Theology and Philosophy, College of St Mark and St John, Plymouth. His books include *Truly a Person, Truly God* (1990), *Liberating Sex: A Christian Sexual Theology* (1993), *People of Passion: What the Churches Teach about Sex* (with Elizabeth Stuart, 1997), and *Marriage after Modernity: Christian Marriage in Postmodern Times* (1999). He has also published numerous journal articles and reviews.

D0840686

NEW STUDIES IN CHRISTIAN ETHICS

General Editor: Robin Gill
Editorial Board: Stephen R. L. Clark, Stanley Hauerwas, Robin W. Lovin

Christian ethics has increasingly assumed a central place within academic theology. At the same time the growing power and ambiguity of modern science and the rising dissatisfaction within the social sciences about claims to value-neutrality have prompted renewed interest in ethics within the secular academic world. There is, therefore, a need for studies in Christian ethics which, as well as being concerned with the relevance of Christian ethics to the present day secular debate, are well informed about parallel discussions in recent philosophy, science or social science. *New Studies in Christian Ethics* aims to provide books that do this at the highest intellectual level and demonstrate that Christian ethics can make a distinctive contribution to this debate – either in moral substance or in terms of underlying moral justifications.

New Studies in Christian Ethics

Titles published in the series:

LIVING TOGETHER AND CHRISTIAN ETHICS

ADRIAN THATCHER

College of St Mark and St John, Plymouth

CAMBRIDGE
UNIVERSITY PRESS

PUBLISHED BY THE PRESS SYNDICATE OF THE UNIVERSITY OF CAMBRIDGE
The Pitt Building, Trumpington Street, Cambridge, United Kingdom

CAMBRIDGE UNIVERSITY PRESS
The Edinburgh Building, Cambridge CB2 2RU, UK
40 West 20th Street, New York, NY 10011-4211, USA
477 Williamstown Road, Port Melbourne, VIC 3207, Australia
Ruiz de Alarcón 13, 28014 Madrid, Spain
Dock House, The Waterfront, Cape Town 8001, South Africa

http://www.cambridge.org

First published 2002

Printed in the United Kingdom at the University Press, Cambridge

Typeface Baskerville Monotype 11/12.5 pt.   *System* LaTeX 2_ε [TB]

A catalogue record for this book is available from the British Library

Library of Congress Cataloguing in Publication data

ISBN 0 521 80204 0 hardback
ISBN 0 521 00955 3 paperback

Contents

General editor's preface

This book is the twenty-first in the series New Studies in Christian Ethics. It returns to a crucial issue discussed earlier in the series in Lisa Cahill's well-received *Sex, Gender and Christian Ethics* – namely, how to understand Christian marriage today in a way that is both sensitive to contemporary changes in sexuality and faithful to Christian theology and tradition. Cahill writes as a modern Catholic, whereas Thatcher writes as a modern Anglican, yet they have much in common in the methods and approaches they use and in the conclusions they reach. Both authors clearly identify with Don Browning's Family, Religion and Culture project at the University of Chicago, and in particular with its central aim to defend faithful marriage in a pluralistic world (not least as the best environment for nurturing children), albeit from a liberal theological perspective.

Adrian Thatcher has already established a reputation for thoughtful writing in this area with his books *Liberating Sex* (1993) and *Marriage after Modernity* (1999). He has also shown in his Christology book *Truly A Person, Truly God* (1990) that he is a creative and innovative theologian. Both of these characteristics are present in the two different levels at which *Living Together and Christian Ethics* can be read.

At the first level this is a well-informed book about marriage and sexuality in the modern world. The first chapter shows that Thatcher has read carefully the most recent empirical information about the changing patterns that are occurring throughout the western world. Increasing cohabitation before or without marriage and the phenomenon of children born in a familial context outside marriage are now widespread. The Family, Religion and

Culture project has been instrumental in mapping these changing patterns and alerting people to some of their negative consequences. There is now clear evidence that some academics and informed journalists are beginning to take notice. Adrian Thatcher, however, adds to the debate by highlighting crucial consequential differences between prenuptial cohabitation and non-nuptial cohabitation. It is non-nuptial cohabitation that is damaging both for those who cohabit and for any children that they may have. The experience of those who cohabit with the clear intention of getting married later differs little from those who marry without first cohabiting. Thatcher argues that this difference is crucial for Christian ethics, but has been largely ignored by others.

At the second level this is a book which argues specifically for the reintroduction of betrothal within churches. Here Adrian Thatcher offers a scholarly account of the history and later eclipse of betrothal within Christian churches and a sustained argument for its reintroduction today. He believes that this could be an important way of encouraging and sustaining those couples intending to live together as a prelude to a later marriage service. Unlike some others who have discussed this possibility, Thatcher argues that marriage itself is a process and that a liturgically celebrated betrothal could become a significant symbol of the beginning of that process. This twin perspective of championing the reintroduction of betrothal and of seeing betrothal as already part of the process of marriage then gives Thatcher a filter for reviewing critically a wide variety of church reports in this area. As a result the book offers genuinely new insights and admirably fulfils the two key aims of the series – namely to promote monographs in Christian ethics which engage centrally with the present secular moral debate at the highest possible intellectual level and, secondly, to encourage contributors to demonstrate that Christian ethics can make a distinctive contribution to this debate.

Unsurprisingly there are still questions that remain about Thatcher's radical suggestions about betrothal. As he admits himself, the history of betrothal (with children as young as seven being betrothed) has not always been attractive. It has been strongly associated at times with notions of children as property, of patriarchy and of social control. At other times it was associated with sexual laxity and confusion about marital status. It remains to be seen whether it can be reintroduced into churches without being sullied by these earlier associations. Thatcher believes that betrothal would help churches to distinguish more carefully between, say, faithful and committed cohabitation as part of the process of marriage and faithless promiscuity. He makes an important point here. Conservative Christian approaches to sexuality (which predominate in official church reports) tend to condemn *all* non-marital, and especially homosexual, sexual intercourse without distinction. As a result most young people (heterosexual as well as homosexual, and Christian as well as non-Christian) and many divorced older people are simply condemned. But the question remains of whether or not Thatcher's suggestions about betrothal will be able to convince conservative Christians to be more discriminating.

Whatever the answer to this question, Adrian Thatcher has written a thoughtful and clearly argued book on an important issue which I am delighted to welcome to the series.

ROBIN GILL

Acknowledgments

This book could not have been written without support from many people. I thank Kevin Taylor of Cambridge University Press for his enthusiasm and support for the project when it was no more than a proposal. The College of St Mark and St John is a productive place for theological research, and I am grateful for the support from my colleagues in the Centre for Theology and Philosophy (especially during my research leave in 1999), from the Principal, Dean of Faculty and Committee for Research, and from the staff in the College library. I am particularly grateful to Professor Don Browning for hosting my research visit to the University of Chicago, home of the Family, Religion and Culture project which he directs, and for his kindness in arranging many fruitful contacts while I was there. I am grateful to friends who have read parts of the text and commented helpfully on them. The Revd Dr Duncan Dormor and Prof. Michael Lawler were especially helpful. I received valuable feedback also from Prof. Herbert Anderson, Prof. Don Browning, Dr Jack Dominian, the Revd Greg Forster, Dr David Horrell, Dr Will Large and the Right Revd Dr Kenneth Stevenson. I thank the Revd Canon Reg Harcus for allowing me to include his betrothal rite, in use in his parish church, as an appendix. I am grateful for the very positive responses I have received over the last few years to the main ideas and theses of this book, many from students past and present. They convinced me this book had to be written. I thank Caroline Major for preparing the final version of the manuscript. Most of all, I owe a huge debt of thanks to Grace Thatcher for her support throughout the long writing of the book.

PART I

Living together as a theological problem

CHAPTER I

A guide to living together

Christian theology is necessarily a human, intellectual endeavour which *listens*. It believes that God has spoken decisively in Christ, and that God's Word is yet able to be heard in every generation. Listening, therefore, is a primary virtue in theology. But Christian theology and ethics must also listen to the understanding diligently provided by other, more secular, intellectual endeavours. The word of revelation may be heard there too. Only when theology performs the double act of listening to the voices of its traditions, and the voices surrounding those traditions, is it able to make connections between Christian faith and ordinary life, and perhaps to indicate humbly how the gospel of Christ may be capable of touching and transforming it. Perhaps there is no ethical problem where this double act is as apt as in the case of cohabitation. People in many parts of the world now live together before marriage, after marriage, and instead of marriage, in numbers which have been increasing remarkably for the last thirty years. Sociologists, ethnologists and demographers have made valiant attempts to track, chart and perhaps explain this unprecedented shift in family formation. The results are available for theologians (and everyone else) to study and deploy. The whole of the present chapter is an attempt to listen to secular authors as they describe and explain cohabitation.

By 'a guide to living together' is meant an attempt to provide a detailed sketch of an increasingly common social and sexual practice, in order to bring it into a theological focus. It takes the form of 25 propositions or statements about living together which are intended to shape the theological treatment that the practice receives in the rest of the book.[1] Readers eager to plunge straight into the theological analysis and to discover the core concepts presented by this study should at least skim these propositions before proceeding to chapter 2 (a summary of the argument of the rest of the book is found at pages 74–5). The propositions are offered as assertions which, given the state of current research, are probably true. 'Probably' registers the *caveat* that the pace of the social changes marked by the rise of cohabitation presently appears inexorable and data become redundant quickly. Hypotheses which were presently accepted when the bulk of the research for this part of the book was done (1999) may look inadequate when it is read. Nearly half of the statements (first section) attempt a description of some of the characteristics of cohabitation, followed (in the second section) by some unfortunate consequences and (in the third section) some attempts at explanation. Finally, after this depressing read, there is some good news about cohabitation (fourth section). Inevitably there is some overlap between sections.

COHABITATION: SOME FEATURES

1. In many countries more people enter marriage from cohabitation than from the single state.

Most definitions of cohabitation assume the notion of a 'heterosexual couple who are not formally married to one another living in a sexually intimate domestic relationship under the same roof'.[2] A British definition assumes a cohabiting couple is 'a co-resident man and woman, living together within a sexual union, without that union having been formalised by a legal marriage'.[3] These definitions are insensitive to homosexual couples because the alternative of marriage is unavailable to them. Cohabitation before marriage is an incontrovertible trend. This represents an alarming change over the last 25–30 years. In many states in the USA, 'until

---

[1] Since writing this 'Guide' I have come across Patricia Morgan's *Marriage-Lite: The Rise of Cohabitation and its Consequences* (London: Institute for the Study of Civil Society, 2000), which reinforces several of the empirical claims advanced here.

[2] Gordon A. Carmichael, 'Consensual Partnering in the More Developed Countries', *Journal of the Australian Population Association* 12.1 (1995), 51.

[3] John Haskey, *Trends in Marriage and Cohabitation: Population Trends 80* (Office of Population Censuses and Surveys, 1995), p.6.

recently' (i.e., 1994) cohabitation for the unmarried was actually illegal.[4] Between 1970 and 1980 in the USA, Census Bureau data record a tripling in the number of cohabiting couples, to over 1.5 million, and a further increase of 80%, to 2.9 million couples, between 1980 and 1990. However, these are only the official statistics. So strong are the reasons for concealing cohabitation from the authorities (possible loss of social security, child custody, lack of social acceptability, among others) that the actual number of cohabiting couples in the USA in 1990 was between 3 and 8 million.[5] Clearly this is a broad guess. During that decade, the sharp decline in the numbers of people marrying (not just for the first time) did not lead (at least in the United States) to an increase in singleness or single-households, because people who eventually marry were living together instead.[6] In this respect there has been little change. The numbers of people living together may be changing little: the change is found in the type of arrangements they choose.

The trend towards cohabitation before marriage has been registered in many countries.[7] France may be typical of countries to report, in the mid-eighties, that the 'tide of early marriages' which peaked in mid-century had receded, leaving 'a delayed marriage trend' in its wake. As a consequence, there was said to be 'an expanding life-space in early adulthood where informal premarital unions may flourish'. 'Informal cohabitation generally amounts to a form of "partial marriage" with reproduction actively delayed or avoided.'[8] This author was confident that

---

[4] Monica A. Seff, 'Cohabitation and the Law', *Marriage and Family Review* 21.3–4 (June 1995), 149.

[5] Ibid., 144, citing J. Duff and G.G. Truitt, *The Spousal Equivalent Handbook* (Houston: Sunny Beach Publications, 1990).

[6] Larry L. Bumpass, James A. Sweet and Andrew Cherlin, 'The Role of Cohabitation in Declining Rates of Marriage', *Journal of Marriage and the Family* 53 (November 1991), 913, 924. And see Arland Thornton, 'Cohabitation and Marriage in the 1980s', *Demography* 25.4 (November 1988), 497–508.

[7] For an analysis of European trends, see Duncan Dormor, 'Marriage and the Second Demographic Transition in Europe – A Review', in Adrian Thatcher (ed.), *Celebrating Christian Marriage* (Edinburgh: T&T Clark, 2002).

[8] Elwood Carlson, 'Couples Without Children: Premarital Cohabitation in France', in Kingsley Davis (ed.), *Contemporary Marriage: Comparative Perspectives on a Changing Institution* (New York: Russell Sage Foundation, 1985), p.113. For later confirmation of the trend see also H. Leridon, 'Cohabitation, Marriage, Separation: An Analysis of Life Histories of French Cohorts from 1968 to 1985', *Population Studies* 44 (1990), 127–44.

cohabitors would eventually marry. 'These informal unions', he
wrongly opined, 'will continue to be transformed into traditional
marriages'.[9] By the mid-1970s, a majority of couples marrying in
Geneva, Switzerland, had lived together before marriage and in
Sweden and Denmark 'informal cohabitation' had become 'all but
normative'.[10] In the countries of Southern Europe (e.g., Italy, Spain)
cohabitation has yet to become widespread. If informal cohabitation is extended to include individuals who identify as a couple,
are sexually intimate, but retain separate residences, the numbers
will be much greater. In France this practice has been named 'semi-
cohabitation';[11] in Finland and the Netherlands (and doubtless elsewhere), it is 'living apart together' (LAT).[12] Similarly, the 1991 census in Britain showed that more people, especially young people, are
'living alone', yet many of these 'may only do so for part of the time,
or may indeed live separately but be in permanent relationships'.[13]

A recent study in Britain confirms more people enter marriage from cohabitation than from the single state. A comparison
between first partnerships of two cohorts of women in Britain who
were born in the two specific periods 1950–62 (the 'pre-Thatcher
cohort') and after 1962 (the 'Thatcher cohort') confirms that 'the
primary difference between the two cohorts is that cohabitation
is a much more important route into first partnership for the
Thatcher cohort. By their 26th birthday, over half of the Thatcher
cohort had entered cohabitation, compared with one-quarter of
the earlier cohort.'[14] In Canada, cohabitation is said to have been

9 Carlson, 'Couples', p.128.
10 Ibid., pp.114, 119. And see J. Trost, 'A Renewed Social Institution: Non-Marital
   Cohabitation', *Acta Sociologica* 21 (1978), 303–15.
11 Catherine Villeneuve-Gokalp, 'Vivre en Couple Chacun Chez Soi', *Population* 5
   (September–October 1997), 1059. Within this sub-group, there is to be found 'une cohabitation *intermittente*' and 'une cohabitation *alternée*' (1059–60).
12 J. Hoffmann-Nowotny, 'The Future of the Family', in *European Population Conference 1987,
   Plenaries* (Helsinki: Central Statistical Office of Finland, 1987), pp.113–200.
13 Economic and Social Research Council, *Population and Household Change, Research Results
   1–13* (1997–8), no.7, 'One Person Households in England and Wales and France', p.1.
14 John Ermisch, *Pre-Marital Cohabitation, Childbearing and the Creation of One Parent
   Families* (Colchester: Working Papers of the ESRC Research Centre on Micro-social
   Change, No.95-17, 1995), p.3. The conclusions are based on data drawn from the
   British Household Panel Study. See also Jonathan Gershuny and Richard Berthoud,
   New Partnerships? Men and Women in the 1990s (University of Essex: Extracts from the
   Research Programme of the ESRC Research Centre on Micro-social Change, June
   1997), p.3.

'an irrelevant phenomenon' prior to the 1970s.[15] The 1981 census reported over 700,000 cohabiting couples: by the time of the 1991 census, that figure had risen to 1.4 million, or 10% of all couples.[16] Similar 'spectacular trends' have been recorded in Sweden, Denmark, Norway, Finland, Netherlands, France, Austria, West Germany, Australia, New Zealand[17] and Japan.[18] There has been a longer tradition of informal consensual unions in some countries in South America, especially in the Caribbean basin where they are more common than legal marriages.[19]

2. Cohabitors are as likely to return to singleness as to enter marriage.

Whereas increasing numbers of people arrive at marriage via cohabitation, it is less often realized that increasing numbers of cohabitors *do not marry their partners at all*. By 1985 it had been noticed that in the USA more cohabitors aged 23 and under were returning to singleness than 'upgrading' (so to speak) to formal marriage. 'For men, nearly two-thirds of all cohabiting relationships were terminated within two years of the initiation of the cohabitation; 40 percent were terminated by union dissolution within two years and another 23 percent were terminated because the partners married.'[20] For

[15] David R. Hall and John Z. Zhao, 'Cohabitation and Divorce in Canada: Testing the Selectivity Hypothesis', *Journal of Marriage and the Family* 57.2 (May 1995), 421.
[16] Ibid.: based on D. Larrivee and P. Parent, 'For More and More Canadians, Common-Law Unions Make Good Sense' (Census of Canada article series: 1993). Zheng Wu puts the figure of cohabiting couples at 11%. See Zheng Wu, 'Premarital Cohabitation and Postmarital Cohabiting Union Formation', *Journal of Family Issues* 16 (March 1995), 212–33.
[17] Summarized in detail by Carmichael, 'Consensual Partnering', 54–9. See also A.K. Blanc, 'The Formation and Dissolution of Second Unions: Marriage and Cohabitation in Sweden and Norway', *Journal of Marriage and the Family* 49 (1987), 391–400; and Gigi Santow and Michael Bracher, 'Change and Continuity in the Formation of First Marital Unions in Australia', *Population Studies* 48 (1994), 475–96.
[18] Joy Hendry analyses 'the modern Japanese practice of living together' in her 'Japan: Culture versus Industrialization as Determinant of Marital Patterns', in Davis, *Contemporary Marriage*, p.215. While it 'reflects Western influence' (p.214), it also reflects more liberal (but still patriarchal) attitudes to sex in Japan and it has premodern precedents.
[19] United Nations, *Patterns of First Marriage: Timing and Prevalence* (New York: United Nations, 1990).
[20] Thornton, 'Cohabitation', 504. These conclusions were based on a panel study drawn from records of White children born in the Detroit metropolitan area in July 1961. They were all aged 23 at the time of the research.

women, '60 percent were terminated within two years; 23 percent were terminated through union dissolution and 37 percent through marriage of the partners'.[21] As the age of cohabitation rises, so does the proportion of them marrying, to between 50 and 60%.[22] Only in the late 1980s did it become clear that both of the conventional ways of viewing cohabitation, as informal marriage or as 'the last stage in the courtship process', were seriously misleading.[23] Instead cohabitation was compared with the single life and found to be more like it in several respects.[24] In particular, about two thirds of a research sample (of nearly 13,000 cohabitors) did not have immediate marriage plans, exploding the conventional interpretation that cohabitation is equivalent to being engaged. Conversely, the authors of the study concluded that 'cohabitation for most is a convenient living arrangement for single individuals not ready to make long-term commitments'.[25] Slightly later, but large-scale, research in Britain confirms a similar trend. Results from the Economic and Social Research Council show 'evidence that the outcomes of cohabitation may be changing. Earlier cohorts seem to have been more likely to view cohabitation as a prelude to marriage ... Younger people, however, are more likely than older ones to end cohabitation through separation than through marriage.'[26]

3. Cohabitation has weakened the connection between marriage and parenthood since the 1970s.

A startling discovery was made in the early 1990s which has enormous consequences for family formation well into the third millennium. Jane Lewis and Kathleen Kiernan postulated two major changes in Britain with regard to 'reproductive behaviour' in

[21] Ibid.

[22] Linda J. Waite, 'Cohabitation: A Communitarian Perspective', unpublished paper, University of Chicago (January 1999), 5; Larry Bumpass and James Sweet, 'National Estimates of Cohabitation', *Demography* 24.4 (1989), 615–25.

[23] Ronald R. Rindfuss and Audrey VandenHeuvel, 'Cohabitation: A Precursor to Marriage or an Alternative to Being Single?', *Population and Development Review* 16.4 (December 1990), 705.

[24] The 'respects' studied were childbearing and marriage plans, employment and educational activities, and the cohabitors' own self-identification (ibid., 708–21).

[25] Ibid., 711.

[26] Economic and Social Research Council, *Population and Household Change*, no.1.

the previous 30 years.[27] The first was a widespread separation of sex and marriage which happened in the 1960s. The second was a widespread separation of marriage from parenthood, which happened in the 1980s, gathered pace in the 1990s, and 'has given rise to moral panic about lone motherhood'.[28] The key to both changes is the declining importance of marriage. According to this thesis when an unmarried couple conceived in the 1960s, they generally married. In the early 1970s, when an unmarried couple conceived they generally either married or had an abortion. Living together as a prelude to marriage (aptly named 'nubile cohabitation'), 'began in the 1970s'. In the late 1970s and early 1980s, an unmarried couple upon conception opted increasingly for an abortion or an illegitimate birth. The 1990s has seen a confirmation of this trend. But in the 1990s 70% of women marrying for the first time had cohabited before marriage compared with only 6% in the late 1960s. Cohabitation is therefore 'inextricably linked' both to the decline of marriage and the increase in childbearing outside it.[29]

The weakening connection between marriage and parenthood may be an international trend. Gordon Carmichael risked the generalization (in 1995) that in many of the 'more developed countries' the 'transition to parenthood is held to be a major catalyst to the conversion of cohabiting unions into marriages'.[30] But cohabiting unions are not always converted into marriages. Most of the data used to support the claim were collected in the 1980s, and the extent of the separation of marriage from parenthood may have been insufficiently appreciated then. The pattern just described within Britain clearly fits trends from the USA and other countries. The ingredients are simply stated. They are: an increase in sexual activity without reference to marriage which has been charted extensively; a rise in the age of first marriage (currently 29 for men and 27 for women in the UK); the increasing availability of reliable

---

[27] Jane Lewis and Kathleen Kiernan, 'The Boundaries Between Marriage, Nonmarriage, and Parenthood: Changes in Behavior and Policy in Postwar Britain', *Journal of Family History* 21 (July 1996), 372–88. And see Jane Lewis, *Marriage, Cohabitation and the Law: Individualism and Obligation* (Lord Chancellor's Department Research Secretariat, 1999), p.10.

[28] Lewis and Kiernan, 'Boundaries', 372.   [29] Ibid.

[30] Carmichael, 'Consensual Partnering', 75.

contraception; increasing recourse to abortion when contraception fails or is unused; and the vanishing stigma attached to cohabitation. Couples *desiring* children may simply not see the advantages of marriage in either personal or economic terms.

4. Some people choose cohabitation as an alternative to marriage, not as a preparation or 'trial' for it.

A hint of this discovery was dropped earlier when it was noted (proposition 2) that people who leave a cohabiting relationship are as likely to return to singleness as to enter marriage. However, there are more disturbing trends to unearth about the endings of cohabitations. Many of these cannot be satisfactorily explained by couples who abandon plans to marry. They never had such plans. They chose cohabitation because it was an *alternative* to marriage.

Kingsley Davis offered a candid explanation for the extent of cohabitation in the USA (in the mid-1980s) which had little to do with marriage. He thought it was 'an ephemeral pairing based on sexual attraction'. Cohabitation allowed 'young people *considerable postponement* of marriage without loss of a convenient sexual partnership'.[31] He ruled out the likelihood that cohabitation was a 'trial marriage', since revised divorce laws allowed disillusioned marriage partners, discovering apparent incompatibility after the wedding, to extricate themselves from marriages without difficulty. Rather, cohabitation was characterized by a sexual freedom which might be more tellingly compared with that of adultery and the keeping of mistresses in earlier times. There was little thought of marriage in the intentions of most cohabitors.

Some researchers in the USA have shown that the very publicness of a wedding ceremony symbolizes a transition which many unmarried couples are, at least initially, reluctant to make. The ceremony is itself an expression 'of the long-term commitment between partners'.[32] The reluctance to enter into the deeper commitment

[31] Kingsley Davis, 'The Future of Marriage', in Davis (ed.), *Contemporary Marriage*, p.38 (emphasis added).

[32] Robert J. Willis and Robert T. Michael, 'Innovation in Family Formation: Evidence on Cohabitation in the United States', in John Ermisch and Naohiro Ogawa (eds.), *The Family, the Market and the State in Ageing Societies* (Oxford: Clarendon Press, 1994), p.10.

of marriage was for some respondents due to doubt about whether they wished to marry *at all*. Insofar as the cohabitation was a 'trial', it was not a trial which aimed at assessing partner compatibility for future marriage, but a trial for assessing whether the state of living together was to be preferred to the state of remaining single.[33] Others were thought to be combining the pleasurable aspects of living together with the shunning of 'the commitment and permanence associated with marriage and the family'.[34] Others regarded cohabitation as a trial-marriage. They were conscious of the extent of divorce, anxious to avoid ending their marriages through divorce, and believed that living together first was an acceptable and effective way of testing compatibility.[35]

5. 'Trial-marriages' are unlikely to work.

A clear majority of young people in the USA 'agreed' or 'mostly agreed' with the statement, put to them in 1991–5, that '[i]t is usually a good idea for a couple to live together before getting married in order to find out whether they really get along'.[36] This growing belief may be rooted in the near universal aspiration of people intending marriage that their unions be durable and happy. On an optimistic assessment of these arrangements, known as the 'weeding hypothesis', only 'those cohabiting couples who find themselves to be well suited and more committed to marriage go on to marry'.[37] The rest weed themselves out or are weeded out by the experience. However, the extent of the support for living together as a 'trial' for marriage is not justified by its success in securing the goods sought. It seems rather to rest on a set of dubious cultural myths. Evidence

---

33 David Popenoe and Barbara Dafoe Whitehead, *Should We Live Together? What Young Adults Need to Know about Cohabitation before Marriage: A Comprehensive Review of Recent Research* (The National Marriage Project, New Jersey: Rutgers, The State University of New Jersey, 1999), p.4.

34 Rindfuss and VandenHeuvel, 'Cohabitation', 722.

35 Willis and Michael, 'Innovation', pp.10–11. Research was carried out in 1986 when the link between cohabitation and marriage was considerably stronger (and cohabitation less normative) than it is today.

36 Popenoe and Whitehead, *Should We Live Together?*, p.4.

37 See Lynda Clarke and Ann Berrington, 'Socio-Demographic Predictors of Divorce', in John Simons (ed.), *High Divorce Rates: The State of the Evidence on Reasons and Remedies, Vols. 1–2* (Lord Chancellor's Department Research Secretariat, 1999), vol.1, p.16. See the sources cited there.

from several countries shows that 'couples who cohabit prior to marriage have a higher risk of marital dissolution'.[38] We have just had occasion to query, in a cohabitation arrangement, what is actually being 'tried'. David Popenoe and Barbara Whitehead warn:

Cohabitation does not reduce the likelihood of eventual divorce; in fact, it may lead to a higher divorce risk. Although the association was stronger a decade or two ago and has diminished in the younger generations, virtually all research on the topic has determined that the chances of divorce ending a marriage preceded by cohabitation are significantly greater than for a marriage not preceded by cohabitation.[39]

However, while their warning remains salutary, there are good grounds for thinking, at least in western Europe, that the association between cohabitation and marital breakdown is becoming weaker (below, propositions 16 and 17).[40]

There is also a fairly obvious conceptual difficulty with 'trial-marriage'. If compatibility for life is what is being tried or assessed, there must be opportunity for leaving the trial, in case it yields unsatisfactory results. But marriage itself does not allow such opportunity since it is for life. The unconditional love which in Christian marriage reflects Christ's love for the Church (Eph. 5:25) cannot be nourished in a context where it can be terminated if 'things don't work out'. As Jack Dominian says, 'Human relationships are built on the principles of availability, continuity, reliability and predictability and these are conditions found in the parent–child relationship and in marriage.'[41] But in a trial-marriage all these qualities are compromised. So a trial-marriage is not a marriage.

6. Cohabitation may be a union which is different in kind from marriage.

We have already noted the finding that cohabitation may be more like singleness than marriage. Further research has produced a stronger version of the difference between the two institutions, and concluded that, in many cases, there is a difference *in kind* between them. It remains customary to regard cohabitation as a relationship similar to marriage, except with regard to the duration and

[38] Ibid.   [39] Popenoe and Whitehead, *Should We Live Together?*, p.4.
[40] Kathleen Kiernan, 'Cohabitation in Western Europe', *Population Trends* 96 (1999), 25.
[41] Jack Dominian, *The Church and the Sexual Revolution* (London: Darton, Longman and Todd, 1971), p.32, and see p.34.

the degree of commitment involved.[42] But the assumed comparison between cohabitation and marriage may have seriously misled
researchers who have persisted in seeing cohabitation as 'short-
duration marriage',[43] 'a stage of courtship',[44] etc. There has been
considerable disagreement over this point. 'An alternative view' of
cohabitation, articulated by cohabitors themselves, is 'that cohabitation is a distinct institutional form, a "looser bond", with different
goals, norms and behaviors'.[45] Robert Schoen and Robin Weinick
believe that in the USA, the behaviour of cohabiting couples in
respect of three key indicators (fertility expectations, non-familial
activities and home ownership) firmly establishes that 'cohabitors
resemble single persons more than married persons'.

If living together more resembles singleness than marriage, there
are clear implications for the understanding of partner selection. If
someone is looking for a live-in partner with whom to share a life
which *remains importantly a single life*, then he or she will not be looking
for a potential bride or bridegroom. As the researchers say, 'Because
partner selection is influenced by the kind of relationship that is
sought, the "informal marriage" and "looser bond" perspectives
on cohabitation imply different patterns of partner choice.'[46] On
this view, of course, marriage is a relationship different *in kind* from
cohabitation. 'While cohabitors anticipate time together, married
persons anticipate a lifetime. A different kind of relationship calls for
a different kind of partner.'[47] This research provides good support
for the view that cohabitations and marriages need not be located
on a single continuum, even if many cohabitors eventually marry
their partners.

7. Men are less committed to their female partners and much less committed to children.

By the mid-1990s Frances Goldscheider and Robin Kaufman
had shown that 'the substitution of cohabitation for marriage is
a story of lower commitment of women to men and even more so of

---

[42] See Willis and Michael, 'Innovation', and the extensive literature they cite.
[43] Ibid., p.10.
[44] E. Thomson and U. Colella, 'Cohabitation and Marital Stability: Quality or Commitment', *Journal of Marriage and the Family* 54 (1992), 259.
[45] Robert Schoen and Robin M. Weinick, 'Partner Choice in Marriages and Cohabitations', *Journal of Marriage and the Family* 55 (May 1993), 409.
[46] Ibid.   [47] Ibid., 413.

men to women and to their relationship as an enduring unit'.[48]
While men wanted sex and female companionship, they did not
want them within a family-making context, and they also valued
the amassing of consumer items which took economic preference
over household commitments. Men have 'greatly increased aspirations for expensive consumer goods such as new cars, stereophonic
equipment, vacation homes, and recreational vehicles' and they
prefer these to the responsibilities of settling into a new family.
The authors find that 'although marriage is declining in centrality in both men's and women's lives, the centrality of parenthood
is declining far more in men's lives'. There has been 'a retreat
from children' and most of it has been on the part of men. There
is evidence, they say, that 'men increasingly view children and
fatherhood primarily as responsibility and obligation rather than
as a source of marriage, happiness or stability'.[49] Since there is less
commitment to a cohabiting than to a marital union, it would seem
to follow that there is more unfaithfulness in the former. Although
cohabitors *expect* their partners to be faithful, they are much less
likely to be faithful than married partners.[50]

Recent research (1997) carried out in Norway (where 45% of
children are born outside marriage) also identifies a lack of commitment of many cohabitors to their union. However, this lack
of commitment is differently explained. A majority of unmarried
couples with children had no plans to marry. Asked why, they explained this attitude 'partly by the less easy dissolution of a marriage'. They considered their union to be 'different from marriage
in terms of *commitment and stability*'.[51] The lack of commitment involved in living together, which contrasts with the commitment
expected by marriage, is explained by the belief (however mistaken
it may turn out to be) that cohabitation actually delivers a higher

---

[48] Frances K. Goldscheider and Gayle Kaufman, 'Fertility and Commitment: Bringing
Men Back In', *Population and Development Review* 22 (supp.) (1996), 89 (emphasis added).

[49] Ibid., 90. They complain that men are generally not considered in fertility studies and
that little is known about men's attitudes to fathering generally.

[50] Linda J. Waite and Kara Joyner, 'Emotional and Physical Satisfaction in Married,
Cohabiting and Dating Sexual Unions: Do Men and Women Differ?', in E. Laumann
and R. Michael (eds.), *Studies on Sex* (Chicago: University of Chicago Press, 1999).

[51] Øystein Kravdal, 'Wanting a Child without a Firm Commitment to the Partner:
Interpretations and Implications of a Common Behaviour Pattern among Norwegian
Cohabitants', *European Journal of Population* 13 (1997), 269 (emphasis added).

quality relationship than marriage. Marriage was thought to make it 'more difficult to resume single life or form another relationship (and perhaps also reduce the probability that attractive alternatives actually appear, since a married person may tend to be considered "reserved")'.[52] There was also evidence that those cohabitors who wanted to have children but did not want to marry 'were less likely than others to consider a parental break-up to be very deleterious for the child'.[53]

8. Cohabitors with no plans to marry report poorer relationship quality than married people.

A sample of over 13,000 individuals taken from the United States' National Survey of Family and Households (1987–8) was used to compare relationship quality between married and co-habiting couples. Quality was measured across five dimensions – disagreement, fairness, happiness, conflict management and interaction.[54] The researchers found 'a modest but significant difference' in the first four of the five dimensions. 'Those in cohabiting unions have poorer relationship quality than their counterparts in marriages. Cohabitors experience disagreement with greater frequency than their married counterparts. Cohabitors report more depression and less satisfaction with life than married people.'[55] As Linda Waite explains:

The key seems to lie in being in a relationship that one thinks will last. Marriage is, by design and agreement, for the long run. So married people see their relationship as much more stable than cohabiting people do. And for any couple, thinking that the relationship is likely to break up has a dampening effect on the spirits. The result – cohabitors show less psychological well-being than similar married people.[56]

But it is in the area of domestic violence that the poorer relationship quality of cohabitation when compared to marriage becomes most obvious. Domestic violence is an acute problem in

---

[52] Ibid., 281. Other reasons given for resistance to marriage included dislike of its formal status, and the time and money costs of a wedding.

[53] Ibid., 269, and see 281–7.

[54] Susan L. Brown and Alan Booth, 'Cohabitation Versus Marriage: A Comparison of Relationship Quality', *Journal of Marriage and the Family* 58 (August 1996), 673.

[55] Waite, 'Cohabitation'.   [56] Ibid., 25–6.

many societies, and the rigid gender stereotypes associated with it are, sadly, sometimes engendered by religions.[57] It would, however, be completely wrong to assume that, having avoided patriarchal marriage and settled for the less formal and potentially more egalitarian relationship of cohabitation, the chance of becoming a victim of violence was less. Waite's analysis shows that 'even after controlling for education, race, age and gender, people who live together are 1.8 times more likely to report violent arguments than married people', and that '[c]ohabitors with no plans to marry are *twice* as likely to report couple violence as either married or engaged couples'.[58]

9. Cohabitation after marriage is sometimes a substitute for remarriage and often precedes it.

So far only premarital cohabitation has been considered. However, cohabitation after marriage is equally widespread and important. It explains the drop in remarriage rates in the USA and Canada, at least in the 1980s.[59] By the mid-1980s non-marital cohabitation was preferred to remarriage among divorced people in Sweden and Norway.[60] In the UK, around 30% of women marrying for the second time in the late 1960s had cohabited first: in the early 1990s, the number had increased to about 90%.[61] Postmarital informal unions last longer than premarital ones.[62] Religious affiliation was thought to be irrelevant to the decision to cohabit after marriage, presumably because if the disapproval of divorce within the churches did not prevent divorce, similar teachings would be unlikely to prevent the formation of a non-marital

---

[57] Margaret Bendroth, *Fundamentalism and Gender* (New Haven: Yale University Press, 1994), p.116. And see Elisabeth Schüssler Fiorenza and M. Shawn Copeland (eds.), *Concilium: Violence Against Women* (Maryknoll, N.Y.: Orbis Books, 1994).

[58] Waite, 'Cohabitation', 14–15. The figures are based on data from the US 1987/99 National Survey of Families and Households (author's emphasis). See also Brown and Booth, 'Cohabitation', 674–6.

[59] Zheng Wu and T.R. Balakrishnan, 'Cohabitation After Marital Disruption in Canada', *Journal of Marriage and the Family* 56 (August 1994), 723–4.

[60] Blanc, 'Formation and Dissolution of Second Unions'.

[61] John Haskey, 'Families: Their Historical Context, and Recent Trends in the Factors Influencing Their Formation and Dissolution', in Miriam E. David (ed.), *The Fragmenting Family: Does It Matter?* (London: IEA Health and Welfare Unit, 1998), p.23.

[62] Bumpass, Sweet and Cherlin, 'The Role of Cohabitation'.

union.[63] Alternatively, divorced people may feel that in the eyes of the churches, their lives have already shown signs of irregularity and failure, so religious affiliation weakens or vanishes.

10. In some developing nations a new form of cohabitation has appeared alongside traditional informal unions.

Work done in 1991 on the Longitudinal Fertility Survey in Caracas, Venezuela, indicated 'the emergence of a different type of consensual union' more typical of developed societies.[64] The 'traditional' type of consensual union is 'associated with rural origins, low levels of education, low female independence, low male responsibilities, high fertility, and high instability'. It does not replace marriage but remains a version of marriage for people who remain beyond the touch of state bureaucracies, the influence of churches, or the wealth required for starting a family. By contrast the modern type is similar to cohabitation practised in North America and elsewhere. It is 'prevalent among more educated women'; it is 'an alternative to marriage among couples who enter into a consensual union as a trial phase before legal marriage, or those who choose cohabitation as an alternative to being single'.[65] For the cohort of women (aged 25–29 at the time of the survey), the number in consensual unions outnumbered the number in legal marriages by nearly half.[66] The Venezuelan study indicates the extent of the spread of modern cohabitational practice to developing countries together with the attendant upheavals and problems.

11. There are ethnic variations in the willingness to cohabit, and in the outcomes of cohabitation.

There are two points to be emphasized, one about the extent, the other about the meaning, of cohabitation, considered as a part of a broader picture of informal kinship arrangements. In the USA in the early 1980s it was found that among Puerto Ricans 59% of

---

[63] Wu and Balakrishnan, 'Cohabitation', 731.
[64] Emilio A. Parrado and Martin Tienda, 'Women's Roles and Family Formation in Venezuela: New Forms of Consensual Unions?', *Social Biology* 44.1–2 (September 1997), 6.
[65] Ibid.   [66] Ibid., 7.

non-marital births occurred within informal unions.[67] In the late 1980s, a growing body of research confirmed that African Americans are more likely to cohabit than Whites, and both African American and Puerto Rican women are more likely to bear children within such unions than are non-Hispanic Whites.[68] In short, 'both the prevalence and the meaning of cohabitation differ by race and ethnicity'.[69] Between 1960 and 1996 the proportion of Black babies born to unmarried mothers (whether single or cohabiting) rose from 22% to 70% of the total.[70]

Reference to poverty and high rates of unemployment is thought to provide only a partial, albeit important explanation. '[F]or a complete explanation one must look beyond economics to history and culture.'[71] These may include 'long-standing group differences in the organization of family life', 'extended family ties' and 'well developed extended kin networks, often involving coresidence' which 'have served as important mechanisms for coping with economic hardship'.[72] Non-Hispanic Whites are more accustomed to living in nuclear families than other groups. When they experience cohabitation it still tends to be for relatively brief periods. However, informal unions have long played a more central role in other groups, leading to the argument that 'black families are not necessarily centered around conjugal unions, which are the *sine qua non* of the nuclear family. Among Blacks, households centered around consanguineal relatives have as much legitimacy (and for most people, as much respectability) as family units as do households

[67] N. Landale and S. Hauan, 'The Family Life Course of Puerto Rican Children', *Journal of Marriage and the Family* 54 (1992), 912–24.

[68] Wendy D. Manning and Nancy S. Landale, 'Racial and Ethnic Differences in the Role of Cohabitation in Premarital Childbearing', *Journal of Marriage and the Family* 58 (February 1996). And see Wendy D. Manning, 'Marriage and Cohabitation Following Premarital Conception', *Journal of Marriage and the Family* 55 (November 1993), 839–50.

[69] Manning and Landale, 'Racial and Ethnic Differences', 63, 75. See further references there.

[70] Morehouse Research Institute and Institute for American Values, *Turning the Corner on Father Absence in Black America* (Atlanta and New York: 1999), p.10.

[71] Andrew Cherlin, *Marriage, Divorce and Remarriage* (Boston: Harvard University Press, 1992), p.107.

[72] Manning and Landale, 'Racial and Ethnic Differences', 65.

centered around conjugal unions.'[73] Among some Whites even in
the modern period, e.g., convicts deported to Australia from Britain
and Ireland,[74] families in frontier territories in the USA,[75] and rural communities in many countries, access to bureaucracies which
would formalize irregular unions has been unavailable. In New
Zealand and Australia the indigenous Maori and Aboriginal populations 'are culturally more attuned to consensual partnering than
the European majorities'.[76]

It may therefore be fairly claimed that the nuclear family for a
variety of reasons is less historically rooted in some ethnic traditions than in others. That much may be said in advance of any
consideration of slavery. The influence of the dominant economic
system was at its most brutal in the institution of slavery, where
conditions for marriage were difficult or impossible. A recent analysis of the causes of father absence in Black America is applicable
equally to the less formal kinship arrangements within that community. Drawing attention to the legacy of slavery and the racism
and economic discrimination that followed it, the authors say:

The legacy of slavery is tragically relevant to the issue of Black fatherhood,
for the conditions of slavery in the United States provided exactly the
opposite of what is required in order to preserve the fragile bond between
father and child. By law, the male slave could fulfill none of the duties of
husband and father. The institution of slavery created a sub-culture where
all the societal norms, mores, expectations, and laws, instead of helping to
connect men to their offspring, forcibly severed the bonds between fathers
and their children.[77]

73 N. Sudharkasa, 'African and Afro-American Family Structure: A Comparison', *Black Scholar* 11 (1980), 54–5.
74 Gordon A. Carmichael, 'From Floating Brothels to Suburban Semirespectability: Two Centuries of Nonmarital Pregnancy in Australia', *Journal of Family History* 21 (July 1996), 281–316. And see M. Sturma, 'Eye of the Beholder: The Stereotype of Women Convicts, 1788–1852', *Labour History* 34 (1978), 3–10.
75 Seff, 'Cohabitation', 142.
76 Carmichael, 'Consensual Partnering', 64, citing Gordon A. Carmichael, 'Living Together in New Zealand: Data on Coresidence at Marriage and on *de facto* Unions', *New Zealand Population Review* 10.3 (1984), 41–54; and A. Gray, 'Aboriginal Marriage and Survival', *Journal of the Australian Population Association* 1 (1984), 18–30.
77 Morehouse Research Institute and Institute For American Values, *Turning the Corner*, p.10.

The authors were divided on the causes of father absence, some identifying contemporary economic conditions as the principal cause, others the continuing influence of slavery on attitudes and behaviour. Both are doubtless to some extent responsible. In these circumstances any understanding of cohabitation has to explore how it has become locked into traditions of marital informality, together with the continuing and horrendous influence of slavery and the disproportionate burden of unemployment born by ethnic minorities.

COHABITATION: SOME CONSEQUENCES

In the previous section some properties of cohabitation were described. In this section some consequences of cohabitation are described, principally for children, but also for their parents and society.

12. The increase in cohabitation has contributed directly to the increase in the number of children of single parents.

Little has so far been said about children or about how they fare in cohabitation arrangements. They fare worse than their parents. First, there is a strong connection between the increase in cohabitation and the increase in single-parent families. This has been noticed only recently. That is because researchers have typically treated non-marital pregnancies as pregnancies of *single* mothers, whereas many so-called single mothers are in fact in cohabiting relationships when they become pregnant. The connection between pregnancy and cohabitation at conception began to be made during the 1980s.[78] But does the rise in number of cohabiting couples really lead to more children being born, not merely outside marriage, but outside the cohabiting relationships in which they were conceived? Yes. Recent research in the UK (1997) proves the connection dramatically. It indicates that 'about two-fifths of one parent families headed by never-married mothers are created through childbearing within cohabitation followed by dissolution of the cohabitational union'.[79] In Britain there are now more single

[78] Lewis and Kiernan, 'Boundaries'.   [79] Ermisch, *Pre-Marital Cohabitation*, abstract.

pre-married, than single post-married mothers.[80] One in five of all children are children of one-parent families.

Cohabitation then, is a *source* of single-parent families. In the UK, for every twenty cohabiting couples, eleven marry each other, eight split up without marrying, while one remains together and unmarried after ten years.[81] Of cohabiting couples who are pregnant, half get married. It is the other half that cause concern. Gershuny and Berthoud comment: 'The other half of the cohabiting couples split up before their child has left primary school. Four out of ten separate before the child even starts school. The women become "single" mothers, though they might be considered "separated". In fact two out of five women who become "single" mothers do so via a cohabitation that does not survive.'[82] The position is similar in the USA. Over a third of all cohabiting couples have at least one child, and 'fully three quarters of children born to cohabiting parents will see their parents split up before they reach age sixteen, whereas only about a third of children born to married parents face a similar fate'.[83]

13. Cohabitors with children are very likely to split up.

Unmarried couples with children are much less likely to proceed to marry than couples without children. Work done on the Canadian Family and Friends Survey in 1990 showed that the 'presence and number of children within cohabitation have a strong negative influence on separation for both sexes' and 'a strong negative effect on the transition to marriage'.[84] Work done in Britain for the Research Centre on Micro-social Change (1997) concluded that

[D]irect comparison between first children born in a cohabitation and those born in a marriage shows that the former are much more likely to end up with only one parent. Starting from the birth of the first child, half of the cohabiting parents have separated within ten years, compared

[80] 'Single lone mothers eclipsed divorced lone mothers in relative numbers from the beginning of the 1990s.' See John Haskey, 'One-Parent Families and their Dependent Children in Great Britain', in Reuben Ford and Jane Millar (eds.), *Private Lives and Public Responses* (London: Policy Studies Institute, 1998), p.28.

[81] Gershuny and Berthoud, *New Partnerships?*, p.4.

[82] Ibid., p.5.   [83] Popenoe and Whitehead, *Should We Live Together?*, p.7.

[84] Zheng Wu and T. R. Balakrishnan, 'Dissolution of Premarital Cohabitation in Canada', *Demography* 32.4 (November 1995), 528.

with only an eighth of parents who were married before the baby was born.[85]

14. Children raised by cohabiting couples are likely to be poorer than children raised by married parents.

The difference is very marked. In fact, 'cohabiting couples are economically more like single parents than like married couples'.[86] A comparative study of the poverty rate (in the USA in 1996) of children of cohabiting and of married parents showed that '[w]hile the poverty rate for children living in married couple households was about 6%, it was 31% for children living in cohabiting households, much closer to the rate of 45% for children living in families headed by single mothers'.[87] Another study shows two-parent families have mean levels of wealth six times as high as cohabiting couple families.[88] In the United States in 1990, 2.2 million children lived in cohabiting couple families. Data from the 1990 census gave information about parental income and showed that the income of cohabiting couples resembled more the income of single-parent families than of married couples. The 'mean income of male cohabiting partners is substantially lower – almost one half lower – than the mean income of males in married couples. Children in married-couple families (at least in the USA) appear to be better off economically than children in cohabiting-couple families because of the education and income of their parents, rather than simply because they share a residence with two adults.'[89] Neither is the deficit merely economic. While the literature on single-parent families 'acknowledges their resilience and commitment', it 'also shows how the life-chances of children are impaired in a number of specific respects'. Married-couple families are 'more likely to foster wellbeing', and to demonstrate to children the values of 'trust, faithfulness and love'.[90]

---

[85] Gershuny and Berthoud, *New Partnerships?*, p.5.
[86] Popenoe and Whitehead, *Should We Live Together?*, p.8.
[87] Ibid., p.9, summarizing Wendy D. Manning and Daniel T. Lichter, 'Parental Cohabitation and Children's Economic Well-Being', *Journal of Marriage and the Family* 58 (November 1996), 1009.
[88] LingXin Hao, 'Family Structure, Private Transfers, and the Economic Well-Being of Families with Children', *Social Forces* 75 (1996), 269–92.
[89] Manning and Lichter, 'Parental Cohabitation', 1009.
[90] Keith White, 'The Case for Marriage', *Third Way* 19.1 (February 1996), 12.

15. Children of cohabiting couples are more likely to be victims of abuse.

We have already noted (above, proposition 8) that cohabiting couples are more violent to each other than married couples. Robert Whelan's study, based on British data in the 1980s, claimed that children of cohabiting parents were 20 times more likely to be subject to child abuse. If children lived with their mother and their mother's boyfriend who was not their father, they were 33 times more likely to suffer abuse than if they lived with their parents.[91] 'The most unsafe of all family environments for children is that in which the mother is living with someone other than the child's biological father. This is the environment for the majority of children in cohabiting couple households.'[92] Jon Davies envisages an imaginary foetus approaching a life assurance agent about a policy which is most likely to provide him or her with a happy life. The advice given is to get born to a married couple who love each other, and

Avoid, if you can, such 'families' as your biological mother living with a man who is not your father: that tends to be dangerous for you (and for your mother). Money helps, but at every level of society a monogamous, married couple as the family unit will help *a lot* more. It will help you do well at school, to keep out of trouble with the police, and, by example and precept, will teach you the basics of getting on with people, friends and strangers, to learn the necessary sociabilities of proper altruism and sensible egotism, to learn to listen and to talk, to have the courage to get things wrong ...[93]

16. People who live together before they marry may be more likely to divorce than people who marry directly from the single state.

Many studies have shown that 'living together before marriage substantially increases the chance of divorce for a couple'.[94] It was shown (in 1995) that 'premarital cohabitors in Canada have over

---

91 Robert Whelan, *Broken Homes and Battered Children: A Study of the Relationship Between Child Abuse and Family Type* (London: Family Educational Trust, 1993).

92 Popenoe and Whitehead, *Should We Live Together?*, p.8.

93 Jon Davies, 'Neither Seen nor Heard nor Wanted: The Child as Problematic. Towards an Actuarial Theology of Generation', in Michael A. Hayes, Wendy Porter and David Tombs (eds.), *Religion and Sexuality* (Sheffield: Sheffield Academic Press, 1998), p.332.

94 Hall and Zhao, 'Cohabitation', 426–7. See the many sources cited there.

twice the risk of divorce in any year of marriage when compared with noncohabitors'.[95] By the early 1990s the assumption that cohabitation had a negative effect on subsequent marriage was taken as generally true, and given a name – 'the cohabitation effect'. Further hypotheses were then devised and tested to determine why the cohabitation effect occurred.

The three main explanations were based on the separate ideas of duration, causation and selection. The first is the claim that cohabitors who subsequently marry and then divorce will have spent a longer overall time together than those who marry directly from the single state, so like is not being compared with like.[96] This hypothesis is now generally rejected as an over-simplification. Even when the length of marital unions of couples who formerly cohabited is recalculated from the beginning of their living together, their overall unions are shorter than those of married people whose unions are measured from the time of marriage.[97] The *causal* hypothesis claims that the actual experience of living together outside marriage 'could undermine the legitimacy of formal marriage and make divorce seem more palatable if one runs into marital difficulties at some future date'. Causal hypotheses are notoriously difficult to substantiate but some studies claim to show that the experience of cohabiting 'reduces commitment to marriage'.[98] The selection hypothesis claims cohabitors are 'a select group of people who differ in salient ways from those who do not cohabit'. The differences may include unconventional family ideologies, exposure to parental divorce, lack of concern about marital status and low religiosity.

However, detailed testing of selectivity in Canada showed only that it was 'unable to materially account for the cohabitation

[95] Ibid., 425; and (based on 13,495 respondents in Canada), Wu and Balakrishnan, 'Dissolution', 521–32.

[96] J.D. Teachman and K.A. Polonko, 'Cohabitation and Marital Stability in the United States', *Social Forces* 69 (1990), 207–20.

[97] See A. DeMaris and K.V. Rao, 'Premarital Co-habitation and Subsequent Marital Stability in the United States: A Re-assessment', *Journal of Marriage and the Family* 54 (1992), 178–90.

[98] See Hall and Zhao, 'Cohabitation', 422. They cite W.G. Axinn and A. Thornton, 'The Relationship Between Cohabitation and Divorce: Selectivity or Causal Influence?', *Demography* 29 (1992), 357–74; and Thomson and Colella, 'Cohabitation', 259–67.

effect'.[99] The authors were left affirming both the cohabitation effect – people who cohabit before they marry *are* more likely to divorce – and the inability of any available hypothesis to explain it. Other researchers also deny there is a cohabitation effect to explain. Willis and Michael, for example, using a national sample of 32-year-olds in the 1980s in the United States, conclude: 'There is no great apparent difference in the stability of the marriage dependent on whether it was preceded by a cohabitation.'[100] Similar results have been reported from France and Australia.[101] There is now, however, a more convincing version of the causal hypothesis which may remove the confusion.

17. The experience of cohabitation may change partners' attitudes to marriage.

The disagreement about the cohabitation effect may be explained by the age of the data on which the link between cohabitation and divorce is based. For example, cohabitation even in the early 1980s was sometimes taken as a sign of revolt against traditional marriage. Now that cohabitation has become more socially acceptable and even normal in many countries, it can hardly remain a token of protest. Attitudes towards marriage will clearly influence marital stability. People who resort quickly to divorce may be less likely to hold that marriage is an irrevocable state than married couples who stay together. Some people may hold a similar relaxed attitude to entering marriage and to leaving it. Popenoe and Whitehead suggest that the relaxed attitude to cohabitation (less commitment than in marriage, less reluctance to terminate it than in marriage) is carried over into marriage when cohabitors eventually marry. 'Once this low-commitment, high-autonomy pattern of relating is learned, it becomes hard to unlearn.' If this suggestion is true, it may also be true that the marriages of serial cohabitors are particularly at risk. 'The experience of dissolving one cohabiting relationship generates a willingness to dissolve later relationships. People's tolerance for unhappiness is

---

99 Hall and Zhao, 'Cohabitation', 426.   100 Willis and Michael, 'Innovation', 18.
101 Carmichael, 'Consensual Partnering', 74, citing H. Leridon, 'Cohabitation', and M. Bracher, G. Santow, S.P. Morgan and J. Trussell, 'Marriage Dissolution in Australia: Models and Explanations', *Population Studies* 47 (1993), 403–25.

diminished, and they will scrap a marriage that might otherwise be salvaged.'[102]

There is clearly a need for more research to be done into the relationship between cohabitation prior to marriage and the propensity to divorce. In the meantime this hypothesis accepts and begins to explain the cohabitation effect. It is based on how the experience of cohabitation impacts upon cohabitors during cohabitation and their subsequent attitudes to marriage. It is hardly likely that attitudes to marriage on entering it are uninfluenced by cohabitation, if it has happened. New research suggests that attitudes to marriage are negatively influenced by cohabitation. The experience of cohabitation impacts on attitudes to marriage, making marriage less likely, or if it happens, less successful.[103] Popenoe and Whitehead conclude: 'The act of cohabitation generates changes in people's attitudes to marriage that make the stability of marriage less likely. Society wide, therefore, the growth of cohabitation will tend to further weaken marriage as an institution.'[104] There may then be a serious compound effect of cohabitation on the wider societies where it is practised. If so, this becomes a strong reason for arguing that the process of legal recognition of cohabitation should be halted.

18. The extent of cohabitation may reinforce the belief that all intimate relationships are fragile and transient.

The possibility exists, then, that the understanding of marriage as a long-term, irrevocable commitment is being eclipsed by the belief that intimate relationships are almost inevitably ephemeral. It has been plausibly claimed that the high rate of union dissolution among cohabiting couples may 'reinforce the view that intimate relationships are fragile and temporary, thereby reducing the expectation that marriage is a lifetime relationship and commitment'.[105] This claim is similar to the causal version of the cohabitation effect, except that it operates as a longer-term generalization about the

---

[102] Popenoe and Whitehead, *Should We Live Together?*, p.5.
[103] e.g., Alfred DeMaris and William MacDonald, 'Premarital Cohabitation and Marital Instability: A Test of the Unconventional Hypothesis', *Journal of Marriage and the Family* 55 (May 1993).
[104] Popenoe and Whitehead, *Should We Live Together?*, p.5.
[105] Axinn and Thornton, 'The Relationship Between Cohabitation and Divorce', 361.

deleterious impact of cohabitation as an accepted social practice upon attitudes to marriage. Anthony Giddens' influential notion of 'the pure relationship' has been used as an explanatory hypothesis for the increasing fragility of all (Canadian) intimate relationships, marital and non-marital.

A pure relationship is 'a situation where a social relation is entered into for its own sake, for what can be derived by each person from a sustained association with another; and which is continued only in so far as it is thought by both parties to deliver enough satisfactions for each individual to stay within it'.[106] David Hall advances the hypothesis that 'couples who cohabit prior to marriage are signalling an inclination on the part of one or both partners to form a pure relationship'.[107] Hall found that 'women who lived common-law before their first marriage have a 33 percent greater risk of divorce at any time in their marriage than the reference group of women who did not cohabit before their first marriage'.[108] However, he denies the association between cohabitation and divorce (the cohabitation effect). It is 'statistically insignificant'. Rather, marital break-up can be explained by the pure relationship. 'Favourable views on pure relationships account for the high risk of marital instability previously attributed to premarital cohabitation ...' Premarital cohabitors 'are more likely to exit from their marriages for the same reason they lived common law – their favorable attitudes regarding pure relationships. To the extent that these attitudes give form to their marriages, their marriages will resemble the inherently unstable pure relationships described by Giddens.'[109] On this view there is a serious crisis for marriage and family life and it is found in 'the attitudes regarding intimacy that a person brings to their intimate relationships', whether cohabitation or marriage. These attitudes may cause long-term social

---

[106] Anthony Giddens, *The Transformation of Intimacy: Sexuality, Love and Eroticism in Modern Societies* (Cambridge: Polity Press, 1992), p.58. For a detailed analysis of the term, see Adrian Thatcher, *Marriage after Modernity: Christian Marriage in Postmodern Times* (Sheffield and New York: Sheffield Academic Press and New York University Press, 1999), pp.47–50.

[107] David R. Hall, 'Marriage as a Pure Relationship: Exploring the Link Between Premarital Cohabitation and Divorce in Canada', *Journal of Comparative Family Studies* 27.1 (Spring 1996), 3.

[108] Ibid., 9.   [109] Ibid., 10.

damage. The more people form pure relationships, the less inclined they may become to enter permanent mutual partnerships.

COHABITATION: SOME EXPLANATIONS

The previous section described some of the consequences of cohabitation for children, for their parents, and (since cohabitation weakens marriage as a family form) for societies where cohabitation is common. An obvious further question arises: why do people do it? There are at least two kinds of answers that may be given: one referring to recent social trends; the other to longer-term and broader historical trends which invite the use of general and contestable terms like 'individualism' or 'capitalism'. Each is considered in turn.

19. Cohabitation is clearly linked to sexual, social and economic changes.

When one writer attempted an aetiological overview of cohabitation in the early 1980s (in the USA), he referred to sexual, social and economic changes. More people were having sex outside marriage. This was due to the availability of contraception and abortion. Women wanted careers and these impeded marriage but not cohabitation, which was best understood as a 'contemporary extension of the courtship process'.[110] Couples were more cautious about becoming married because of the 'increased propensity to divorce' and cohabitation offered them 'the opportunity to terminate a relationship without the messy legal tangles'.[111] Conspicuously there was little awareness in the analysis of cohabitation as an alternative to marriage, and no attempt to set cohabitation in a broader theoretical, economic or sociological framework.

Fifteen years on it is no longer possible to regard cohabitation as an extension of the courtship process, for neither courtship nor cohabitation need have an end in view, that of engagement and marriage. The availability of reliable contraception has largely taken away the fear of pregnancy. Indeed it is often claimed that contraception has separated fertility from sexuality altogether: pleasure

---

[110] Graham B. Spanier, 'Cohabitation in the 1980s: Recent Changes in the United States', in Davis (ed.), *Contemporary Marriage*, p.97.
[111] Ibid., p.100.

and procreation can now be differentiated at will. These claims are, of course, premature and exaggerated. Contraceptive failure, even among careful users, is alarmingly high. Nine per cent of women using reversible contraceptives become pregnant during their first year of use, and the 'typical woman who uses reversible methods of contraception continuously from her 15th to her 45th birthday will experience 1.8 contraceptive failures'.[112] What matters is the *belief* that pregnancy can be avoided, and that should it result, abortion may be available. Contraception has removed a hitherto strong belief that sexual intercourse belongs to marriage. Contraception allows unrestricted sexual intercourse while making both children and marriage optional.

These changes in sexual behaviour have been accompanied by other far-reaching changes to do with gender, education and work. Expectations about respective gender roles and spheres of work for men and women, bequeathed to us by the industrial revolution, weakened throughout the twentieth century. In several countries, the number of women in universities equals that of men. Women expect, and get, jobs and careers which are impeded by marriage. Women will marry later if they marry at all. Marriage is no longer required as a means of subsistence for women, because their growing economic independence removes their need to depend on husbands. And if marriage is chosen, there is likely to be an insistence (even if it is not fully honoured) on its egalitarian character, where the total inventory of household duties is negotiated and shared. While sightings of the 'new man' may still remain sparse,[113] the movement toward more egalitarian marriages is becoming harder to resist. These are some of the circumstances surrounding the 'expanding life-space' between puberty and marriage, and cohabitation cannot be properly examined without it.

20. Cohabitation may be the product of a long-term trend towards individualism.

There is surprising lack of agreement among researchers over whether the concept of individualism can be used at all in the

---

[112] James Trussell and Barbara Vaughan, 'Contraceptive Failure, Method-Related Discontinuation and Resumption of Use: Results from the 1995 National Survey of Family Growth', *Family Planning Perspectives* 31.2 (March/April 1999), 64.

[113] Lewis, *Marriage, Cohabitation and the Law*, p.4.

attempt to explain the range of behaviour associated with cohabitation. One researcher claims: 'The empirical evidence on intimate relationships does not reveal any clear trend towards individualism, either at the level of activities or mentalities. The reality seems to be considerably more complicated.'[114] Another says individualism has been 'identified by most theorists as the key, ongoing, ideational change of the century'.[115] There is a major disagreement between 'pessimists' and those who take a 'more nuanced' view[116] about the matter.

Ron Lesthaeghe and Johan Surkyn, in common with many social critics, have posited an 'era of individualism' that drives the upsurge in cohabitation.[117] Individualism here means that the interests and desires of the individual will take precedence over the interests and desires of one's partner, family, or social group. They locate people's choices about, in particular, fertility, within broader economic change (of the kind just mentioned), and 'ideational change' which gives meaning to their lives.[118] The central feature of ideational change in recent decades, they say, is 'disenchantment with institutional regulation' which manifests itself in the processes of secularization and what they call 'individuation'. Historically churches have had a major influence in the 'institutional regulation of individuals' lives through the collective assertion of norms that restrict individualism ... and through the psychological internalization of sanctions ranging in format from guilt to damnation'.[119] However, the influence of the churches has been seriously curtailed, especially in Europe, allowing greater freedom, pluralism and tolerance. With the weakening of regulation and religious sanction, unprecedented space is opened up for individual choice. Individuation may be defined as the process whereby a person becomes

---

[114] Ibid.
[115] Jenny Reynolds and Penny Mansfield, 'The Effect of Changing Attitudes to Marriage on its Stability', in Simons (ed.), *High Divorce Rates*, p.8.
[116] Lewis, *Marriage, Cohabitation and the Law*, p.20.
[117] R. Schoen and D. Owens, 'A Further Look at First Unions and First Marriages', in S. J. South and S. E. Tolnay (eds.), *The Changing American Family: Sociological and Demographic Perspectives* (Boulder and Oxford: Westview Press, 1992). pp.109–17.
[118] Ron Lesthaeghe and Johan Surkyn, 'Cultural Dynamics and Economic Theories of Fertility Change', *Population and Development Review* 14.1 (March 1988), 3.
[119] Ibid., 13.

more aware of himself or herself as an individual self or agent.[120] Choices will increasingly be made with reference to peer groups and decreasingly with reference to institutional authorities and norms.

The European Values Studies[121] are thought to provide detailed confirmation of the influence of both secularization and individuation on family formation. Other researchers move from the empirical conclusion that cohabitation is much more like singleness than marriage, to the moral conclusion that 'in the United States, at least, cohabitation partially sprang out of the *ideology of individualism*, despite its action of coupling two individuals'. They add: 'If the ideology of individualism is the spiritual father of the rise in cohabitation, then we should not be surprised that cohabiting unions are of relatively short duration.'[122]

According to the pessimists individualism may have become 'cancerous' in the body of middle America.[123] Baroness Young in the British House of Lords said in 1996: 'For one party simply to decide to go off with another person ... reflects the growing *self-first disease* which is debasing our society.'[124] Other writers commonly associate individualism with the rise of competitive, free-market values. They argue, worryingly, that these values 'cannot be contained within the market place and will inevitably filter into other aspects of life, e.g., sexual behaviour. The growth of a "consumer culture" reinforces the dominant ethos of choice in relationship options, and continues to undermine tradition.'[125] According to the 'more nuanced view' the behavioural evidence which would support the pessimistic view can be analysed in other ways. The evidence is found, on the male side, in the failure of many men to maintain dependent partners and children, and on the female side, in the increasing economic

[120] This might more properly be called 'individualism'. Individuation, more accurately, is what makes a thing one of something. Nevertheless I have retained the term used in Lesthaeghe's and Surkyn's paper.
[121] Lesthaeghe and Surkyn, 'Cultural Dynamics', 23–31.
[122] Rindfuss and Vandenheuvel, 'Cohabitation', 722–3 (emphasis added).
[123] R. Bellah, R. Madsen, W. Sullivan, A. Swidler and S.M. Tipton, *Habits of the Heart: Middle America Observed* (Berkeley: University of California Press, 1985), p.vii (cited in Lewis, *Marriage, Cohabitation and the Law*, p.19).
[124] Cited in Lewis, *Marriage, Cohabitation and the Law*, p.19 (emphasis added).
[125] Reynolds and Mansfield, 'The Effect of Changing Attitudes', p.8.

independence of women. But the male failure to maintain need not be analysed 'in terms of male flight'.[126] Economic deprivation, or 'structural change', may be 'as or more important a factor than male irresponsibility and selfishness'. It may be, concludes Jane Lewis, 'that (possibly selfish) individualism is the outcome rather than the determinant of changes in economic and social behaviour'.[127]

Social critics who deploy the term pejoratively sometimes overlook several inconvenient features of it. For example, it has been happening for a very long time. Lawrence Stone thinks there was a 'critical change' in family life from 'distance, deference and patriarchy' to what he calls 'Affective Individualism'. But this happened in the early modern period, and may have been occurring 'in the *last thousand years* of Western history'.[128] Again, the rise of individualism within modernity takes place alongside a positive revaluation of the individual person and his or her rights and needs, regardless of rank or race, and this has brought profound moral gain.[129] Even the pessimists agree individualism 'has been a positive force in bringing about greater gender equality and opportunity'.[130] Again, individualism is 'carried' and 'freighted' by churches which emphasize conversion and the individual's private relationship to God. It is also possible that cohabitors intending marriage simply woke up to the fact that the early years of marriage were often childless, so the requirement to validate them by marriage before they arrived became weaker. Individualism as an explanatory conceptual tool is perhaps more effective when it is used to critique selfish behaviour, together with an atomistic attitude to the wider society or community of people which it often assumes. Don Browning and his co-authors provide an important contrast between 'ordinate' and 'inordinate individualism'. Ordinate individualism is virtuous and is expressed by a proper 'self-regard' which is nonetheless

---

[126] Lewis, *Marriage, Cohabitation and the Law*, p.23, and see also p.21.

[127] Ibid., p.26.

[128] Lawrence Stone, *The Family, Sex and Marriage in England 1500–1800* (London: Weidenfeld and Nicolson, 1979), p.4 (emphasis added).

[129] This is magisterially argued by Charles Taylor in his *Sources of the Self: The Making of the Modern Identity* (Cambridge: Cambridge University Press, 1989).

[130] Reynolds and Mansfield, 'The Effect of Changing Attitudes', p.38.

expressed 'within an ethic of community'.[131] But individualism of the inordinate kind, which places one's own satisfactions above those of others, sometimes with ruthless determination, is a vice which threatens mutuality and militates against the negotiation of long-term and loving relationships.

21. Cohabitation is more likely to occur where religious belief is weak.

The contribution of the decline of religious belief to a cultural climate favouring cohabitation has already been noted. Research from nine countries and three continents indicates this conclusively.[132] A study based on over 13,000 adults in the USA found that '[p]ersons with no religious preference and Jews have a much higher level of approval of cohabitation than any of the other groups'.[133] Christians most likely to approve of cohabitation were Episcopalians, followed by Roman Catholics and Presbyterians, while the 'fundamentalist groups all have lower than average levels of approval of cohabitation'. The finding is expected, but it is helpful to spell out why Christian influence is still able to deter cohabitation. Research conducted on data collected from White people born in Detroit showed that 'young women who attend religious services several times a week have a cohabitation rate only 14% as large as those who never attend', and those who attended less than once a month were more than three times as likely to cohabit as those who attended once a week.[134] Religious people are exposed to strong negative sanctions against cohabitation, and these are strongest where there is a declaratory tradition of preaching which reinforces sectarian identity by prescribing members' conduct.

---

[131] Don S. Browning, Bonnie J. Miller-McLemore, Pamela D. Couture, K. Brynolf Lyon, and Robert M. Franklin, *From Culture Wars to Common Ground: Religion and the American Family Debate* (Louisville: Westminster/John Knox Press, 1997), pp.51, 59.

[132] See Carmichael, 'Consensual Partnering', 62 and the references there.

[133] Based on the 1987–8 National Survey of Families and Households. See James A. Sweet and Larry L. Bumpass, 'Religious Differentials in Marriage Behavior and Attitudes' (National Survey of Families and Households Working Paper 15, Madison: Center for Demography and Ecology, 1990), p.11.

[134] Arland Thornton, William G. Axinn and Daniel H. Hill, 'Reciprocal Effects of Religiosity, Cohabitation, and Marriage', *American Journal of Sociology* 98.3 (November 1992), 641.

Among Roman Catholics in France, 50% of church attenders (regular and irregular) entering first unions in the early 1980s cohabited first, compared with 70% of non-attenders.[135] Perhaps this finding shows that Catholic young people are at odds with the official teaching of their church about cohabitation, as well as contraception and abortion. Cohabitors who remain in disapproving religious groups experience conflict which is likely to result in their leaving.[136] Cohabitation, unlike other sexual relationships which can be hidden, is public behaviour which attracts censure from many Christians. Going directly from singleness to marriage elicits religious approval and actually increases religious involvement,[137] while cohabitation is still strongly associated with less religious people. But the impact of belief on behaviour is a difficult area of study. Interviews for the research just cited were carried out in 1980 and 1985. Twenty years on, a greater polarization of religious attitudes can be expected. On the one hand, fundamentalist groups will further emphasize the sin of sex before marriage, while less literalist and conservative individuals and churches may gradually assimilate some forms of cohabitation as an established normative practice.

This picture is confirmed in another volume in the New Studies in Christian Ethics series, *Churchgoing and Christian Ethics*. Robin Gill analyses data from the British Household Panel Survey, which in 1994 asked respondents the additional question whether they agreed with the statement, 'The Bible is God's word and every word in it is true.'[138] Three categories of Christians were then distinguished, those who 'strongly agree' with the statement (the 'biblical literalists'), those who 'agree' with it (the 'intermediate group'), and those who 'neither agree nor disagree', 'disagree' or 'strongly disagree'[139] with it (the 'biblical non-literalists'). The literalist group differed 'sharply from the whole sample' in the belief that 'it is wrong to cohabit'. Seventy-three per cent of the (306) biblical literalists strongly agreed with the statement 'cohabitation

[135] Catherine Villeneuve-Gokalp, 'From Marriage to Informal Union: Recent Changes in the Behaviour of French Couples', *Population: An English Selection* 3 (1991), 81–111.
[136] Thornton et al., 'Reciprocal Effects', 630.
[137] Ibid., 643.
[138] Robin Gill, *Churchgoing and Christian Ethics* (Cambridge: Cambridge University Press, 1999), p.100.
[139] Ibid., p.117.

is wrong', compared with 50% of the intermediate group, but only 25% of the (451) biblical non-literalists.[140] However, as Gill adds, even among the literalists, many were 'reluctant to say that cohabiting is actually wrong'.[141]

22. Cohabitation may also be linked to new employment patterns and the 'world economic system'.

The decline of religious belief in the west is frequently associated with its economic system, so it is not surprising that some analyses of the demise of families in the west identify that system as a principal cause. On this view, capitalism is the big corruptor – cohabitation is an index of the economic selfishness and *modus vivendi* that capitalism everywhere produces. Its very transience and informality symbolize the corrosive effects of the economic order on durable kinship arrangements. The capitalist 'world economic system' is said to be responsible for 'individuation from social groups, erosion of kin group functions and authority, and various types of mobility'.[142] Industrialism led to greater economic adequacy (for some!) which in turn undermined patriarchy and the nuclear family by providing, independently, 'greater elaboration and formalization of such areas as education, law, social services, health care, media and recreation'. The demand for labour was responsible for the movement of women into paid work. The combination of increased economic adequacy together with 'some erosion of the old belief constellation and less reinforcement for its practice' undermines the nuclear family and its religious supports.[143] The flexibility and mobility required by employers or accepted by employees in their search for advancement militates against settlement in local communities and the discharge of parental responsibilities. Within this milieu cohabitation appears attractive. It is provisional, informal, and terminable (just like employment contracts). It is unencumbered (at least initially and generally) by children and

---

[140] Ibid., pp.118–19. [141] Ibid., p.121.

[142] Thomas Brockmann, 'The Western Family and Individuation: Convergence with Caribbean Patterns', *Journal of Comparative Family Studies* 18.3 (Autumn 1987), 471. I do not develop Brockmann's provocative contrast between western family forms and Caribbean family forms under the conditions of slavery. Both forms are said to have been negatively influenced by 'capitalism' in strikingly similar ways.

[143] Ibid., 472.

so provides the pleasures of sexual love, the opportunity for full-time double careers and high spending on consumer and leisure goods.

This analysis labours under similar difficulties encountered by the individuation hypothesis. Just how old is capitalism? Are its effects on the family comparable with the effects of alternative systems? If it operates causally on behaviour, are not the effects it delivers, like other systems, morally mixed? Moving from the level of generalization to narrower, particular effects, factors such as the increase in private affluence or the state of the housing market play an enormous part in the growth of cohabitation. An obvious example of this is the increasing tendency of sons and daughters to leave their childhood home and set up independent households of their own prior to becoming married. This is a very recent development which affluence makes possible. There may be other, more pernicious influences of economic forces upon the moral life of individuals. Does consumerism mesmerize us into thinking that changing sexual partners (as serial cohabitors do) is a process akin to changing cars or dishwashers? Has regular sexual intercourse among the unmarried become a satisfaction that is supplied by the market of informal gender relations, using cohabitation as a mechanism of distribution?

COHABITATION: AT LAST SOME GOOD NEWS

So far, all indications about cohabitation suggest it is a state of affairs to avoid. The implications of this will be discussed in chapter 2. There are, however, some positive outcomes of cohabitation. All of them concern cohabiting couples who eventually marry.

23. Cohabitors with plans to marry report no significant difference in relationship quality to married people.

Once the distinction among cohabitors is made between those with and those without plans to marry, the differences in relationship quality noted earlier (above, proposition 8) disappear. The same researchers who report lower relationship quality among cohabitors specifically exclude those intending to marry. 'Cohabitors *with marriage plans* are involved in unions that are not qualitatively different from those of their married counterparts.'[144] Indeed in one of the five areas on which relationship quality was based, 'interaction' quality (defined as 'reported frequency of time spent alone with the partner or spouse in the last month') was higher for intending marriers than for marrieds. The finding led the researchers to conclude that for this group of cohabitors 'cohabitation is very much another form of marriage'.[145] Cohabitors intending marriage 'likely view their current living arrangements as a stepping stone to marriage or as a temporary arrangement until marriage is practicable'.[146]

24. People who live together with their partner before they marry value fidelity almost as much as married people do.

European Union research in 1993 showed that 66.5% of married respondents and 62.9% of cohabiting respondents endorsed the statement, 'Getting married means committing yourself to being faithful to your partner.' However, less than half of those who had previously cohabited and were currently cohabiting or single, endorsed the statement.[147] This finding contributed to the conclusion that 'it is the issue of commitment which appears to be central to understanding the greater instability of marriages preceded by cohabitation'.

25. The stability of cohabitation and marriage may be measured by the beliefs and attitudes partners bring to each.

The point of importance is that high among the factors which determine whether a particular cohabitation develops into a marriage lie the beliefs, hopes, attitudes and aspirations of the partners themselves. It is these, rather than the fragile nature of cohabitation, the attitudes rather than the institution, which influence the

[144] Brown and Booth, 'Cohabitation', 674 (emphasis added).
[145] Ibid., 677. The group was actually 76% of the total of over 13,000 individuals surveyed (using data from the 1987–8 National Survey of Family and Households). In the 1990s the numbers of cohabitors with marriage plans progressively diminished.
[146] Ibid., 671.
[147] *Eurostat, 1995*, in Reynolds and Mansfield, 'The Effect of Changing Attitudes', pp.16–17.

likely marital outcome. While pure relationships represent and already reflect short-term, instrumental attitudes, so cohabitations which intend marriage also reflect attitudes essential to the maintenance and flourishing of marriage. 'What does appear germane to marital and familial stability are the attitudes regarding intimacy that a person brings to their intimate relationships.'[148] The good news lies in the lack of contamination of the intention of the permanent commitment by anticipating the marital union. The same attitudes sustain each. For serial cohabitors, though, the acceptance of transience sets in (above, proposition 17).

In assessing cohabitation as an informal institution, it is important to recognize that the attitudes brought into it are complex, changing and sometimes unacknowledged even by the cohabitors themselves. Researchers have overlooked 'the complexity of consensual partnering'. Carmichael sums up the task for future cohabitation research by acknowledging the different strands of the complexity awaiting clarification:

It straddles courtship and the early stages of marriage, deferring marriage but also displacing to varying degrees engagement, 'going steady', and even, if convenience dominates and commitment is minimal, experimental dating. For some it is also a long term marriage substitute. At any given time it has different meanings to different participants: alternative to being single; precursor to marriage; substitute for marriage. And these perceptions can change and differ between parties to the one relationship.[149]

These remarks conclude the 'guide' to cohabitation. This chapter has attempted to indicate something of the complex, shifting, nature of cohabitation. It will quickly become out of date, but for now it must remain the basis for theological analysis, reflection and response. These tasks are now overdue and will be taken up in the next chapter.

[148] Hall, 'Marriage', 10.
[149] Carmichael, 'Consensual Partnering', 69.

CHAPTER 2

Living together: a preliminary theological analysis

The previous chapter was a 'pre-theological' attempt to understand an international social phenomenon prior to beginning theological analysis and reflection upon it. A whole book might be devoted to the selection of appropriate methods, principles, and applications. It may help to confess to the reader that the present author affirms mainstream Christian faith, and believes the Christian tradition is far too revelatory and insightful to be left to so-called 'traditionalists'. I say the creed cheerfully and thankfully (and as a practising Anglican, frequent opportunities arise). I have set out elsewhere the loyalties to which I believe any Christian theologian should adhere as a determining and liberating influence.[1] However, an author's prior commitments are no substitute for a clear account of the adopted method for dealing with an ethical problem.

So: the theological analysis gets started by contrasting the negative results of the guide to cohabitation with what Christians understand by salvation (first section). The analysis soon reaches a crossroads. A basic distinction is required between two types of cohabitation, 'prenuptial' and 'non-nuptial' (second section): thereafter one type only (prenuptial) becomes the preoccupation of the book. What will be called throughout the book 'the marital norm' is advocated, but because of the difference between norms and 'rules' what is the general norm for sexual relations in Christianity need not also be the rule in every case of sexual relations (third section). Next, what will be called 'the betrothal solution' is introduced as the prospective solution to the churches' difficulties

---

[1] Adrian Thatcher, *Marriage after Modernity: Christian Marriage in Postmodern Times* (Sheffield and New York: Sheffield Academic Press and New York University Press, 1999), pp.12–26.

with prenuptial cohabitation (fourth section). Christian marriage
cannot be fully understood without understanding the part betrothal has played in it: indeed, the whole of part 2 of the book is an
exercise in retrieving it in order to show how (in part 3) the recovery
of betrothal is essential to the pastoral, theological and liturgical
renewal of marriage. There is ample precedent within Christian
tradition and practice for regarding the betrothed as already *having
begun marriage*. A version of a recognizable theology of liberation
is next invoked (fifth section). It will be shown how, in the pressing
context of the sexual ethics of developed nations, it yields surprising, indeed, counter-intuitive conclusions, for parents, children and
societies. Chapter 2 ends (sixth section) by anticipating the pastoral,
theological and liturgical conclusions where the argument of the
book will arrive.

FOUND WANTING?

Living together is disapproved of in the *official* documents of the
churches and by many theologians. Some even condemn the practice completely, invoking the nomenclature of promiscuity and fornication. One fierce Reformed theologian (writing in 1999) would
refuse Christian weddings altogether to sexually experienced people. He deplores the fact that 'thousands of ministers not only allow
brides who are not virgins to wear white, but even bless with the rites
of Christian marriage young couples who admit to and have not re-
pented of their premarital sexual intimacy'. Clergy who 'grant the
blessing of God to couples who have spurned God in their sexual
conduct' are said to be acting disgracefully.[2] A clergyperson accuses
a couple who had lived together for three years before asking him
to officiate at their marriage of adultery and of failing to understand 'the biblical view' of marriage.[3] A liberal rabbi who frankly
acknowledges that most Jewish couples live together before they
marry describes the problem which the bride's status poses for
completing the marriage document. Conservative and Orthodox

---

[2] Jeffery E. Ford, *Love, Marriage, and Sex in the Christian Tradition from Antiquity to Today* (San
Francisco: International Scholars Publications, 1999), pp.115–16.

[3] Arthur A. Rouner, Jr., *Struggling With Sex: A Serious Call to Marriage-Centered Sexual Life*
(Minneapolis: Augsburg, 1987), p.28.

Jews continue to write the word *betultah* ('virgin') on the certificate, thereby risking a lie. Rabbi Gold would not refuse marriage to a couple who had lived together first but he thinks the traditional wording should be retained. Why? Because to change it would be 'to give up on an ideal that Jews have tried to maintain for thousands of years', and this would serve as a shameful failure for the whole of the Jewish faith, serving 'as a public statement that the majority of Jewish brides are no longer virgins'.[4] They are not, of course, but Gold thinks it is 'legitimate to maintain the legal fiction' that they are. This questionable solution brings into view the acute difficulty raised for the Jewish tradition by this wholesale departure from accepted norms. Christians will find this Jewish difficulty highly redolent of their own problems.

Official church teaching cannot bring itself to sanction cohabitation before marriage. The unanimous teaching of the churches is that sexual intercourse must be confined to marriage. The *Catechism of the Catholic Church* requires engaged persons to 'reserve for marriage the expressions of affection that belong to married love': while it admits into discussion the term 'trial marriage', it calls such unions 'liaisons' and condemns them because they 'can scarcely ensure mutual sincerity and fidelity in relationship between a man and a woman'.[5] The Orthodox churches strongly disapprove of cohabitation. The recent teaching document of the Church of England, *Marriage* (1999), affirms that '[s]exual intercourse, as an expression of faithful intimacy, properly belongs within marriage exclusively' (below, p.107).[6] It is in the sexuality reports of the Lutheran, Presbyterian, Episcopalian and other churches (discussed in detail in chapter 3) that some pastoral accommodation of living together is found, yet none of these reports ever became official documents of the churches that produced them. There is, then, near unanimity in the official teachings of the churches that living together before marriage is wrong.

4 Rabbi Michael Gold, *Does God Belong in the Bedroom?* (Philadelphia: Jewish Publication Society, 1992), pp.70–1.
5 *Catechism of the Catholic Church* (London: Geoffrey Chapman, 1994), 2350 (p.503), and 2391 (p.512), citing *Familiaris Consortio*, 80. Text in e.g., *Apostolic Exhortation: The Role of the Christian Family in the Modern World* (Boston: St. Paul Books and Media, 1993).
6 *Marriage: A teaching document from the House of Bishops of the Church of England* (London: Church House Publishing, 1999), p.8.

A cursory look at the guide to cohabitation in chapter 1 appears to confirm the wisdom of Christian traditions of thought about the matter. An approach to the problem through a patient attempt to understand it, prior to consulting the wealth of the Christian traditions of marriage, has not exactly yielded much by way of commendation. Cohabitation cannot generally be seen as anticipating marriage, since around half of cohabiting couples do not marry. Little research has been done on the emotional pain, misunderstanding, inconvenience, and financial and property chaos into which the ending of these informal unions often plunges former partners. There will have been little thought of endings when these partnerships began. The descriptions of some of the features, consequences and causes of cohabitation did not amount, on straightforward humanitarian grounds, to an endorsement of the practice. Let us now introduce an explicitly theological consideration, based loosely on the Christian doctrine of salvation. God wills that all people should be touched by and share in the salvation that is God's gift in Christ. How does cohabitation look from the perspective of the salvation God wills all people to enter?

The question is intended to register that, according to Christians, God loves us such that God wills always what is best for us. God wills our flourishing.[7] Our failure to flourish cannot be a matter of divine indifference. There are many metaphors which help to probe the mystery of salvation. 'Flourishing' is one of them. Salvation 'encompasses all that heals and enhances human life'. It is 'life in the maximal sense', that is 'real life, all that it is to be fully alive, all that makes for a life worth living'.[8] In both Greek and Latin, it can mean 'either being brought to safety from a position of peril, or a making whole and healthy, or both'.[9] Above all, it is the sharing in God's triune life, where Persons abound in the communion of love. There has been a restoration of fractured relationships between people and people, and between people and God, which has been brought about in the Person and work of Jesus Christ. God then, we might

[7] See part 2, 'Flourishings', of David Ford's *Self and Salvation: Being Transformed* (Cambridge: Cambridge University Press, 1999).
[8] Doctrine Commission of the Church of England, *The Mystery of Salvation* (London: Church House Publishing, 1995), pp.40, 45.
[9] Ibid., p.121.

say, wills that all our relationships, and especially intimate ones, should be models of the restoration and renewal of relationships which are found in Christ. In relation to the fullness of salvation God offers, do these new, temporary family units enable people to experience the healed and renewed relationships that God wills for everyone, whether married, single, in between, straight, lesbian or gay? There are few indications that, overall, cohabitation offers them.

This cautious judgment receives further verification as soon as the well-being of children is taken into account. The phrase 'retreat from children' (above, p.14, proposition 7) might refer not only to the desire to avoid having them, but also to the retreat from protect-ing their interests as they are born into or are otherwise propelled (nearly always against their wishes) into broken or non-traditional homes. On the broad demographic level, cohabitation is heavily implicated in the separation of parenthood from marriage. No-one is prepared to say that extra-marital parenthood represents an ad-vance of children's interests. At the level of individual family units, children are much more likely to lose out. There is more violence in non-traditional than in traditional households and children are much more likely to be victims of it. Cohabitors with children are much more likely to split than married couples, and children who are raised, however supportively, other than by their biological par-ents, fare worse on all counts and measurements yet devised.

An initial, negative, theological judgment against cohabitation receives further support from the longer-term explanations for its arrival (above, pp.28–36). If individualism, consumerism and sec-ularization help to fill out the background to cohabitation, then it is not difficult to trace parallels with theological analyses of how the world is. Individualism is easy to link with forms of human behaviour which neglect neighbour-love and mutuality and for that reason are regarded as 'sinful'. The boundaries between healthy self-love and aggressive self-assertion are difficult to draw. While Christians in wealthy countries have not been slow to avail them-selves of the benefits of the economic system under which they live, there is a strong and justified suspicion in Christianity that the lure of material goods can dangerously corrupt the will and the soul. If, then, a link were to be established between attitudes of cohabiting partners towards each other and towards cohabitation in general, and attitudes which were shaped by consumerism and participation in market forces, such a link would be seen as a vindication of Christian vigilance against the corrupting power of Mammon over all forms of human intimacy. But the proven association between lack of religious faith and cohabitation may weigh heaviest of all for many Christians (above, proposition 21). There is good reason to associate the lack, or loss, of religious commitment with cohabitation, at several levels. Secularization as a long-term trend may be thought to have weakened the institution of marriage alongside the weakening of the churches in most areas of the world. 'Cohabiting reduces religious attendance, while going directly to marriage increases the religious involvement of young people.'[10] Not only is there a unanimity in disapproval among conservative Christians, any attempt to question its basis or wisdom is likely to be seen as unwelcome, unnecessary and destructive.

There is also a strong apparent concurrence between theological and secular opinion over cohabitation. The National Marriage Project in the United States is a fine example of a non-religious body which, having considered all the appropriate research, felt able to offer advice to potential cohabitors, not on religious, but on broad health grounds, to avoid cohabitation. Specifically they are advised (i) to consider not living together before they marry (because it may be harmful as a 'try-out'); (ii) not to make a habit of cohabiting (because it is likely to diminish well-being and the likelihood of forging a lifelong partnership); (iii) to limit cohabitation to the shortest possible term (thereby allowing a shorter time for the 'low-commitment ethic' to take hold); and (iv) never to cohabit if children are involved (for a whole battery of reasons, not least the 'higher risk of sexual abuse and physical violence, including lethal violence').[11] Since there is much support among churches for these views, why disturb the emerging consensus, especially as it appears

[10] Arland Thornton, William G. Axinn and Daniel H. Hill, 'Reciprocal Effects of Religiosity, Cohabitation, and Marriage', *American Journal of Sociology* 98.3 (November 1992), 643.
[11] David Popenoe and Barbara Dafoe Whitehead, *Should We Live Together? What Young Adults Need to Know about Cohabitation before Marriage: A Comprehensive Review of Recent Research* (The National Marriage Project, New Jersey: Rutgers, The State University of New Jersey, 1999), p.2.

to amalgamate religious and non-religious thought in the name of human flourishing?

THE BASIC DISTINCTION—`PRENUPTIAL´ AND `NON-NUPTIAL´ COHABITATION

Perhaps enough has been done already to indicate that Christian faith and cohabitation are incompatible. Perhaps the book should finish at this point, saving paper and readers' time? A crucial distinction will indicate there is still much unfinished business to be undertaken. The distinction is between 'prenuptial' and 'non-nuptial' cohabitation. It was noted (above, p.36) that cohabitors who marry enjoy the same relationship quality as married people, and are no more likely to divorce than cohabitors who break up. Linda Waite insists: 'All cohabiting relationships are not equal; those on their way to the altar look and act like already-married couples in most ways, and those with no plans to marry look and act very different.'[12] These are the exemptions from the otherwise gloomy propositions of chapter 1, and this has only recently become understood. 'There is a growing understanding among researchers that different types and life-patterns of cohabitation must be distinguished clearly from each other. Cohabitation that is an immediate prelude to marriage, or prenuptial cohabitation ... is different from cohabitation that is an alternative to marriage.'[13] Around half of cohabiting couples eventually marry. Just as there is a qualitative difference between those who do and do not intend marriage, so there can be a corresponding difference in theological judgment about the type of relationship being shared. If a couple intends marriage, it is surely a failure of charity to subsume their evolving relationship under the rubric of fornication.

There is, however, a much stronger argument for treating engaged couples in a different category from those who are merely living together. For most of Christian history the entry into marriage

[12] Linda J. Waite, 'Cohabitation: A Communitarian Perspective', unpublished paper, University of Chicago, Jan. 1999, 13. And see The National Marriage Project, *The State of our Unions, 1999* (New Brunswick, N. J.: Rutgers, The State University of New Jersey, 1999), p.11.
[13] Popenoe and Whitehead, *Should We Live Together?*, p.10.

has been by betrothal and marriage has begun, not with a
wedding, but earlier with the *spousals* or betrothal ceremony. While
'engagement' exists as a pale echo of the more formal practice of
former times, the central importance of betrothal in the rite and
process of marriage has been almost entirely, and indeed in some
cases wilfully, lost. Gone with it is the sense of the entry into marriage as a process, liturgically marked and celebrated, and sometimes revocable in cases of serious difficulty or incompatibility.
Gone too is much of the social recognition of the 'in-between' status
of the couple which betrothal formalized. The loss of betrothal is
very much more serious than the disappearance into disuse of a
pointless rite. The sense of the betrothal period as a spiritually
rich and theologically educative phase of a couple's life has been
lost. The recovery of betrothal from its pulverulent obscurity is an
urgent task for theology with highly important outcomes.

Churches worldwide are unanimous in affirming the God-given
character of marriage, and almost overwhelming concern is frequently expressed at its neglect or marginalization. Unfortunately,
when it comes to commending and celebrating marriage, the
churches appear mainly *unaware* of a large slice of tradition which, if
reappropriated, would provide much assistance in coming to terms
with the present marital crisis. There is also little understanding
of the enormous changes to the institution of Christian marriage
which the churches have sanctioned since New Testament times.
The removal of betrothal is one of them! In the second millennium, marriage became a sacrament; it incorporated priests and
ministers; it absorbed companionate love; it has made exit from
itself permissible in one way or another; it is even beginning to
recognize the full equality of partners. The sense of change which
the recovery of the history of Christian marriage provides releases
into contemporary discussion both a fresh dynamism and a sense
of gratitude to God that further development of the basic form of
marriage is not only legitimate but necessary and inevitable for the
institution's health. I think the recovery of earlier (and, indeed, biblical) understandings of the entry into marriage is essential to the
future of marriage as a new millennium begins. While the churches
are vigorously and rightly commending Christian marriage in a
largely post-Christian era, their efforts are hampered because the

full spread of Christian teaching about the entry into marriage is neither appreciated nor communicated. Neither do marriage liturgies any longer celebrate the fullness of marriage as once they did.

All that is signalled at this stage is that there is a large hiatus in the teaching of the Western churches on the entry into marriage. This hiatus has become routinized to the extent that it is no longer even dimly envisaged as a hiatus: it is not envisaged at all. Yet there is an obvious point of connection between those millions of prenuptial cohabiting couples and part of the Christian tradition which has become overlooked. The celebration or solemnization of marriage in church is not, historically speaking, the beginning of marriage (despite what canon law says). It is the point within a couple's marriage beyond which there can be no turning back. While this point is certainly a high point in the couple's growing union, the assumption that the union *begins* at this point has gravely weakened the churches' efforts in commending marriage in the present late modern or postmodern period.

There are some signs that the hiatus in the theology of marriage is being recognized, but these are slender. A far-sighted review of cohabitation in a Church of England report in 1995 concluded: 'The wisest and most practical way forward therefore may be for Christians both to hold fast to the centrality of marriage and at the same time to accept that cohabitation is, for many people, a step along the way towards that fuller and more complete commitment'[14] (below, p.102). But this report was only grudgingly noted by the General Synod and never commended or adopted. Sadly the report did not draw (partly because of lack of space) on either the history or theology of marriage, and, as the quotation clearly shows, it regarded 'prenuptial cohabitation' as a state apart from, although leading to, marriage. The work of the liturgist and Anglican bishop Kenneth Stevenson on betrothal and marriage liturgies and the persistence of the betrothal rite, to this day, in the churches of the East, establishes beyond doubt the centrality of betrothal to marriage. Stevenson himself advocates the reinstatement of betrothal in Western traditions. He thinks that '[s]uch a

---

[14] *Something to Celebrate: Valuing Families in Church and Society* (Report of a Working Party of the Board for Social Responsibility, London: Church House Publishing, 1995), p.115.

format has the advantage of spreading the sacrament of marriage over a far wider terrain than it has occupied for many centuries. It could demarginalize our marital practice and rescue it from trivialization.'[15] Tucked away in one of his analyses of marriage rites is the explosive suggestion that the widespread practice of cohabitation is providing the right conditions for bringing back the betrothal rite. It is possible, he says, 'that when betrothal was used as an option in later medieval and Counter-Reformation France, it inaugurated (imperceptibly) what we would nowadays call "trial marriages"'. But speaking next of what the Church might do in order to bring about the liturgical renewal of marriage at the present time, he adds, 'What the Church does when faced with such a phenomenon could result in a revival of a kind of betrothal rite.'[16] It will be argued presently that there are also great theological, social and pastoral gains from the 'deep excavation' of betrothal that is beginning to be undertaken.

There have been other signals that the present theology and practice of marriage is due for re-investigation in the light of extensive premarital cohabitation. One pastoral theologian in the 1980s held that engaged couples living together before the ceremony were 'in one sense ... married already, but not ceremonially, not publicly'.[17] For this writer, misgivings about the practice gave way to a sense of positive opportunity. Marriage remained for cohabiting Christian couples 'one context for growth of people toward the fullness of personhood God wants through Jesus Christ'.[18] Living together before the ceremony was an opportunity for a couple to acquire skills they would need to support the marital sharing which was soon to be a pledged common life, while the responsibility of the Church remained to provide realistic marriage preparation for couples whatever their living arrangements. Another theologian addressing the problem of premarital sex held that the pre-wedding

---

[15] Kenneth Stevenson, 'The Marriage Service', in Michael Perham (ed.), *Liturgy for a New Century: Further Essays in Preparation for Revision of the Alternative Service Book* (London: SPCK/Alcuin Club, 1991), p.59.

[16] Kenneth W. Stevenson, *To Join Together: The Rite of Marriage* (New York: Pueblo Publishing Company, 1987), p.191.

[17] David A. Scott, 'Living Together: Education for Marriage?', *Journal of Pastoral Counselling* 18 (1983), 48.

[18] Ibid., 47.

phase of a couple's history was *educative*, enabling them to 'to divest the myths that surround each partner and prepare for the partnership of covenant'.[19] Both these writers (and many more) are best understood as signalling that the practice of marriage as it is found among the churches is unable to cope with the onslaught unleashed on it by cohabitation. They are right to signal this. Equally there remains in the tradition an alternative way of conceiving the beginning of marriage which *need not have* the consequence of affirming the educational appropriateness and goodness of premarital sex. For, in specific senses yet to be developed, a betrothed couple is already married.

The writings of the Roman Catholic couple Evelyn and James Whitehead have long advocated a processive understanding of beginning marriage. They say:

Understood as an institution, marriage has been a state that one either did or did not inhabit. Legally, a person is either married or not married; there is no in-between. The Christian Church, influenced by this legal orientation toward marriage, came to view matrimony as an either/or institution. Christian ambivalence about sexuality found a clear resolution in this institutional view of marriage. Outside this well-defined state no sexual sharing was permitted; once inside this institution, one could even demand one's sexual rights. There seemed no gradualness or development in this commitment; one was either in or out. The periods of engagement and of marriage preparation were anomalies; little effective attention and ministry could be given to these 'borderline' events.[20]

They believe that 'any notion of marriage as a passage with stages of deepening intimacy and commitment' is bound to meet with fierce resistance, even though it is verified by the lives of countless engaged couples. The reason is it 'threatens the conventional Christian understanding that all genital expression is forbidden before marriage'.[21] While they do not mention betrothal specifically, their account of the beginning of marriage confirms the starting point of the present inquiry. The hiatus they complain of, the

[19] Stuart D. McLean, 'The Covenant and Pre-Marital Sex', in Charles Amjad-Ali and W. Alvin Pitcher (eds.), *Liberation and Ethics: Essays in Religious Social Ethics in Honor of Gibson Winter* (Chicago: Center for the Scientific Study of Religion, 1985), p.111.
[20] Evelyn Eaton Whitehead and James D. Whitehead, *Marrying Well: Possibilities in Christian Marriage Today* (New York: Doubleday, 1981), p.98.
[21] Ibid., p.132.

inadequacy of legal definitions of the married state, the lack of recognition of growth into marriage, the evacuation of religious meaning from engagement and its displacement to the margins of ecclesial and social significance, are all addressed and satisfied by the recovery of the betrothal tradition.

There are also fairly obvious *pastoral* reasons why prenuptial cohabitation is able to be more positively regarded in the churches than at present. These have to do with the widening gap between puberty and marriage; the negative experience of marriage which leads some people to suspect and even fear it; and finally the possibility that Christians who break with tradition by living together before marriage do so because of a discernment which deserves respect and awaits integration into a developing theology of marriage. The belief that people should not have sexual intercourse before they marry remains the official teaching of the churches, even though it is now almost universally disregarded, and very widely disregarded (and unadmitted) among the churches' membership. At the same time the age of people at first marriage is rising steadily (to 29 for men, and 26.9 for women, in Britain in 1997). One very conservative church generously acknowledged the unprecedented gap between puberty and marriage. 'The 10-year span between sexual maturity and marriage creates a difficult situation in which to preserve chastity, a situation different from the biblical era.'[22] In fact the gap is likely to be fifteen years or more. What expectations of premarital chastity are actually expected by the churches of their young members during this period? Jack Dominian rightly dismisses the expectation of complete abstinence from sexual intercourse as unrealistic and unlikely to be re-established. This, he says, is 'a dilemma that Christianity has to face. Youthful marriages are bad for the stability of marriage. Just as those entering the priesthood are encouraged to be older and more mature, so marriages need the same maturity. Sexual energy, however, is at its peak in the late teens and early twenties.'[23]

[22] Church of the Brethren: Excerpt From 'Annual Conference Statement On Human Sexuality From A Christian Perspective' (1983), in J. Gordon Melton, *The Churches Speak on Family Life: Official Statements from Religious Bodies and Ecumenical Organizations* (Detroit: Gale Research Inc., 1991), p.63. The puberty gap of course is now nearer 20 than 10 years.

[23] Jack Dominian, 'Marriage Under Threat', in Charles E. Curran and Richard A. McCormick, SJ (eds.), *Readings in Moral Theology No.8: Dialogue About Catholic Social Teaching* (New York: Mahwah, 1993), p.446.

An Episcopal Church report (below, p.92) sensitively observes: 'Many in contemporary culture begin and establish a career at a later age than formerly. Marriage also tends to occur later. These two developments combined with convenient methods of birth control, the earlier onset of puberty and the absence of chaperonage, significantly lengthen the period when sexuality will be expressed outside of marriage.' The Church is warned to 'order its teachings and corporate life so as to guide and sustain persons whose lives are touched by these realities'.[24] Some churches are prepared to acknowledge that some cohabitors are actually on the run from marriage. For them, marriage is a problem for, and no solution to, their life plans. A Church of Scotland report recognized 'that the Church has, in much of its traditional utterance and practice, accepted and reinforced a patriarchal account of family structures which makes women subservient to men'. Problems within marriage, 'including widespread uneasiness and criticism about the institution as such, stem from the legacy of these past and present structural problems with the evolution of marriage'.[25]

Now it is quite possible that all unmarried and premarried cohabitors are simply morally wrong and Christian cohabitors unanimously and sadly unfaithful in their practice. That too is the official view. But it is also possible that when such a mis-match occurs between traditional, official teaching of the churches and the convictions and practices of many of their members, there is a deficiency in that teaching which requires the teaching to be re-examined. Such an admission need not lead to the conclusion that the tradition was wrong, nor that any departure from it represents faithless accommodation or capitulation to the secular or humanistic milieu. It might simply indicate that unexpected realignments can and should be made between tradition and culture, and that sometimes these are prompted not by faithless abandonment of tradition but faithful recovery of it. One such realignment is prompted by Gill's findings (above, p.34) that three quarters of 'non-literalist' Christians did *not* think it wrong to cohabit and that even among the literalists a change of attitude

---

[24] 'Episcopal Church: Excerpt from the "Report of the Task Force on Changing Patterns of Sexuality and Family Life" (1987)', in Melton (ed.), *Churches*, pp.72–3.
[25] Church of Scotland Panel on Doctrine, *Report on the Theology of Marriage* (1994), pp.273–4. See also *Something to Celebrate*, p.111.

is under way. Such Christians, whether right or wrong in their practice, require pastoral support. That they are uniformly wrong is a presumption which is likely to alienate them from their congregations. This book outlines a way of thinking about prenuptial cohabitation which, based in history and in the contemporary theology of marriage, is able to remove the alienation and replace it with a positive account of the presence of God in the growing together of couples prior to the wedding ceremony.

A study of marriage breakdown in Ireland in 1993 concluded that those couples who applied for annulment to a marriage tribunal and who had lived together before they married, experienced 'marital difficulties before the marriages took place', yet they married anyway. The author concludes that 'the view that premarital cohabitation serves to enhance the courtship process is not supported by the present study'.[26] Does this study provide evidence that prenuptial cohabitation is harmful? Not necessarily. Some of the harm done may be due to the residual resistance to cohabitation, probably stronger in Ireland than anywhere in Europe. However, the same author, complaining that couples 'drift into marriage' from engagement, whether or not they are living together, thinks that '[a] possible strategy to counteract this tendency is the introduction of a formal, public celebration of engagement'. Such an event, he continues, 'could take place at a set interval before the marriage ceremony and focus on emphasising the process involved in the couple building their relationship and discussing their future'.[27] So the study actually calls for the reintroduction of betrothal, except that that term, and the practice associated with it, has been lost to view. The solution required is, in fact, an old one.

The distinction picked up in the sociological analysis of cohabitation, between prenuptial and non-nuptial types, will be preserved in the rest of the book. The possibility of some kind of 'fit' between premodern and late modern prenuptial practices is exciting and will receive detailed treatment. From this point onwards, prenuptial cohabitation moves centre stage. That is why a little more needs to be said now about the tensions the idea brings with it. Prenuptial

[26] Albert McDonnell, *When Strangers Marry: A Study of Marriage Breakdown in Ireland* (Blackrock, Co Dublin: Columba Press, 1999), p.67.
[27] Ibid., pp.169–70.

cohabitation assumes an intention by both parties to proceed to unconditional promises, yet intentions change and are slowly and mysteriously formed. How strong does an intention have to be? Are not intentions unverifiable, whereas public vows (as in marriage) are obviously witnessed and recognized? If prenuptial cohabitation can be brought under the rubric of beginning marriage, then this form of living together can be transferred from the domain and terminology of sinfulness and fornication, to the domain of marital beginnings, and therefore of hope, preparation and mutual growth. While such transfer may seem implausible and undesirable, the book will unveil a hallowed tradition of entry into marriage which will make negative judgments about prenuptial cohabitation much less secure.

AFFIRMING `THE MARITAL NORM´

The thorniest question for the sexual teaching of the churches from the 1970s through to the new century has been whether heterosexual marriage remains the sole context for full sexual expression, or whether other norms for regulating it are available. While many denominational reports have recommended widening the scope of legitimate sexual experience beyond married people to include co-habitors, single people, and lesbian and gay people (usually as long as they are not clergy), the mood of denominational authorities, councils, synods and governing bodies has nearly always veered back to a traditional formulation of the traditional heterosexual teaching. The resilient conservative temper in these matters has given rise to charges that the traditional teaching is now affirmed for a different reason. It is a convenient way of dealing with a related issue, viz., proscribing homosexual sexual experience. The traditional teaching for heterosexual people, 'no sex outside marriage', now has new relevance in a related area. It conveniently proscribes all same-sex sexual activity because it does not and *cannot* take place within heterosexual marriage. As Marie Fortune angrily accuses the churches:

Although these studies have concluded that there is no real basis for the condemnation of homosexuality, denominational conventions have repeatedly rejected their own studies and continue to rationalize their condemnation of homosexuality based though it is on prejudice and homophobia. These denominations maintain the dictum of sexual activity only within heterosexual marriage as the *sine qua non* of sexual ethics and deny gays and lesbians the legal or ecclesiastical option of marriage, creating an intentional Catch-22 which they hope will discourage same-sex sexual activity. Then they explain that it is okay to *be* gay or lesbian (citing research evidence that some people are born this way) as long as gays and lesbians are not sexually active.[28]

While there is much justification for the anger expressed over the treatment lesbian and gay people have received in denominational quarrels over the last twenty years, there must be some doubt whether Fortune's position, and that of many lesbian and gay theologians, is the one that will finally achieve its goal, viz., justice for lesbian and gay people within the churches. Their solution is that marriage remains a stumbling block within the entire area of Christian sexual ethics. While a minority of Christians may prefer it, what matters most is an ethic of justice and right-relation for all Christians, whatever their orientation. Egalitarian marriage might just scrape in as an example of right-relation. It is hard to see how, on the various versions of this view, marriage will not be further marginalized and optionalized, and therefore further weakened.

So the question whether marriage is necessary for full sexual relations is now entangled in other debates, sometimes bitter and destructive, about lesbian and gay partnerships and the exclusion of these from recognition, ratification or blessing. However, there is good reason to think that a false dichotomy has been set up – between marriage and alternatives to marriage – which overlooks an alternative way of dealing with the issue. The alternative way seeks the recovery of the great flexibility of marriage both for remaining the sole context for full sexual expression while at the same time embracing several of the groups of people whose unions cause controversy in the churches. Marriage is broad enough and sufficiently well established within the Christian tradition to shoulder the burden – if indeed it is a burden – of accommodating the religious and spiritual needs of prenuptial cohabiting couples, and

[28] Marie Fortune, *Love Does No Harm: Sexual Ethics for the Rest of Us* (London: Continuum, 1998), pp.23–4.

of lesbian and gay couples who intend lifelong unions and to whom marriage is denied. The former group is accommodated by the recovery and practice of betrothal. Betrothal, as the evidence will conclusively show, is the beginning of marriage, not merely the prelude to it, as the marriage of Mary and Joseph indicates. Marriage is not so much extended to embrace the betrothed. Rather our modern and restricted understanding of marriage has needed to be extended in order for us to realize that the betrothed are *already* encompassed by it.

Much has been written about lesbian and gay unions (and as a straight, married man I remain diffident about adding more to what I have already written about this topic[29]). However, the solution to the global problem for the churches of prenuptial cohabitation also suggests itself in answer to the continuing global problem for the churches of lesbian and gay unions. In the one case the flexibility of Christian marriage is used to advantage by being extended, with ample historical precedent, to the betrothed. In the other case, the same flexibility is able to be used to embrace the lifelong covenants sealed between same-sex partners, which are not merely *analogous* to heterosexual marriages, but, as chapter 9 will show, can be incorporated into the ever-moving, dynamic, Christian marital tradition. Before both 'sides' in these disputes write off this solution, what might be called 'the extended marriage solution', they need to ask whether marriage in all its fullness, richness and historically proven potential for adaptability has even been registered, still less tried. The robustness of marriage as the solution to these acute problems is well brought out by Joseph Monti in his detailed and superb treatment of marriage in his *Arguing About Sex*. Since his treatment throws much light on the recent sexuality debates in the churches it is important to examine and respond to it now.

Monti's work deserves fuller treatment than can be given here, so attention will be drawn only to features which help to build the argument of the present work. He notes there is more required from fidelity to Christian tradition than the mere recapitulation of it. If faithful repetition only were required, there would be no need to construct a sexual ethic, only to hand one down hoping it

[29] Thatcher, *Marriage after Modernity*, chs.9 and 10.

would be received by grateful individuals and congregations. 'The denominations are forgetting how the obligation of fidelity must be dialectically engaged with the equal obligation of contemporaneity – how Christian life must make sense in its own time, must be truthful and right-making, and promote the good in whatever world we find ourselves.'[30] Since the Church is a trans-historical body, it spans more than one 'cosmological world',[31] and so cannot remain identified with any, and especially not with our, cosmological world. There is ample precedent for a positive estimation of non-Christian sexual morality in the tradition, as the historical appreciation and incorporation of Stoicism shows. Christian exegetes should beware the 'geneticist residue' within the tradition, i.e., the damaging assumption that however different and novel are our questions, 'we are called always to judge the present in terms of the past'. Modernity has emphasized the particularity, the historicist and relativizing character of all moral questions, so repetition of earlier answers prior to contemporary engagement with the questions is a Platonic evasion, a nostalgic abiding in mythical permanence.[32]

Christian self-understanding, continues Monti, is 'always framed by the *external* stories of others – those different from us who challenge our penchant to claim that we have, so to speak, given birth to ourselves'. It is claimed (following Richard Niebuhr) that the Church must tell two stories, which are dialectically related to each other, the internal and external stories. While the internal story is more obviously familiar and visible, it is often forgotten that this story cannot only be internal since it involved and involves critical conversation beyond the church with the wider society and culture. 'The cosmological and cultural environments of the Church are neither accidental nor only "external", but foundational for what is commonly termed [Christian] "self-identification".'[33] The dialectic has immediate relevance to the Church's theology of marriage. Just because Monti holds the *conservative* position that Christian sexual ethics are identified by marriage, the dialectic between the internal and external stories requires him, as an act of fidelity

---

[30] Joseph Monti, *Arguing About Sex: The Rhetoric of Christian Sexual Morality* (New York: State University of New York Press, 1995), p.5.
[31] Ibid., p.21.   [32] Ibid., pp.26–7, 34.   [33] Ibid., pp.45, 47, and see 86–9.

alike to tradition and to contemporaneity, to engage those who are marginalized by this aspect of the Church's internal story. So, 'if heterosexual marriage is to remain normatively identifying in the sexual morality of the Church, then it can only do so through critical conversations with those who are not married and not heterosexual. In this way heterosexual marriage as the Christian norm for sexual normality will find its identifying strengths as well as its limits – will have the "rest of its story" told.'[34]

When Christians live the reign of God, anticipating God's future and exercising fidelity to Jesus Christ through fidelity to tradition and contemporaneity, they stand in the tradition and they also move it along. A model is needed for understanding this process, and the one provided is that of an advancing spiral. Remembering, reading and affirming the Christian tradition is like belonging on

an advancing spiral that constantly loops back as a precondition of advancement. This looping remembrance sets a continuity with the past that is internally necessary for the shape of the spiral and its advancement toward an anticipated future. However, when set in motion, such advancing spirals create new and discontinuous centers and radii. With this continuing recombination of the dimensions of continuity and discontinuity that mark historical experience, an historical foundation and model for critical discourse and argument is attained.[35]

The looping spiral is an excellent model for getting to grips with the continuity and discontinuity involved in growing traditions of faith. If the Church's understanding of marriage is also conceptualized as an advancing spiral, the continuities and discontinuities with past understandings are given something of a visual image. The exercise of 'steadfast love', it is suggested, 'is constant, but there are many different ways of expressing it across cultures'.[36] Steadfast love gives the spiral of marriage its shape and direction: the different culturally conditioned ways of expressing it provide the 'discontinuous centers'.

The task of hermeneutics is set between continuity and discontinuity, between fidelity to tradition and to contemporaneity. It is said to consist of two 'moments' or processes, one familiar, the other less so. The first is exegesis – 'what appears at the literal threshold

---

[34] Ibid., p.48, and see p.90.   [35] Ibid., p.61.   [36] Ibid., p.65.

and surface of fact and language is only an invitation to the deeper recesses of human lives and historical ages that must be probed and sorted out'. Even the best of exegesis will enjoy only limited success. The second moment is 'reconstructive', since 'we will want to know how much sense, coherence, meaning, truth, and right can be brought forward in terms of our own age and its challenges to the renewal of Christian faith and life'.[37] Now despite apparent liberal and deconstructive tendencies in Monti's assessments of Christian arguments about sex, he identifies marriage as belonging firmly within the strand of continuity of the spiral model. If marriage were to be marginalized in favour of a different sexual ethic, then, he thinks, the very character of Christian identity would change. But marriage can only be fully affirmed when the Church has external conversations with the unmarried and those who are barred from marriage. To remove, or consciously to weaken, marriage would be to do disservice to the tradition, indeed to de-centre it irrevocably. Rather, a more cautious but positive option remains. Within the continuities provided by the traditional Christian ethic, sex only within marriage, other possibilities remain.

Of further assistance to us is Monti's careful distinction between *norms* and *rules* and his argument that norms become operational for the Christian community in metaphor, symbol and sacrament. What is it to affirm marriage as the only relationship wherein full sexual experience is permitted? There is an 'analytic mistake' here waiting to be made. Norms are distanced from the moral life; rules operate closer to home. A major flaw in the denominational conversations about sexuality is said to be the 'collapse' of 'the distinction and distance between norms and rules'. Norms disclose and generate 'values for orienting the moral life': rules are 'proximate', providing guidance 'in particular situations and circumstances'. When the two are confused 'critical moral reflection becomes confused and dysfunctional'. An example of the confusion is the norm 'Always tell the truth'. This is a norm so deep that it helps to form character and promote moral goodness. However, if the norm is appropriated 'as an absolute rule of literal speech – a regulation of literal behaviour in any and all circumstances, the norm

---

[37] Ibid., p.98.

becomes dysfunctional. Since preference for a literal understanding of moral norms has become 'a modern idolatry', the dysfunctional collapse of the difference between norms and rules is difficult to prevent. Marriage is a norm, but not a rule: 'In upholding the norm of heterosexual marriage as a rule of behaviour in any and all situations and circumstances, many denominations are making the same analytic mistake of confusing ethical norms and moral rules.'[38]

Finally, the relation between norm and rule allows flexibility in the way obedience to the rule through moral decisions gives expression to the regulating power of the norm. While marriage remains the norm of sexual behaviour for Christians, the embodiment of the values of the norm may, it turns out, reside in relationships other than marriage. This is a further important feature of Monti's argument (which I am about to disclaim). The 'orbit of the norm is flexible enough to sometimes change what has traditionally been included and excluded'. Using marriage once more as an example of a norm, he claims:

It is possible to argue that in principle, and on the basis of abiding and effective values of love and commitment revealed by the norm of marriage, that sexual intimacy may be morally responsible in certain material conditions and situations other than marriage and heterosexuality because the same values are being effected as goods. In these cases, the sacramental effectiveness of the Church's norm has been extended functionally to these states of affairs.[39]

Only fragments from the sustained discussion of the character of arguments about sex have been prised from Monti's long and difficult book. The distinction between norm and rule overlaps carefully nuanced descriptions of metaphor, symbol and sacrament, and ideals, images and models. I have confined the discussion to norms and rules to avoid complexity and unnecessary ramification, and to home in on a particular issue – the meaning of the Christian advocacy of marriage within sexual ethics. (Even the illuminating section on principles and their relation both to norms and rules[40] has been excluded.) I hope the fragments together serve to illustrate the possibility of a *via media* or much needed mediating path between Christians who see marriage as an inflexible rule and those who

[38] Ibid., pp.115–16, 160, 121.   [39] Ibid., p.154.   [40] Ibid., pp.132–9.

reject it as a norm *and* as a rule. There remains the question (which recurs in chapter 9) whether in sanctioning relationships other than marriage, the norm of marriage is compromised. However this question may be answered, the answer is *emphatically not essential* to my own developing argument about prenuptial cohabitation. The Christian community will not be asked to sanction cohabitation via the route of accepting the transfer from marriage to cohabitation of certain marital values which, because they may appear in some form in marriage-like relationships, allow such relationships to be seen as quasi-marriages. These transfers run the risk of appearing to sanction alternatives to marriage. I have no need of this argument because there is an altogether better, stronger (and more traditional) one. Marriage belongs to premarital cohabitors already because, by their intention to marry, they have already embarked on the process that leads to the solemnization of the matrimony already begun. Although it has yet to be shown, this is sound, although forgotten, Christian teaching.

It is not expected that the marital norm will be popular among the different groups and theologies to be found in the churches. It will be disliked by conservatives because, while it appears disarmingly and even cunningly traditional, the difference between a norm and a rule prevents the exclusionary use of marriage that is customary among conservatives and denominational authorities. Theological liberals will dislike it because it will appear to dissipate what fragile 'progress' has been made in establishing Christian sexual ethics on a different basis. Lesbian and gay people may dislike it most of all, because the churches have never extended marriage to them: indeed at the present moment marriage is being actively used against them (as Marie Fortune has pointed out). To all of them I can only plead the fullness of marriage, rather than the partial versions which have shaped most of the recent quarrels. I have not attempted to explain here what I mean by the 'fullness' of marriage. My recent *Marriage after Modernity* is devoted to that task, and another work in the New Studies in Christian Ethics series, Lisa Sowle Cahill's *Sex, Gender and Christian Ethics*,[41] admirably

[41] Lisa Sowle Cahill, *Sex, Gender and Christian Ethics* (Cambridge: Cambridge University Press, 1996), esp. ch. 6.

explores the theological meanings of marriage in relation to sexuality, gender and Christian thought.

The previous section made a basic distinction (between prenuptial and non-nuptial cohabitation) which will become foundational for the argument of the book. The present section established a second foundation, the marital norm. A third foundation is 'the betrothal solution'.

THE `BETROTHAL SOLUTION´

Churches have wavered over whether full sexual expression is to be confined to marriage. The solution just suggested is that sexual intercourse should be thus confined to marriage as a *norm*, and that premarital cohabitation is capable of being 'covered' by marriage as either a norm or a rule. Marriage is sufficiently encompassing to cover premarital cohabitation because marriage begins not with a wedding but with betrothal.[42] This will be called 'the betrothal solution' and its relation to marriage developed in the present section. An advantage of this solution is that fidelity to the traditional teaching is retained, while fidelity to contemporaneity demands that all cohabitors, whatever their status vis-à-vis marriage, are taken with great seriousness. Some churches, acting from good pastoral intentions towards sexually active but unmarried heterosexual members, have played with a different solution which involves alternative norms. The present section will suggest that the 'betrothal solution' offers a better prospect of legitimizing theologically the full acceptance by congregations of at least some of those who are having sex 'before' marriage. Since this solution has not generally been advocated, it will shortly be tested (in chapter 3) against some important church documents for preliminary confirmation.

One author whose writings have edged towards the betrothal solution during the last four decades is the contemporary Roman Catholic psychiatrist, Jack Dominian. What appears in

---

[42] This is a solution that might have aided the Australian Anglican writer, Muriel Porter, in her fine study, *Sex, Marriage and the Church: Patterns of Change* (North Blackburn, Victoria: Dove, 1996). She, unusually, is well aware of the church's forgotten betrothal practice (e.g., pp.9, 123), yet in her proposals for change, she does not argue for its reinstatement, nor for the adoption of marriage as a norm.

an undeveloped and embryonic way in his writings will be shown
to deserve a full systematic explication and defence. As early as
1967 Dominian was castigating the Catholic Church for worrying
too much about premarital chastity and too little about the many
other factors crucial to making marriages work.[43] A little later he
was nudging Christians to ask 'whether it is permissible to lump all
premarital sexual intercourse together and condemn it on a single principle of lowered moral standards reflecting a hedonism of
the age'. This approach he dismissed as 'naïve and irrelevant'.[44]
In 1985 couples living together before marriage were said, more
guardedly, to be in a state of 'compromise', enjoying intimacy while
postponing commitment.[45] In 1989 he proposed that the morality
of sexual intercourse should be assessed by 'four criteria of love,
procreation, pleasure, relief of tension'. Sexual intercourse, he has
consistently held, 'is an act of love in which the human and the
divine meet and it is the central act of prayer in that couple's life'.[46]
However, in this analysis he applied the criteria to *cohabitors* as well
as to the married.

Dominian admitted that '[i]n so far as such a couple have not undertaken a formal ceremony of marriage, they are in fact formally
fornicating'. However, on the basis of the criteria he set out, he was
willing to acknowledge that 'they are in fact in a state of committed love which is marriage'.[47] Anticipating an adverse reaction he
argued:

The concept that they are married without going through a formal ceremony is not a leap of the imagination or an externalizing liberal handout.
There is a deep-seated theological tradition that the essence of marriage
is to be found in the commitment and donation of a man and a woman
of their person to each other in a committed relationship which is consummated by intercourse.

---

[43] Jack Dominian, *Christian Marriage: The Challenge of Change* (London: Darton, Longman and
   Todd, 1967).
[44] Jack Dominian, *The Church and the Sexual Revolution* (London: Darton, Longman and Todd,
   1971), p.31: and see also Jack Dominian, *Sexual Integrity: The Answers to AIDS* (London:
   Darton, Longman and Todd, 1987), pp.72–4.
[45] Jack Dominian, *The Capacity to Love* (London: Darton, Longman and Todd, 1985), p.84.
[46] Jack Dominian, 'Masturbation and Premarital Sexual Intercourse', in Jack Dominian and
   Hugh Montefiore, *God, Sex and Love* (London and Philadelphia: SCM Press and Trinity
   International, 1989), pp.29, 30.
[47] Ibid., p.34.

Marriage is not conferred by a priest, but by the couple themselves. Drawing on the ample historical precedent of valid clandestine marriages, he argues that the 'public dimension of the wedding ceremony' remains strongly desirable because it safeguards the commitment the couple make to each other. However, a ceremony was not necessary for the validity of marriage for most of Christian history, and a clear inference may be made from the uncertain status of the informal but valid unions of the past, to the uncertain status of informal unions today.[48]

Dominian returns in a later article to the subject of 'couples committed to each other in love, with marriage as their object'.[49] In the language used in the present book, they are prenuptial cohabitors. This time he identifies the state of living together with the intention to marry as 'a state of betrothal'. While betrothal is not further defined, the ground for affirming these couples as betrothed is again that the ministration of the church is unnecessary for the validity of the marriage. 'It is they who make the marriage, not the Church; their commitment to one another is the marriage. The wedding is the public witnessing by the Church and society of that mutual commitment which they have made to one another.'[50] It is tentatively suggested that the Song of Songs provides biblical precedent for the celebration of sexual love prior to formal marriage. Some scholars believe the Song 'is a celebration of physical and sensuous communion between what is most likely to be a betrothed couple'. Finally, the practice of sexual intercourse in the betrothal period is sanctioned by precedent. 'The obligation to marry before a priest and witnesses in church, and *to avoid all premarital sex before*, is a late phenomenon after the Council of Trent. Sex following betrothal and before marriage, as a way of expressing commitment to each other, has a long history.'[51]

Dominian is one of the few writers to advance the betrothal solution to the theological problem of unmarried cohabitation, and to do so as an informed practising Christian. His wisdom as an eminent Christian psychiatrist and marital therapist adds weight to the solution, which will be developed historically and systematically in the present work. I applaud this solution but foresee

[48] Ibid., pp.34–5.   [49] Dominian, 'Marriage Under Threat', p.447.
[50] Ibid., pp.447–8.   [51] Ibid., p.448 (emphasis added).

several difficulties with it as it stands. First, the distinction between prenuptial and non-nuptial cohabitation would have been useful, but its significance was not generally understood in the 1970s and 1980s. (In his most recent work he uses the distinction, and declares that while prenuptial cohabitation is 'not the fully comprehended view of marriage and therefore in some sense incomplete', it is also 'moral'.[52]) Since criteria exist for judging the moral goodness of sexual intercourse without recourse to the institution of marriage, what is the link between these criteria and marriage? Is the love expressed by sexual intercourse before the ceremony theologically acceptable because it can pass the criteria which may be theologically derived from marriage, or is it acceptable because it is deemed to *be* marriage, already begun with betrothal?

Dominian holds that 'the essence of marriage is to be found in the commitment and donation of a man and a woman of their person to each other in a committed relationship which is consummated by intercourse'. This allows him to deny that the essence of marriage is formal consent, or *only* formal consent, and if the essence of marriage is not consent, then presumably a formal ceremony is not required for it to be expressed or witnessed. I think Dominian is right (and brave) to claim this, but if the claim can stand, it will first need to be shown that the medieval synthesis that 'consent *makes* the marriage' (and the consummation of it achieved by sexual intercourse *ratifies* it), is defective. Since practically all versions of Protestantism and Roman Catholicism after (as well as before) the Council of Trent rely on the consent theory, and canon law insists on it, it will be necessary to show that the common reasons for doing so were inadequate (they *are* inadequate – below, p.227.) But the role of consent in the present context is different. The designation of consent as 'commitment', coupled with 'donation', appears to be to allow the legitimacy of private or informal marriage, however undesirable, where *formal* consent is not essential to the continuing commitment which is the marriage. While this position brings irregular premarital unions within the ambit of marriage, it may be vulnerable to the criticism that it does so by bestowing the status

---

[52] Jack Dominian, *Let's Make Love: the meaning of sexual intercourse* (London: Darton, Longman and Todd, 2001), p.108.

of marriage honorarily upon them. Betrothal historically is a real beginning of marriage, and should be differentiated from private or informal marriage.

A difference between informal marriage and betrothal is that the former required two witnesses to hear the couple exchange vows in the present tense for its validity, while the latter could be formal, semi-formal or informal. Since parents and family were generally involved in betrothal, and agreements were made between the couple and their families regarding the marital home, property, dowry, etc., betrothal is better regarded as a public act, whether or not accompanied by a ceremony. It is important not to see prenuptial cohabiting couples as *de facto* betrothed. This is to overstate the case. Even if couples who are 'engaged' believe that engagement makes love-making morally permissible, they are unlikely to understand engagement as a real beginning of marriage (since almost no-one believes this any more). The betrothal solution enables Christians who are prepared to grasp it to relate to cohabiting couples in a very different way. Indeed once the historical importance of betrothal is grasped, the current absence of it is likely to be seen as a weakness in the churches' ministry to, and support for, couples contemplating marriage.

Many betrothed couples had sex before their nuptial ceremony, as Dominian knows. Evidence from the church courts shows the church disapproved of it, and spasmodically attempted to prevent it. However, many betrothed couples (we may surmise) did not have sex until the marriage ceremonies were completed. It should not be assumed that the precedent for having sex in the betrothal period automatically justifies present liberties, although past and present practices can be helpfully compared. One factor which prevailed in premodern and early modern betrothed unions, and which can *not* be assumed today, is the insistence (which communities were generally able to enforce) that, should pregnancy result, the couple proceed to the nuptial stage of their union. A further problem arises in relation to contemporary practice: how do couples know when they are 'committed to each other in love', i.e., when they reach the justifying moment of moving in together and expressing their commitment in sexual intercourse? If betrothal, or what counts as betrothal, is the 'marker' for the point of beginning marriage, presumably the marker must have a public character, be verifiable and witnessed by others?

The betrothal solution will be developed in the remaining chapters. It is the third foundational principle of the present work, alongside the basic distinction (above, p.45) and the marital norm (above, p.53). The betrothal solution is forged in the heat of the convergence between, as Monti might put it, the internal story of marriage and the external story of those who are being marginalized by it. It will be offered as a major contribution to the solution to the problem of the theological and spiritual status within the churches of premarital cohabitors, which has the potential to restore them unambiguously into the communal life of the church, and to transform the ministry the church provides for them in the form of marriage preparation. The term is of foremost importance in contributing to an overdue re-think of the processes of beginning and entering marriage. The betrothal solution does not depend on there being actual betrothals or on the introduction of earlier or new betrothal rites (although these will be advocated in due course). The term invites comparisons between premodern and postmodern customs of entering marriage which will be theologically fruitful. It stands as a possible major contribution to the never-completed revision of the Christian theology of marriage, with particular relevance for couples living together who wrongly suppose they have placed themselves beyond the limits of Christian teaching and divine grace.

LIVING TOGETHER AND LIBERATION

There is much to be said for a liberationist perspective on cohabitation which links the non-nuptial version of it to social and structural sin. No attempt is made explicitly to adopt Third World methodologies in the resolution of First World problems:[53] indeed since grinding poverty remains the experience of most of the practitioners of Third World liberation theologies, an apology may be due for what appears as a trivialization of suffering. What is meant by

[53] For creditable attempts to do this see e.g., John Vincent, 'Liberation Theology in Britain, 1970–1995', in C. Rowland and J. Vincent, *Liberation Theology UK (British Liberation Theology 1)* (Sheffield: The Urban Theology Unit, 1995), pp.15–40.

a liberationist perspective is that liberation theologies deploy a particular terminology in relating the gospel to oppressive social and political contexts, and few if any First World theologians have yet to notice that the method and vocabulary of liberation has peculiar explanatory power in relation to the breaking-up of families and the shared misery of failing alternative lifestyles. How?

These theologies arise from the experience of *oppression*. There are *victims*, whose plight is caused by *injustice* or *structural sin*. Victims are powerless, and generally voiceless. This injustice is capable of passing itself off as natural, normal and unchangeable. However, Jesus Christ comes to reverse routinized injustice. He announces *good news* to the poor (Luke 4:18), fills the hungry with good things and sends the rich away empty (Luke 1:53). With the arrival of the reign of God *liberation* from oppression and the simultaneous *transformation* of societies and individuals begins. The church, the liberated community, lives a *praxis* or shared programme of action which strives to implement God-given liberation practically. It takes little imagination to see how the sufferings of children in First World countries, affected adversely and innocently by the actions of their biological parents, especially fathers in temporary liaisons, together with the required transformations of their lives, are able to be brought sharply into focus by means of the learned vocabulary of liberation. While such suffering may not begin to rival in intensity and extensity the suffering of children caused by poverty throughout the world, suffering it remains, and a way of liberation is available.

We have already seen (above, p.13, proposition 7) that male co-habitors are much less committed to their children than married men; that non-nuptial cohabitation is a supplier of single-parent families (above, pp.20–2, propositions 12 and 13); and that children of cohabiting but unmarried parents are much more likely to be exposed to poverty, violence and abuse (above, pp.22–3, propositions 14 and 15). There is a detailed catalogue of neglect and suffering caused to children by parents, especially fathers, abandoning them. Four children out of every ten in the United States currently sleep in a home other than that of their biological father,[54] and more

---

[54] Morehouse Research Institute and Institute for American Values, *Turning the Corner on Father Absence in Black America* (Atlanta and New York, 1999), p.6.

than half of all children in that country will spend a significant portion of their childhoods living apart from their fathers.[55] It is not suggested that non-nuptial cohabitation is responsible for all child suffering, neither is it suggested that children of married parents all escape suffering, or that children of single parents will fail to thrive. Evidence-based probabilities cause us to draw attention to pointless unnecessary suffering which puts children in non-traditional families at greater risk.

These probabilities justify, and directly trigger, what I have called elsewhere 'a theology of liberation for children',[56] although, as we shall see, oppression is by no means confined to them. Clearly children count as victims if they are brought into the world unwanted, or are abandoned by their natural fathers, or are incorporated, nearly always against their wishes, into new or step-families, or are brought up within domestic arrangements which are known to be less successful or to offer less security. They are powerless to prevent this, and generally voiceless. When they speak, it is generally of fear, guilt, loss, grief, anger, even 'life in exile'.[57] Oppression is no less real if its agents are members of the child's own family instead of impersonal political or economic forces. The injustice suffered is structural to the extent that disrupted childhood is now passed off to children themselves in soap operas, comedies and even cartoons as a natural, indeed normal, sequence of events, while the power of the social expectations both of cohabitation before marriage and divorce after it make both occurrences more likely.

The gospel reverses these fatalistic expectations in the name of a higher power, that of divine love. One form of God's liberation from injustice comes from parents whose commitments to each other and to their children remain firm. These commitments may be a conscious expression of divine love, mirroring God's commitment to humanity in Christ. This is liberative *praxis* indeed. The *praxis* of the community of faith will include commitments to

---

55 David Blankenhorn, *Fatherless America: Confronting Our Most Urgent Social Problem* (New York: Basic Books, 1995), pp.1, 18–19.

56 Thatcher, *Marriage after Modernity*, pp.142–70.

57 This phrase was used in the testimony of Elizabeth Marquardt who describes her experience of growing up after her parents divorced and each of them subsequently married twice more. See her *The Moral and Spiritual Experience of Children of Divorce* (University of Chicago Divinity School: Religion, Culture and Family Project, 1999).

their children and to practical assistance to parents and children in need because of disturbance or break-up. The social and personal transformations which the gospel can yet bring about include the complete reframing of heterosexual sexual relationships in such a way that the arrival of children is received as a joy and a gift, and contraception for the betrothed a means of postponing rather than preventing them.

It is possible to develop the liberation perspective upon living together, and apply it directly to the experience of potential co-habitors, especially women, with or without children. Non-nuptial cohabitation turns out to be a 'remarkably poor bargain' for mothers as well as their children.[58] 'The separateness of cohabitors' lives also reduces their usefulness as a source of support during difficult times', and this 'lack of sharing ... disadvantages the women and their children in these families relative to the men, because women typically earn less than men and this is especially true for mothers'.[59] Cohabitors seeking freedom from the constraints and gendered expectations of formal marriage in informal unions will not find the freedom equitably dispersed. Men are the principal beneficiaries, leading Linda Waite to adjudge that '[t]he increasing trend toward consensual partnering in the West, seen by many as an emancipation from rigid concepts of marriage, may represent *a new enslavement* rather than freedom for women'.[60]

Secular advice to women not to cohabit has already been noted. Religious advice concurs, and the liberationist perspective adds to the advice critical sharpness. Some liberationist perspectives assume the presence of ideology (a set of beliefs which misrepresent the interests of many, perhaps a majority, of people) and the existence of false consciousness (people being duped into accepting as true, false beliefs which misrepresent their interests). It is easy to make the case that there exists both an ideology that misleadingly offers non-nuptial cohabitation as a liberation from the obligations and constraints of patriarchal marriage, and that women who enter it are in a state of false consciousness that misrepresents their interests. An example of the huge influence of such an ideology is

---

[58] Maggie Gallagher, *The Age of Unwed Mothers: Is Teen Pregnancy the Problem?* (New York: Institute for American Values, 1999), p.28.
[59] Waite, 'Cohabitation', 9–10.   [60] Ibid., 26 (emphasis added).

revealed by a research report on twenty undergraduate textbooks on marriage and the family in use in the USA in 1997. The report concluded the books 'convey a determinedly pessimist view of marriage', omitting many of its advantages, downplaying its benefits, and repeatedly suggesting that marriage is 'more a problem than a solution'. Almost all of the books were found to 'shortchange children, devoting far more pages to adult problems and adult relationships than to issues concerning child well-being'. Finally, the books were 'typically riddled with glaring errors, distortions of research, omissions of important data, and misattributions of scholarship'.[61] This finding is easily capable of being read and understood as evidence of a baleful ideology which operates against lifelong marriage.

The discovery that informal sexual arrangements should operate against the interests of women should surprise no-one. There are plenty of precedents in recent history. Hundreds of women in Victorian Britain cohabited with their prospective husbands on the basis of the promise of future marriage which, upon pregnancy, was withdrawn, generally leaving women desperate, stigmatized, disowned and financially ruined.[62] Men had no compunction against lying about their marital intentions, or, when sued for breach of promise, complaining, in a classic case of the double standard, that 'once the plaintiff agreed to sleep with the defendant, she had failed the crucial character test by proving herself unchaste'.[63] The increasing availability of condoms in the early twentieth century, together with strident campaigning for their social acceptability, was not welcomed by all the early feminists. Some of these women believed that the weakening of the fear of pregnancy which condoms began to bring about, removed from women the principal reason for refusing unwelcome sexual advances from men, within marriage and without. The solution they advocated was not contracepted sexual intercourse but the complete reformation of sexual

---

[61] Norval Glenn, *Closed Hearts, Closed Minds: The Textbook Story of Marriage* (New York: Institute for American Values, 1995), p.3.

[62] Ginger Suzanne Frost, 'Promises Broken: Breach of Promise of Marriage in England and Wales, 1753–1970', PhD dissertation, Rice University (1991), especially pp.230–3.

[63] Ibid., p.230.

relations between men and women.[64] An identical argument is equally valid against the current panoply of contraceptives including Norplant and the so-called 'morning after' pill. Cohabitation and contracepted extra-marital sex have already shown themselves to involve significant risks for women. Their bodies are made yet more readily available to men, while they themselves and possibly their children carry the consequences. This is surely a clear case of false consciousness which must be countermanded by patient truth-telling regarding the facts and making attractive the genuinely liberating alternative of the Christian marital ethic.

The twin motifs of salvation (above, p.42) and liberation will be retained in the foreground of the book. Christians must never lose sight of the fact that they are loved with an everlasting love. Our health and well-being is desired not just for our own sakes but for God's sake. False consciousness and structural sin can damage us. Liberation from these perils is open to us by God's grace. While not a foundation principle for this study like those discussed in the present chapter, the healing influence of Christian liberation is never far away.

SETTING OUT THE ARGUMENTS

It is now time to make clear the rest of the agenda for the book. The argument rests on what the elementary logic textbooks call affirming the antecedent or *modus ponens*. Such arguments work with conditionals. They begin with 'If ...' (the antecedent) and end with 'then ...' (the consequent). What makes a conditional argument formally *valid* is affirming the antecedent. Arguments which affirm the antecedent have the form, If *x*, then *y*: *x*: therefore *y*. A valid argument can still be useless if its premisses are not true. But validity is at least a start. The argument of the rest of the book can be seen as an attempt to affirm a series of antecedents in a simple way.

[64] See Sheila Jeffreys, *The Spinster and Her Enemies: Feminism and Sexuality 1880–1930* (London and New York: Pandora, 1987), chs. 1 and 2. I explore the strange commonality between radical feminist and papal arguments against contraception in my 'A Strange Convergence? Popes and Feminists on Contraception', in Lisa Isherwood (ed.), *The Good News of the Body: Sexual Theology and Feminism* (Sheffield: Sheffield Academic Press, 2000), pp.136–48.

Suppose someone believes (as this author does) that the loss of betrothal is an impediment to the churches' understanding and practice of marriage; that the recovery and reinstatement of betrothal would make an immense difference to the preparation for, and celebration of, marriage in the churches; and that it would strengthen the churches' commendation of marriage at a time when it is increasingly trivialized and disregarded. It then becomes open to argue, *If* betrothal can be reinstated, *then* certain consequences follow. Anyone arguing this way will try to affirm the antecedent, to show that betrothal can be reinstated. Then, if the premises of the argument are true, the argument is sound and worthy of respect. Several such arguments of this kind will be advanced, which have pastoral, theological and liturgical consequences. In short, they can be stated like this:

If betrothal can be reclaimed, *then* there is a new basis for reaching out to some of the many thousands of cohabiting couples *within* the churches who appear to be living in open defiance of the churches' teaching.

If betrothal can be reclaimed, *then* marriage preparation in the churches has a new basis.

If betrothal can be reclaimed, *then* much controversy in the denominations about cohabitation and sex before marriage can be defused.

If betrothal can be reclaimed, *then* marriage liturgies can better express the meaning of marriage as a rite of passage.

If betrothal can be reclaimed, *then* the theology of marriage as a process of growth towards God and one another can be better promoted.

These skeletal arguments have considerable consequences. For example, the pastoral ministry to young people living together before marriage would be transformed by betrothal. The charge of fornication, frequently levelled against such persons, would be seen to be based on poor theology. The destructive consequences of negative judgments on these fledgling unions, loss of membership and frequently of faith, would be avoided. Couples could be challenged early about their intentions, and if they are marital, a simple rite, celebrated in the home or at church, could be offered them, and clear counsel could be offered if they are not. Pastoral interventions would be free from clerical embarrassment, or feigned ignorance of the living arrangements (remember Rabbi Gold), or the insistence on restoration through repentance or penance, and sometimes that the new domestic unit be broken up before the marriage ceremony.[65] Severity of judgment would be retained (for good reason) for non-nuptial cohabitors, and even in these cases the entry into marriage through betrothal would assist the positive and tactful exposition of the churches' teaching.

There could be 'a catechumenate for marriage' (below, p.237), that is, the preparation for marriage might be compared formally, not just analogically, with the process of teaching and learning of adults who have come to faith in Christ and are preparing for baptism. As faith precedes and anticipates baptism, so the *spousals* or betrothal ceremony precedes the *nuptials* or solemnization of marriage. At this point the marriage is brought before God for blessing. That blessing will be invaluable for the marriage since at the same point the couple's promises to each other become unbreakable. Evidence will be brought forward to show that after betrothal fell into disuse, theologians in the Western churches read the tradition as if it had never existed, thereby (sometimes deliberately) concealing it from view. That remains the position in Protestant and Catholic churches. Any conversation about betrothal, unless it is strictly historical and academic, generally meets with incomprehension.

The recovery of betrothal will be assisted by the many betrothal liturgies which remain, and which in the East are used to this day. Kenneth Stevenson sets some of these out in *To Join Together: The Rite of Marriage*. A rite in use in an English parish church forms an appendix to this book. There is simply no excuse for ignorance about the persistence of a betrothal liturgy through the Christian tradition, and about its origin in Jewish, Greek and Roman practices (like most of the marriage ceremony) (below, chapter 5). In Orthodox churches the betrothal liturgy survives intact, but as part of the single occasion which is the marriage (below, p.159). Stevenson suggests that a contemporary betrothal rite might be

---

[65] For the alarming variety of responses to cohabitation within the churches, see Jeffery J. VanGoethem, 'Pastoral Options With Cohabiting Couples', PhD thesis, Dallas Theological Seminary (1998).

located within the mass, as part of the common worship of the local congregation.[66] Another contemporary writer suggests that in churches where banns are called, the importance of banns 'could be extended by making the first occasion of the calling of Banns a fuller Betrothal ceremony in which the couple formally announce their intent and their families and the congregation, as representative of society at large, also acknowledge their role and responsibilities'[67] (see Appendix).

Several writers claim that marriage is a rite of passage. If a rite of passage is to function successfully in the group whose rite it is, it will need to be capable of separating the recipients from the rest of the group and marking their transitional status before reincorporating them into the group once more (below, p.239). The truncated rite of marriage in use in most Western churches is, on this view, *incapable* of performing this all-important function. Influenced by medieval theology and canon law the marriage rite has come to emphasize the exchange of consent as the main meaning of marriage, with the possible consequence that the rest of the rite is seen as little more than an appropriate embellishment for the all-important central event of verbal exchange in the presence of witnesses. The 'deep structures' of the marital passage rite are not allowed to come to the surface in these liturgies.[68] The revision of the liturgies would thereby display the deeper truths and meanings of marriage. They would potentially restore to marriage the sense of growth and journey and greatly expedite the churches' proclamation and commendation.

But the antecedents must first be affirmed before any of these conclusions can follow. In other words, betrothal must first be reclaimed. This is how it will be done. Armed with the basic distinction, the marital norm and the betrothal solution, chapter 3 will show how the damaging arguments about cohabitation and sexual intercourse in relation to marriage, conducted among the denominations in the last twenty-five years, might have been defused if the principles enunciated in this chapter, together with a strong sense

---

[66] Stevenson, *To Join Together*, p.212.

[67] A.R. Harcus, 'The Case for Betrothal', in Adrian Thatcher (ed.), *Celebrating Christian Marriage* (Edinburgh: T&T Clark, 2002).

[68] Stevenson, *To Join Together*, p.8.

of the tradition of betrothal, had been applied. The usefulness of the principles, in particular the betrothal solution, to ongoing arguments about sex, will be demonstrated, bringing chapter 3 and part 1 to an end.

Part 2 is the reclamation of betrothal. Chapter 4 begins with the betrothal of Mary and Joseph and spreads to the betrothal and marriage practices of the Jews, Greeks and Romans contemporary with Jesus. The marital theology of the New Testament, especially its bridal mysticism, will be shown to assume the practice of betrothal. Its incorporation in the traditions of East and West will be noted, and the detailed treatment it receives in the writings of Thomas Aquinas will be observed and carried forward to contemporary discussions of it. Chapter 5 concentrates on liturgy and law. Some betrothal rites and practices of the churches will be noted and the theological understanding expressed by them unravelled. The huge influence of canon law in marital practice in the late medieval and early modern periods will be described in order to indicate its continuing influence and to suggest how that influence might be channelled today. Chapter 6 asks, given the significance of betrothal in earlier periods, what happened to it? Reasons for its demise in Catholicism and Protestantism are given, together with an assessment of the impact of its absence on the impoverishment of marriage. The theology of marriage, it will be shown, unfolds in modernity as if betrothal had never been.

Part 3, 'Extending the marital norm', returns to the present period. Chapter 7 notes how marriage has been influentially regarded as a path of holiness. It shows how the betrothal solution would make the path an easier one to follow. Alternative, but traditional, interpretations of both the exchange of consent (second section), and the meaning of consummation (third section) are offered. The theological material excavated in part 2 makes this a particularly rewarding and exciting task. Chapter 8 compares Roman Catholic and Protestant proposals for 'a catechumenate for marriage', and argues that the hardening of Tridentine orthodoxy, even since Vatican II, vitiates this progressive move. Chapter 9 begins (albeit very briefly) to examine what happens when the marital norm is extended beyond prenuptial couples to other groups of people who are not married but who are sexually active.

CHAPTER 3

Testing the betrothal solution

The term 'marital norm' conveys the conviction that, within the Christian faith, marriage is the norm (but not necessarily the rule) for full sexual experience: the term 'betrothal solution' conveys the conviction that, if betrothal were retrieved, it would provide the comprehensive solution to the problem of prenuptial cohabitation. The aim of this chapter is to show that the betrothal solution fills a hiatus in Christian sexual ethics that is unlikely to be met in any other way. Before the work of retrieving betrothal is carried out in part 2, the utility of both norm and solution will be tested against some of the intense debates over sexuality in the churches over the last twenty-five years. A minor aim is to achieve familiarity with some of the sexuality reports in order to prepare for a fuller, contemporary theology of betrothal in chapters 7 and 8. Some of the sexuality reports are ambivalent about retaining marriage as the norm, and while some mention betrothal, none adopts the betrothal solution explicitly. The advantage of hindsight will be used to show that the marital norm is too important to be abandoned, and the betrothal solution is too useful to remain buried in obscurity. These two principles would have enabled clearer guidance to be produced, and they might have provided common theological ground between the different factions. If the argument is sound, the pain of division in the denominations may yet contribute to a more long-term and satisfying answer to some of the questions exercising Christians in the last three decades of the twentieth century. Several reports from the United States (second section) and Britain (third section) will be examined in order to identify the weakening of the marital norm and the emerging lacuna in the churches' teaching about living together that betrothal is able to fulfil. The first section introduces the possibility, derived from Lutheranism, that betrothal is the beginning of marriage, and no mere prelude to it.

IS BETROTHAL MARRIAGE?

Western churches and societies influenced by them now believe that engagement is an intention to marry some time in the future, not the beginning of marriage. This belief is undoubtedly a reduction of a richer, more biblical view (part 2). An episode in the history of the Lutheran Church (Missouri Synod, USA) in the mid twentieth century helps to unravel the complexity of the question 'is betrothal marriage?' While the Missouri Lutherans are somewhat isolated within the spectrum of North American Lutheranism, their handling of this question was insightful and bold.

The Lutheran Church (Missouri Synod)

A book used by Lutheran pastors since 1912 confirmed, largely on the basis of the Mary and Joseph narrative in Matthew 1, that 'engaged people are married people'. Marriage is 'entered by engagement'. Marriage is described as a covenant,

made between two people by the fact that they promise something to each other, that they solemnly promise to enter this covenant. Therefore also the marriage covenant is established by the promise which a man and a woman give to each other in marriage and will love and honor each other as spouses. This promise is called engagement. But before such engaged people live together as married people, it is necessary that their engagement should be confirmed publicly in order that all may know that these two people are now man and wife and that they desire to live together thus. This is accomplished by the wedding ceremony.[1]

Engagement, then, according to an accepted manual of the church, was the beginning of marriage. There is no distinction between the validity of promises in the future tense (promising to marry) and in the present tense (marrying). The couple, *although*

---

[1] Georg Mezger, *Entwürfe zu Katechesen über Luthers Kleinen Katechismus*, 2nd edn (St. Louis: Concordia Publishing House, 1907), p.50, cited in Paul B. Hansen, Oscar E. Feucht, Fred Kramer, Erwin L. Lueker, *Engagement and Marriage: A Sociological, Historical, and Theological Investigation of Engagement and Marriage* (St. Louis: Concordia Publishing House, 1959), pp.3–4.

married, are not expected to live together. Their engagement was as much for everyone else's sake as it was for their own. Families, neighbours and friends are given time to acknowledge the couple intend to live together, and the wedding ceremony completes the marriage. This was not, of course, the understanding of engagement outside that church, and so horror was expressed that young Lutherans could 'mingle freely with those to whom engagement means nothing more than a conditional promise of future marriage, which may be broken without penalty or disgrace if either of the parties to the engagement experiences a change of heart'. Proof that engagement really was marriage in the teaching of this Lutheran church is found in the sanction against breaking engagement. An attempt to do so was regarded as adultery against one's fiancé(e), and treated as such.[2]

The church asked its seminaries to report on whether engagement was 'really tantamount to marriage'. One said 'no', the other 'yes'. Their reports could not be reconciled, and a further report was commissioned. The record of this controversy provides a remarkable trace of the premodern and early modern tradition of entry into marriage; a trace, moreover, which still has the power to disrupt conventional understanding and practice.

According to one group of seminarians betrothal is said to be 'the entrance on the married state', 'the first stage of their married life', etc. It is 'not a promise of future marriage'. The 'rightful and valid betrothal' of Mary and Joseph, and everyone afterwards, 'is a marriage in essence'. There remains a difference between betrothal and 'consummated marriage' which is said to lie 'not in the *essence* of marriage, but in its *use*; not in the possession, but in the enjoyment of the specific rights of husband and wife'. This view is found to be taught by scripture.

We are bound by God's Word, therefore, to give as our firm conviction that 'betrothal' and 'marriage', as spoken of in the Word of God, are identical in essence and differ only as does the *possession* of privileges and their *use*. This the church of today must firmly maintain in the face of the chaotic conditions which the crumbling morals of this age are causing.[3]

---

[2] Hansen, et al., *Engagement and Marriage*, pp.5–6.
[3] The Springfield Seminary, Illinois, reported in ibid., pp.8–10.

Betrothal then, is a genuine beginning of marriage, but problems emerge. What theological point could there be in a period of *married* life when the possession, but not the use, of marital privileges was required by the church's discipline? It is hard to see what is meant by claiming engagement and marriage are 'identical in essence' when in one only, sexual intercourse is allowed, and each is clearly a different event in the couple's life-cycle, one beginning the other; one temporary, the other lasting for the whole of life. The essence of marriage, it is assumed, is consent, yet does not the object of consent differ in each case? The rule 'no sex before marriage' now becomes 'no sex *within* marriage until the ceremony'.

The opposite case, against the marital status of engagement, was based on three considerations. First, while God instituted matrimony, 'there is no indication that He ordained betrothal' which is 'of human origin'. Second, scripture was said to uphold marriage as a lifelong institution, but 'there is no such pronouncement with respect to betrothal'. And third, 'Since the church must not bind upon the consciences of her people that which the Lord does not Himself expressly demand, it is our opinion that betrothal, or engagement, must not be regarded as tantamount to marriage.'[4] But the first two reasons assume what they set out to prove, viz., that marriage and betrothal are separate institutions. Presuppositions about engagement, current at the time, are arguably brought to scripture and 'discovered' there. One might also wonder, if express dominical demands are the criteria of moral action, how Christians make up their minds about most things. Both seminaries hold there should be no sexual intercourse during engagement: they disagree over whether engagement is marriage.

An attempt to reconcile these contrary opinions was made in a joint statement (in 1953) which defined engagement as 'the mutual consent or pledge of a man and a woman to belong together but not the execution of the pledge'. Consent exchanged in engagement 'binds the man and woman before God. Breaking this promise is a violation of the law of love and of the will of God regarding the sanctity of marriage.' If it happens, 'whether before or after the marriage is consummated, the program of church discipline and

---

[4] The Concordia Seminary, St. Louis, reported in ibid., pp.6–7.

the efforts to restore remain identical'.[5] The distinction between a pledge and its execution replaces the distinction between the possession and uses of privilege. The church is to treat engaged people *as if* married, and simultaneously to expect them to refrain from exercising the privileges that marriage confers. They are married, in that the pledges exchanged at engagement are regarded as 'binding'. They are married if the essence of marriage is consent. Yet, if marriage confers the right of sexual intercourse, married they are not.[6]

There are difficulties with both positions and the attempt to reconcile them. This last attempt failed 'to distinguish adequately between a promise regarding a future marriage and the exchange of marriage vows'.[7] A further, exhaustive report, published in 1959, concluded, 'There are no direct *commands* whatever, either in the Old Testament or in the New Testament, concerning the way in which marriage is entered.' The scriptures are said to 'speak in basic general terms of marriage but refrain from systematic or legal formulations'.[8] The church is free to issue its own guidance about this matter. The report admits 'that much of what we treasure in Christian marriage customs and ceremony, ring, wreath, veil, and even the religious ceremony itself – for which there is no demonstrable precedent in ancient Jewish law and custom – have come to us from heathen Rome, having been adopted and adapted by the Christian church'.[9] It effectively quashes the counter-intuitive inclinations of those Lutherans who affirmed, against contrary opinion in church and state, that marriages begin with engagement. This strategy, however, overlooks the contribution of the Bible, and particularly the Mary and Joseph story, to the position being relativized and abandoned. A contemporary reader

5 Ibid., p.10.
6 As the authors explain, 'Even though betrothals are considered by the post-Reformation canon law to be equivalent to marriage, a number of laws very definitely proclaim the evil of exercising the privilege of marriage before the actual ceremony . . . The only regulation consistent with the consent theory is that of the Swedish ordinance of 1527, which says that if a man has sexual intercourse with a woman to whom he is betrothed he shall not be punished, since the couple is already married in the sight of God.' See Hansen, et al., *Engagement and Marriage*, p.76.
7 Ibid., p.13.
8 Ibid., pp.20–1. The report mentioned is the work of Hansen, et al., cited here.
9 Ibid., p.45.

might express surprise that such a position, that engagement is marriage, was ever advocated. What do the positions described in this section say cumulatively about the view being discarded? Lutherans were saying that marriage did and did not begin with betrothal: that betrothal was demanded and not demanded by the Word of God; that marriage was ordained by God and that betrothal was not; that vows made at betrothal are irrevocable and that they are not; that betrothed couples are to be treated as if married. Why? And why should couples who were truly married and able to live together be expected to refrain from having sex?

There is a simple explanation for this chaotic assemblage of contradictions. There is an earlier Christian tradition that betrothal is a real beginning of marriage; that there were two ceremonies not one (with considerable time between); that frequently sexual relations began in the betrothal stage; that betrothal promises were revocable for good cause; that promises made at marriage were irrevocable for any cause. Betrothal waned because of moves against it by Catholics and Protestants (at different times) because of abuses stemming from false promises of marriage, and the desire, not without ambiguity, to police the entry into marriage with reforming vigour. The belief that marriage begins with betrothal is clearly biblical (below, pp.119–30). Those conservative Lutherans who affirmed this belief strike an unusual colour in this spectrum of evangelical, Protestant views. Their fidelity to scripture enabled them to resist finding there the truncated version of marriage designed by European modernity.

Their position, however, is not a viable option today, if it ever was. The belief that the *betrothal* vows are indissoluble is explained by the collapse of betrothal and marriage into a single event during and after the Reformation (below, p.196). If there is but a single marriage ceremony, then clearly the vows must be irrevocable. The expectation that betrothed persons might be fully married, yet not live together or have sex, is a consequence of retaining the biblical and traditional view that betrothal provides the entry into marriage, while maintaining the horror of the sheer extent of sexual promiscuity that Luther and the Reformers found, and acted against. Having acted against abuses of the twofold system, it was unthinkable for the Reformed churches ever to relax their tightened grip on entry to marriage by a single ceremony.

But the issue was not laid to rest by the 1959 report. The Missouri Synod produced a further report, *Human Sexuality: A Theological Perspective*, in 1981, and the ambiguities of earlier controversies remain. On the one hand, the report clearly affirms the marital norm. 'Sexual intercourse engaged in outside of the marriage relationship is forbidden by the Scriptures and must be condemned by the church.'[10] This blanket condemnation also includes 'arrangements whereby couples live together without being married. Even when the partners feel themselves united by a deep bond of love and intend to be married at some point in the future ("engagement"), the same judgment must be made.' On the other hand, the possibility that there may be a 'commitment to a complete, lifelong sharing of life in marriage' without, or before, a ceremony is actually recognized and affirmed. The report continues:

> Because marriage is not essentially a legal or ecclesiastical matter, it is possible, however, for a man and woman to give themselves physically to each other, affirming to each other and to the public their consent to share their future lives in a permanent union, recognizing that their union might be fruitful *and to do this without a public ceremony*.[11]

Consent makes the marriage even when the marriage is not ratified by church or state. As the report explains, 'Such a relationship in reality constitutes marriage (common-law marriage) and cannot be called fornication.'

Common-law marriage is not recommended, but it is accepted. The report finds two minor problems with it. Informal marriage is not rejected because it is not marriage, or because the absence of ceremony makes it fornication. The *caveats* are that it may 'involve an element of deceit' – cohabitors may appear to be 'living in a single state' when they are not; and they may be setting aside 'the regular societal safeguards which have been established for the protection of the rights and interests of all the parties involved',

---

[10] Lutheran Church – Missouri Synod, 'Excerpt from "Human Sexuality": A Theological Perspective', in J. Gordon Melton (ed.), *The Churches Speak on Family Life: Official Statements from Religious Bodies and Ecumenical Organizations* (Detroit: Gale Research Inc., 1991) p.97.

[11] Ibid. (emphasis added).

and this in some states was still illegal.[12] The report denies sexual intercourse to engaged couples before the ceremony, and yet it allows sexual intercourse to people who are informally married without ceremony! A note explains: 'The nature of commitment in the sequence of engagement and marriage is a twofold one: the promises involved in engagement (betrothal) are made with a view to the pledges given as part of the marriage ceremony, where the promise to live together as one flesh is given in public.'[13] The argument appears to be that betrothal promises (the use of 'betrothal' is significant) are not promises of marriage but promises to marry. So the betrothed are not married and sexual intercourse is forbidden to them. But people who consent to live together permanently are to be regarded as married without betrothal or formal marriage because the required ingredients of a valid marriage are in place. The betrothed cannot have sex, but the unbetrothed can! The earlier position is again reached, and for similar reasons. Reformation horror at premarital sex is compounded with recognition of the earlier tradition of betrothal which made the occasion of pre-ceremonial sex common.

The Missouri Lutherans are clearly in touch with their roots. To say the least, they maintain an unusual position in the sexual ethics of contemporary Protestantism. This position is aided by Luther's view that marriage is a secular matter for the state, not for the church. The church recognizes and celebrates marriage because it is created by God, and is a divinely appointed ordinance, but since Luther follows the Roman Catholic view that the essence of marriage is consent, priestly blessing (and presumably consummation) is not required. There need be no public ceremony, but the consent itself must be public. This position is a version of the betrothal solution. Provided there is an intention of permanence the relationship is a marriage. But it remains unsatisfactory. The concession allowed is really clandestine marriage. Part 2 will indicate the strong historical and theological grounds for reclaiming the view that betrothal *was* the beginning of marriage, while a contemporary version of this traditional view will be worked out in part 3.

---

[12] Ibid., p.98.   [13] Ibid., p.97, note 11.

THE WEAKENING OF THE MARITAL NORM

The United Church of Christ (1977)

Our first example of ambivalence with regard to the marital norm is found in a report for the United Church of Christ in 1977. The overriding principle which governs sexual morality in this report is 'love's justice', and three further principles are enunciated in order to expedite its application. These are that '*Love's justice requires a single standard* rather than a double standard.'[14] There must be a single ethic and standard for unmarried and married people and for homosexual and heterosexual people. 'The same basic considerations of love ought to apply to all.' The second principle is a version of the often invoked principle of proportion: 'The physical expression of one's sexuality in relation to another ought to be appropriate to the level of loving commitment in the relationship.' The rationale for this second principle is that 'human relationships exist on a continuum – from the fleeting and casual to the lasting and intense, from the relatively impersonal to the deeply personal', and 'physical expressions also exist on a continuum'. The morality of the physical expression 'will depend upon its appropriateness to the shared level of commitment and the nature of the relationship'. The third principle, which governs physical expression, is that '[g]enital sexual expression ought to be evaluated in terms of the basic elements of a moral decision, informed by love'. These 'basic elements' are further unpacked by means of the terms 'motive', 'intention', 'act' and 'consequences'.

The obvious question to be addressed to this analysis of sexual activity is, 'Where is marriage?' If the single standard subsumes both married and unmarried people, then marriage is clearly subsumed by the principles which replace it. It cannot therefore be the norm. The attempt to denote the rightness and wrongness of sexual relationships by means of abstract principles has the unintended consequence of further marginalizing marriage. The principle of the 'appropriateness of loving commitment' does not allow for the possibility of self-deception, or provide a public standard, or

[14] United Church of Christ: Excerpt From 'Human Sexuality: A Preliminary Study' (1977), in ibid., p.162 (authors' emphasis).

insist on commitment to children, while marriage provides all these things. Are there degrees of commitment? Can they be measured? That marriage exists for children as well as spouses is barely admitted, for the report says: 'In marriage the procreation of children may at certain times be the intent of intercourse, but statistically those times will be in a small minority, and *even then the desire for children is part of our quest for wholeness*, for wholeness is known in relationships.'[15] Is it unfair to suggest an unfortunate inference: that the place of children in marriage figures mainly in spouses' own desires and quests for their own wholeness?

The marital norm is actually further weakened by the treatment it gets in this report. Christians who want rules, not just principles, for sexual conduct are actually chided. They 'find it important to elaborate more specific rules of sexual love. For example, many would insist that one crucial rule for genital intercourse is that it be confined to the permanently intended covenantal union. Others would agree with the rule but would permit exceptions.' So Christians who adhere to the traditional norm of marriage find themselves no longer standing within a tradition, but clinging to an option, for '[w]hatever option is chosen, we need to remember that rules by themselves can never create love'. An option is an option only when there is a variety to choose from, and there is real variety here. The rule is not allowed to impinge upon conduct or regulate it. It has to be chosen as an option. But if the rule is optional, how can it be a rule? There is no discussion of marriage as a norm instead of a rule. Since marriage has an indeterminate place in the report, the betrothal solution (which relies on it) would have been inoperable.

The Presbyterian Church (USA)

A similar weakening of the marital norm is found in the now notorious document, rejected by the 1991 national General Assembly of the Presbyterian Church (USA), *Keeping Body and Soul Together*.[16] Perhaps there has never been a more positive church sexuality

---

[15] Ibid., p.163 (emphasis added).
[16] General Assembly Special Committee on Human Sexuality, Presbyterian Church (USA), *Keeping Body and Soul Together: Sexuality, Spirituality and Social Justice* (1991).

report for advancing a self-critical understanding of the gender inequalities, patriarchal influences, sexual violence and attempts at social control which can be found in Christian thought and practice, together with a deeply Christian affirmation of people who have suffered from these malign influences or who are found beyond the customary parameters of approved sexual behaviour. However, there can be little doubt that this report further marginal-izes marriage. Marriage is not found in the table of contents. In fact only three and a half pages (out of nearly 200) are devoted to it. It does not feature at all among the 'nine guiding princi-ples' or the 'four theological convictions' which, according to the Chair of the committee that produced the report, undergirded it.[17] In the process of 'learning from the marginalized'[18] readers will soon learn that marriage has also been marginalized by the report. Marriage cannot be the norm for sexual relations. 'A Christian ethic of sexuality is needed that honors but does not restrict sex-ual activity to marriage alone.'[19] 'Justice-love' becomes the 'single standard'. 'Justice-love or right-relatedness, and not heterosexua-lity (nor homosexuality for that matter), is the appropriate norm for sexuality.'[20] The 'diversity of families' must be honored. Structures are necessary but reformable and Christians must 'learn how to affirm and preserve what is valuable in customary family patterns' while learning also how to 'remain open and be appreciative of new forms, new patterns, and new arrangements'.[21] Marriage, or at any rate, 'the right to participate in and receive church, community, and legal support for an enduring, publicly validated partnership in justice-love', should be 'available to same-sex couples, as well as to heterosexual couples'.[22] 'The moral norm for Christians ought not to be marriage but rather justice-love.'[23]

Rarely, if ever, has a report which promised so much in terms of reform, actually achieved so little. The General Assembly did not adopt the report and required the Moderator to send a pastoral let-ter to congregations, affirming, among other things, 'the Scriptures to be the unique and authoritative word of God, superior to all other

[17] John J. Carey, 'The Theological Foundations of the Presbyterian Report', in John J. Carey (ed.), *The Sexuality Debate in North American Churches, 1988–1995* (Lewiston, N.Y.: Edwin Mellen Press, 1995), pp.25–35.
[18] *Keeping Body and Soul Together*, p.20.   [19] Ibid., p.38.   [20] Ibid., p.39.
[21] Ibid., pp.49, 50.   [22] Ibid., p.53.   [23] Ibid., p.56.

authorities' and 'the sanctity of the marital covenant between one man and one woman to be a God-given relationship to be lived out in Christian fidelity'.[24] If the sanctity and centrality of marriage had been upheld by the report writers, much of their reforming agenda might have been retained. The marginalization of marriage made the rejection of the report inevitable. The marital norm was explicitly disowned, and shunned as a means of reaching out to people identified as on the margins of the church and Christian teaching. The possibility of deriving principles and values from marriage such as fidelity, lifelong commitment, mutual love and companionship, and discussing how these values might already be operational in alternatives to marriage, was not entertained. Because the marital norm is abandoned, the betrothal solution to the problem of cohabitation cannot even be considered. Cohabitation is one of the new family forms to which the church must be open and appreciative,[25] but nothing is said about the possible dangers of cohabitation, or its relation to marriage. The sense of history in the report is so weak that the betrothal solution is in any case lost from view.

The Evangelical Lutheran Church in America (1993)

A further example of controversial denominational reports on sexual ethics in the USA is again Lutheran, *The Church and Human Sexuality: A Lutheran Perspective: First Draft of a Social Statement* (1993), produced by the Evangelical Lutheran Church in America. Although I regard this report as the most congruent of all the North American reports on sexuality with the argument of this book, I think both its emphasis on the marital norm and on the betrothal solution could have been considerably more pronounced. These Lutherans acknowledge that '[b]ecause we live with the continuing presence of sin, we need reliable sexual boundaries that protect us and others from the harm we so easily inflict on one another, sometimes out of good intentions'.[26] It is not marriage alone, but 'structures such as marriage' which 'provide a sense of social order'.

---

[24] 'The Church in its Own Life', *Church and Society* (July/August 1991), p.45.

[25] *Keeping Body and Soul Together*, p.50.

[26] Division for Church in Society, Department for Studies of the Evangelical Lutheran Church in America, *The Church and Human Sexuality: A Lutheran Perspective: First Draft of a Social Statement* (Chicago: 1993), p.5.

These boundaries and structures are there because they are good for us, protecting us from harm and encouraging us to act more lovingly. Like the Episcopalian and Presbyterian reports the authors concede these structures can be revised. As with the Episcopalians (p.92) God's Realm (here 'reign') provides the criteria for revision:

All structures, practices, and prohibitions need to be viewed in relation to the revelation of God's reign in Jesus Christ. When God's purposes are not being served, boundaries and structures may need to be re-interpreted or changed. They cannot become more important than the love that human relationships are to embody as a witness to God's love for us (1 Jn 4:7–12). For Jesus, even the observance of the Sabbath was not sacrosanct ...

The bold assertion of the freedom of the church in continuing to reform both its doctrine and its practice is remarkable, and can be attributed to the consciousness of the need for ongoing reformation in the very origins of Lutheranism. 'The Gospel message of freedom allows us to change positions we have held in the past when such change enhances the ministry of the Word of God, as part of the ongoing reformation of the Church.'[27]

Marriage is said to be 'not the only setting in which Christians struggle to live out their faith in relation to their sexuality'.[28] A remarkable empathy is shown towards people who tend to marry later in life, or are single, divorced, widowed, or 'find themselves attracted primarily to another of the same sex, and prohibited from a blessed, legal union'. The report writers eschew the issuing of norms and rules in favour of persuasive guidance. 'We are a community that offers *guidance* to people as they live out their sexuality in a variety of situations. Sexual behaviour is a communal and not a merely private concern. The guidance we offer is intended to be persuasive, not binding or controlling of the conscience, because we recognize the Christian freedom to decide and act responsibly.'[29]

Despite familiar signs of the relativization of marriage, marriage is described and commended as a 'covenant of fidelity'. It provides structure, which in turn 'provides protection and stability for living out our sexuality'. Its qualities include 'mutually self-giving love'. It is 'reflective of the divine faithfulness', and it is said to provide 'a truly safe space – physically, emotionally, and spiritually – where

[27] Ibid., p.17.   [28] Ibid., p.6.   [29] Ibid., p.20 (and see also p.6).

each person feels free to be vulnerable'.[30] A section, 'Growing into Marriage', advises: 'Before entering the covenant of marriage, both persons should have a mature sense of who they are, individually and together, and of their readiness for the commitment marriage entails. As they grow in their friendship and communion, their intimate knowledge of each other is deepened and expressed.' A public commitment 'has both secular and religious significance'. The legal bond helps sustain the marriage. The vows occur 'in the presence of God and the community of faith', and God and the community uphold the couple in their life together.

The section on 'Living Together' was one of several to cause controversy. The report says:

Many choose to test their commitment by living together before getting married. Trial or temporary commitments are not sufficient for developing the total trust and intimate sharing enabled by a binding commitment. Without a binding commitment, good intentions are likely to fail due to the chances and changes of life.

In some situations there may be an enduring commitment to one another with a clear intention to marry at a later date. It is the binding commitment, not the license or ceremony, that lies at the heart of biblical understandings of marriage (Gen.2:24; 24:67). Where there is this commitment, legal sanction and religious blessing of the relationship are important and should be sought.[31]

Very difficult issues are dispatched in these short sentences. While the notion of a trial-marriage is rejected as a sufficient reason for living together, there are other reasons for living together before marriage which are clearly not rejected. Although the report says, 'Without a binding commitment, good intentions are likely to fail', the inference is clear – *with* the binding commitment, the remaining reason for *not* living together before marriage is removed, and this is clearly stated. If the couple's 'intimate knowledge of each other is deepened and expressed' as they grow into marriage, it is difficult to imagine how this happens without having sex, even if they haven't yet moved in together. Once again the theological reason for allowing that the binding commitment is independent of ceremony appears to be the medieval notion that consent makes

[30] Ibid., p.8.   [31] Ibid., pp.9–10.

the marriage. There is a temporal distance between the beginning of a life together which expresses the consent of the couple, and the public ceremony which expresses this consent legally, socially and religiously. Optimistically, the consent theory of the nature of marriage is thought to be biblical. There is an obligation on the couple to undergo a public ceremony, presumably in the near future.

This report commends marriage but remains ambivalent over whether marriage remains the norm for sexual activity within the church. Its pastoral sensitivity to lesbian and gay people, and sexually active single people, leads it towards licensing alternatives to marriage. The possibility of extending marriage through creative extensions of the marital norm is not considered, perhaps because it seemed theologically and politically unfeasible at the time. Warrant for ongoing reformation of doctrine and practice is found in the gospel and the reforming roots of the church. Guidance is offered against trial-marriages, while prenuptial cohabitation is left uncensured. Marriages on this view do not begin with weddings. Sexual experience for prenuptial cohabitors is not 'premarital'; it is merely 'pre-ceremonial'. Consent is formally expressed at the ceremony, but is informally expressed by living together, as long as there is a firm intention to marry. So a theological framework is in place which acknowledges a processive entry into marriage and locates the ceremony as the point whereby the pledges become permanent and unchallengeable.

These are all important steps towards the betrothal solution, but they do not go far enough, and some of them are not entirely in the right direction. As in the Missouri Synod document, the nod towards approval of prenuptial cohabitation is prompted by the memory of informal or clandestine marriages which the church disliked but regarded as legally valid. This prompt is a helpful reminder that ceremonies, whether or not in church, were inessential to marriage. Since millions of valid marriages over time were not marked by a ceremony, these at least cannot be said to have begun with one. But the appeal to this tradition is unsatisfactory. The possibility of secret marriages is one the churches will probably never promote. In their heyday opportunities for deception and termination were legion, and that is one of the reasons why the report gives advice to people beginning their unions in this way to seek legal sanction and religious blessing. There is more to be retrieved from past experience of Christian marriage than clandestinity. Betrothal was always an event, involving families and often, especially in the East, the church, and its recovery will provide a surer foundation for the churches as they wrestle with prenuptial cohabitation than private marriage.

The report was, of course, rejected, and the Director of the Task Force that produced it sacked.[32] Controversy surrounded not merely its treatment of marriage and cohabitation, but of masturbation ('generally appropriate and healthy'), singleness ('advising self-restraint' while ministers were to exercise 'pastoral realism') and, in particular homosexuality.[33] A safer panel, nominated by bishops and church leaders, was quickly set up to replace the Task Force. Within a year a new draft was produced (but never voted on), and its icy tone could be compared with the experience of opening a freezer door. The preamble veers almost to bibliolatry in its question-begging, talking-up of the scriptures as 'the authoritative source and norm (standard for measuring faithfulness) for the *proclamation* of the Church, that is, for the proclamation of God's Word, both the Word of the Law and the Word of the Gospel ... Scripture is the only source and norm for the truth of the Gospel.'[34] It was clearly to be inferred that the earlier report had culpably failed to adhere to biblical norms, and that the church's confident appropriation of these norms was a self-evident matter requiring little further enunciation.

The space subtly opened up for prenuptial cohabitation is now sealed off. The new document also had a short 'Growing into Marriage' section but the possibility of reading this as a tacit affirmation of pre-ceremonial sex was removed. It says: 'As they grow in friendship and in knowledge of each other, their communion is deepened. When they agree to make a permanent commitment to

---

[32] For the details of the furore caused, and the action taken, see *The Lutheran*, January 1994, pp.30–1, 35–7; April 1994, p.33; May 1994, p.35; June 1994, p.35; August 1994, pp.38–45.
[33] *The Church and Human Sexuality*, p.16.
[34] *Human Sexuality Working Draft: A Possible Social Statement of the Evangelical Lutheran Church in America, with Accompanying Documents* (developed by the Division for Church in Society and its Writing Team, October 1994), p.5.

each other, they are ready to enter marriage as a vocation.'[35] Their communion with each other, but not their intimate knowledge of each other, is deepened, and their commitment to marry is not a beginning of marriage but a sign of their readiness to begin it, presumably by having a wedding. The section on Living Together in the earlier document is replaced by a warning: 'Many couples today are living in sexual unions without intending to marry. These relationships are contrary to this church's teaching on the life-long commitment of fidelity in marriage.'[36] The distinction is at last made between prenuptial and non-nuptial cohabitation, but it is not used constructively. Living together is discussed only as non-nuptial cohabitation which is regarded as tantamount to heresy. An awkward veil of silence (evidence of embarrassment and failure of theological nerve?) is drawn over the problem. Marriage is not merely affirmed as the norm for Christian sexual ethics. It is also reaffirmed as a rule for *all* sexual behaviour, including that of single adults. 'This church affirms that sexual abstinence is part of the vocation of a single person.' 'The Church continues to teach that casual or longer relationships involving genital sexual activity outside of marriage are sinful. Living together, for whatever reason, does not provide the full expression and commitment of Christian marriage.'[37] With regard to lesbian and gay Christians, 'This church will continue for now its current policy and practice', and 'will rely for its teachings on the social statements from its predecessor church bodies. This church pledges to pursue with determination continuing study and discussion as it seeks to discern God's will.'[38]

The Episcopal Church, Diocese of Newark (1987)

The tendency to sacrifice the norm of marriage in favour of a more inclusive sexual ethic perhaps reaches new heights in the 'Report of the Task Force on Changing Patterns of Sexuality and Family Life' of the Diocese of Newark in the Episcopal Church of the USA. This report, although only diocesan, raises acutely the issues discussed in this book and so will be examined in some detail. To its great credit the diocese set up the task force to advise it on its

[35] Ibid., pp.14–15.   [36] Ibid., p.16.   [37] Ibid., p.18.   [38] Ibid., p.22.

ministry to three particular groups, '1) young people who choose to live together without being married; 2) older persons who choose not to marry or who may be divorced or widowed; 3) homosexual couples.'[39] 'It is our conclusion', say the reporters, 'that by suppressing our sexuality and by condemning all sex which occurs outside of traditional marriage, the Church has thereby obstructed a vitally important means for persons to know and celebrate their relatedness to God.'[40] Like the report of the United Church of Christ, a single standard for all sexual relationships is affirmed: 'all heterosexual and homosexual relationships are subject to the same criteria of ethical assessment',[41] and the assessment is 'the degree to which the persons and relationships reflect mutuality, love and justice'. The church 'must continue to sustain persons in the fulfillment of traditional marriage relationships both for the well-being of the marriage partners and because such marriage provides the most stable institution that we have known for the nurturing and protection of children'. But any sense that marriage might have priority over other alternatives, or be celebrated as a God-given sacrament or ordinance, is quickly dashed, for marriage turns out to be a hazardous (and dubiously prudential) state of affairs – 'the Church must also recognize that fully intended marriage vows are fraught with risks. Belief that deeper knowledge each of each in marriage will enable the original intentions of love and devotion is not always fulfilled.'

The report recognizes that traditional morality, by providing rules, provides 'structure', and that structure is necessary for order of any kind. 'We cannot live without structure in our relationships; but these structures are subject to continual correction by the image of the Realm of God. If the Church is to err it must err on the side of inclusiveness rather than exclusiveness.' But the structure to intimate relationships provided by marriage is overdue for correction, however painful. 'The church must consider the consequences of calling into question institutional relationships which have permitted the Church to flourish and survive.' Marriage is called into question because it has 'oppressive, repressive and

---

[39] The Episcopal Church: Excerpt from the 'Report of the Task Force on Changing Patterns of Sexuality and Family Life' (1987), in Melton (ed.), *Churches*, p.71.
[40] Ibid., pp.75–6. [41] Ibid., p.76.

exploitative dimensions'. However, while marriage is questioned, the 'cultural ethos that favors self-fulfillment over the dutiful but self-abnegating adherence to conventional marriage and family arrangements' is simply accepted as a social fact. The new task for the church is to 'learn how to continue to affirm the conventional without denigrating alternative sexual and family arrangements'.[42]

It is 'appropriate' that 'whenever persons consider beginning a sexual relationship', they ask:

a) Will the relationship strengthen the pair for greater discipleship in the wider context? Will they be better enabled to love others? Will their relationship be a beneficial influence on those around them? b) Will the needs and values of others in the larger context be recognized and respected, especially the needs of their own children (if any), their parents and their parish community? . . . c) What is the couple's intention regarding the procreation and/or raising of children?

The relationship 'should be life-enhancing for both partners and exploitative of neither'. It should be 'grounded in sexual fidelity', 'founded on love and valued for the strengthening, joy, support and benefit of the couple and those to whom they are related'. With particular regard to cohabiting heterosexual couples, the report mentions the tradition of common-law marriage; explains that young people live together as a trial period before marriage, or as a temporary or permanent alternative to marriage; warns that the church's opposition to cohabitation 'in direct statement and by silent tolerance' has a seriously debilitating effect on the couples, their relationship, their lives and faith; defends ministry to cohabitors as 'an effort to recognize and support those who choose, by virtue of the circumstances of their lives, not to marry but to live in alternative relationships enabling growth and love'; and advocates that 'the Church's focus should be on persons' (i.e., not on institutions), and that all sexual relationships be assessed by their contribution to God's Realm.[43]

The report addresses the needs of cohabiting couples and the theological problems they raise for the churches, with admirable directness, but its solution is far away from the one advocated in this book, based on the marital norm and the betrothal solution.

[42] Ibid., p.77.   [43] Ibid., p.79.

Its most serious failure lies in the inability to see that tradition itself is not static, and that marriage in particular, if viewed historically, is a fine example of just how dynamic Christian traditions actually are. Marriage in the millennium just ended became a sacrament, incorporated priests, absorbed companionate love, and most recently, began to affirm the equality of the sexes. (Further examples of its openness to development are the loss of betrothal, and undeniably, loss of indissolubility.) The repeated use of the term 'traditional marriage' in the document betrays a failure of imagination, a failure to consider moving the tradition on. The term is used pejoratively. It gets in the way. It has already been decided that cohabitors, sexually active singles and homosexual couples are beyond the ethical wisdom of two millennia. In seeking (faithfully) to maintain ministry towards them a break with tradition is required, and courage is required to make the break.

But it is not clear that a break with tradition *is* required. Marriage need not be a liability. There may be a good Christian case for assessing relationships on the basis of mutuality, love and justice, but the question arises whether marriage is capable of achieving this, and achieving it – in an appropriate evolving form – better than its alternatives. Why cannot the undoubted social pressure upon the churches' teaching be used more constructively, as a positive contribution to its reformulation? If assessment of all relationships is to be made according to the criteria of mutuality, love and justice, we need to know how these criteria are applied, verified, and measured. There is an unexamined and unnoticed move in several of the reports from objective to private criteria. Marriage *has* public criteria. It is for ever, for better for worse, for richer for poorer, and so on. It is public, recognized, requires vows to be made in the presence of God, and is offered to God for the divine benediction.

Having agreed that marriage serves children best, the report goes on to say that marriage vows are risky and will be broken by many. The emphasis on support for divorcing parents is of course admirable, but by making 'traditional marriage' one family form among others and offering support for all of them in the name of inclusiveness, the possibility of discriminating between different forms of family is lost. Truth is the casualty, for the evidence shows that children are generally hurt, not helped, by divorce. In fairness, it should be pointed out that the extent of the havoc which divorce generally causes to children was simply unknown, even as late as 1987.[44] The comment about structure being open to correction is evasive. The twin dynamisms of the realm of God and of the struggle of human institutions to keep up with it cannot be used to turn on theological support for *any* change, especially those which arrive unannounced and cause suffering. The well-being or salvation of men, women and children certainly requires mutuality, love and justice. But these goods are more likely to be procured by marriage.

Is it not disingenuous to say the church must consider the consequences of calling into question the institutional relationship of marriage, since it plainly calls this relationship into question without considering the consequences for itself? It doesn't attempt an alternative strategy, developing the tradition that affirms marriage. All the oppressive elements of marriage are capable of being marshalled into arguments for an opposite conclusion, namely the development of a more adequate norm of marriage, one that moves from patriarchy to mutuality, and is actually capable of generating rules which cover the new conditions the report describes. During the 1990s (i.e., after the report) there was a growing awareness that alternative families do not work equally well. While the church needs to learn not to 'denigrate' alternative arrangements, if there is an empirically established consensus that these arrangements are frequently not in the best interests of the people who try to make them work, then in the interests of truth, this must surely be pointed out. It is unforgivable to relativize further the dwindling support for marriage. On what basis is the church's ministry to people with failing marriages conducted, if one set of arrangements is no longer preferred within the Christian community, and counsel is reduced to considering and weighing 'options'?

This report actually denigrates the marital norm. Indeed, insistence on the marital norm has become an obstacle between the unmarried and God. Its advice to all sexually active people is vitiated

[44] David Popenoe's *Disturbing the Nest* (New York: Walter de Gruyter, 1988) was one of the first books to show the declining well-being of children of divorce (see Don S. Browning, Bonnie J. Miller-McLemore, Pamela D. Couture, K. Brynolf Lyon and Robert M. Franklin, *From Culture Wars to Common Ground: Religion and the American Family Debate* (Louisville: Westminster/John Knox Press, 1997), p.55).

by the loss of marriage. With regard specifically to cohabitation, there is little hint of the betrothal solution, only note taken of the past practice of common-law marriage. There is no distinction between prenuptial and non-nuptial cohabitation (the importance of this distinction had not then emerged), and presumably no use for it either. Prospective cohabitors, like all prospective sexually active people, might appropriately address certain questions to themselves (even though they are barely answerable). Ministry to cohabitors is defended, but what might its content be? Ministers will not be recommending marriage, or that assessment of the relationship be based on marital intention. Here is an unfortunate irony: in its determination to provide recognition and support for cohabitors, the question whether, in the light of the church's faith, living together is best for them, is not raised.

The four reports so far considered have weakened or rejected the marital norm. The Lutheran report is the most positive about marriage. The reports are hospitable to cohabitation provided it is judged positively according to particular principles of love and justice. For some, the relationship of living together to marriage is irrelevant, since marriage is part of the problem, and not the solution. We begin to see a pattern confirmed by later reports. There is a crisis in the church's sexual teaching. A group is set up to advise. It reports. Its conclusions recommend changes to the church's teaching in advance of what can be sensibly expected. These changes have their origin in pastoral sensitivity but are advanced in the name of an inadequate or non-existent theology. There is protracted, public, acrimonious debate. The traditionalists affirm the traditional line. Polarization over matters of sexuality within the denominations is confirmed. Initiatives which promise much, deliver little, and those people whose lives challenge the traditional teaching are further alienated from the churches. Do the British sexuality reports handle the polarization more successfully?

PREPARING FOR THE BETROTHAL SOLUTION

At least three documents were produced by the Church of England in the 1990s which deal explicitly (among many other matters in sexual ethics) with cohabitation. One was produced by the House of Bishops and commended by the Archbishop of Canterbury for prayerful study and reflection.[45] One, a working party report with a long section on cohabitation, was heavily criticized.[46] One was an official 'teaching document' (with silver coloured covers) called simply *Marriage*.[47] All affirm the marital norm (although to varying degrees), yet their recommendations on cohabitation would have been much more informed and contemporary if they had deployed the betrothal solution. While the British reports are more careful than the American reports in emphasizing the centrality of marriage, their embrace of the unmarried is more cautious, leading to the risk of alienating the unmarried (i.e., almost half of all adults).

Issues in Human Sexuality *(1991)*

The first of these, *Issues in Human Sexuality*, is well attuned to actual sexual practice in the Britain of 1991. There is frank admission that sexual intercourse increasingly happens shortly after puberty, that it is indulged in for pleasure with 'no requirement of permanence'.[48] The bishops speak of 'a whole range of relationships' which are not marriage, but 'which have some reference, direct or indirect, positive or negative, to the institution of marriage'. In this way they begin with the marital norm and seek to relate, but not necessarily extend, the norm to the non-marital relationships. The range includes

a couple [who] may be lovers, and share much of their lives, but not live together, though the option of doing so eventually is tacitly or explicitly present. Others will live exactly as if married, but refuse to enter into the formal and public marriage relationship. Another couple may agree on a trial marriage, regarding actual marriage and possible parenthood as something that should not be undertaken without some assurance that the parties are compatible. Another couple may be quite clear that they intend to marry, but housing problems or other constraints seem to make that impracticable for the present.

[45] *Issues in Human Sexuality: A Statement by the House of Bishops* (London: Church House Publishing, 1991), p.vii.
[46] *Something to Celebrate: Valuing Families in Church and Society* (Report of a Working Party of the Board for Social Responsibility, London: Church House Publishing, 1995).
[47] *Marriage: A teaching document from the House of Bishops of the Church of England* (London: Church House Publishing, 1999).
[48] *Issues*, p.20.

People in these and other non-marital relationships often overlook what Christian teaching about marriage can give them. God has revealed marriage as 'the way of life within which full physical expression of our sexuality can best contribute to our own maturity and sanctification and that of others'. Secondly, and arising from the elevation of marriage to the norm for all sexual relationships, the bishops hope that marriage will provide 'a direction in which other sexual relationships can and should move, if they are to serve more effectually the true fulfilment of those concerned'. Marriage is positively commended, not least as 'the best home for our children'.[49] 'God's perfect will for married people' is said, echoing tradition, to be 'chastity before marriage, and then a lifelong relationship of fidelity and mutual sharing at all levels'. But the bishops recognize that what they have advocated is an 'ideal' unlikely to be achieved: 'We recognise that it is increasingly hard today for the unmarried generally, and for young people facing peer group pressure in particular, to hold to this ideal.' On the one hand the Church must be 'clearer and stronger in supporting those who are struggling against the tide of changing sexual standards'. On the other hand, 'if we believe in a Gospel of grace and restoration freely offered to all, we need to give this support in such a way that those who may eventually go with that tide will not feel that in the Church's eyes they are from then on simply failures for whom there is neither place nor love in the Christian community'.

The marital norm is unambiguously affirmed, as one would expect from a document written by bishops. The norm is also subtly commended and related to alternative relationships. By offering marriage as 'the direction in which other sexual relationships can and should move' marriage is commended without excluding other relationships or alienating people in them. They are not treated negatively nor labelled as fornication. Since the 'true fulfilment' of all people is willed by God and by the bishops, marriage is offered as a means of realizing this through the values of love, fidelity and commitment which belong to marriage and may already be present in relationships outside it. This is a commendation which is both pastorally and psychologically wise. However, the 'range'

<hr />

49 Ibid., p.21.

of relationships just described which might more obviously lead to marriage knows nothing of the phased entry into marriage through betrothal, and seems disappointingly unaware of the resources available.

The first relationship in the range is 'semi-cohabitation' or 'living apart together' (above, p.6). This is an alternative to marriage. The second is clearly 'common-law marriage'. Earlier generations would recognize the genre as clandestine marriage. The third is a trial-marriage and so not marriage. The fourth is prenuptial cohabitation which, if the argument of this book is successful, may be regarded as the beginning of marriage. While this range of relationships illustrates the diversity of the pastoral problem defenders of marriage have to deal with, it does nothing to clarify how couples enter marriage. Betrothal would help considerably to clarify the status of some of these relationships. The weakest part of the argument lies in the unqualified assertion that 'God's perfect will for married people is chastity before marriage'. It is not that this assertion is not true. Rather it rests on the assumption that we know when marriage begins, and so have a reference point which makes sense of 'before' and 'after'. This assumption is very vulnerable to challenge.

How then are people who live together 'before' marriage to be viewed? Here the bishops descend into what has been called 'a godly, typically Anglican muddle'.[50] There is no distinction between prenuptial and non-nuptial cohabitation. All cohabitation is before marriage. And the immorality of sexual intercourse and living together before marriage is wrong because it falls short of God's ideal. But increasingly, Christian young people will be overwhelmed by the falling tide of changing sexual standards. The gospel of grace, however, will restore them. But this position assumes that while changing sexual standards may be expected outside the church, there is no change inside the church. Although the bishops do not say so, the reason why young people increasingly fall short of God's ideal and the church's teaching is their own weakness of will, and the sinful effect of immorality around them. The pastoral sensitivity which acknowledges people will live together before marriage

[50] Adrian Thatcher, 'Postmodernity and Chastity', in Jon Davies and Gerard Loughlin (eds.), *Sex These Days: Essays on Theology, Sexuality and Society* (Sheffield: Sheffield Academic Press, 1997), p.124.

has not yet caught up with alternative formulations and resolutions of this problem actually licensed by the tradition.

Something to Celebrate *(1995)*

Something to Celebrate provides the most detailed analysis of cohabitation of any of the church-sponsored reports. The General Synod had debated cohabitation in 1992 and a Working Party, already set up to report on a range of issues to do with families, was asked to consider the subject.[51] The Working Party did so. It advocated a positive acceptance of the practice and hinted at theological changes that might accommodate it. It was, of course, heavily criticized, and when the General Synod debated it in 1995, it was reluctant even to 'take note' of it.[52] I have defended the report elsewhere, whilst acknowledging its theological weaknesses.[53] In relation to our two criteria, it will now be shown that the marital norm is affirmed, but the betrothal solution is, at last, implicitly adopted. This is a considerable gain. Unfortunately the betrothal solution is barely grounded in either history or theology, with the result that when the solution was subjected to public debate and criticism (including ridicule by tabloid newspapers), it was rejected without proper opportunity to consider it in relation to recovered traditions of marriage. What was in several ways a traditional document was seen as a precarious departure from tradition.

The authors identify themselves firmly as reformers. They 'believe that one of the tasks facing the Church in the years ahead will be to develop a sexual ethic which embraces a dynamic view of sexual development, which acknowledges the profound cultural changes of the last decades and supports people in their search for commitment, faithfulness and constancy'.[54] Cohabitation is one such change. They recognize that 'marriage "without benefit of clergy" was the reality for the majority in Britain for centuries',[55] and they find four 'concerns' about cohabitation. First, '[t]he traditional Christian understanding situates sexual intercourse firmly

---

[51] *Something to Celebrate*, pp.3, 109.   [52] See *Church Times*, 8 December 1995.
[53] Adrian Thatcher, *Marriage after Modernity: Christian Marriage in Postmodern Times* (Sheffield and New York: Sheffield Academic Press and New York University Press, 1999), p.107.
[54] *Something to Celebrate*, p.109.   [55] Ibid., pp.110–11.

within the context of the bond of marriage and therefore means that any non-married relationship involving sexual intercourse is wrong'.[56] It follows, therefore, 'for those who believe that all sexual intercourse outside marriage is wrong, all cohabiting relationships – whatever their qualities of love, commitment and tenderness – are flawed'. Second, some Christians believe 'cohabitation poses a threat to the institution of marriage and the family as Christians understand them'. Marriage is a solemn covenant entered into before God and witnesses, whereas cohabitation 'tends to be an informal arrangement of a more private kind, involving consent but lacking the unlimited commitment of the vows of marriage'.

A comparison is next made between the processes of entering the two types of relationship. 'Instead of constituting a formal passage into a new social and legal status publicly acknowledged and confirmed, cohabitation is usually a relatively private expression of personal choice, an agreement between the man and the woman alone.' The defect in this private arrangement is not that it is morally wrong, but that it is *incomplete*. Cohabitation, privately negotiated, 'can be seen as a step in the search for a fulfilling relationship. This may be good as far as it goes, but it does not go far enough if it fails to recognise God's desire for "fulfilling relationship" to extend into the family, the Church and the wider society.' Third, prospects for the stability and quality of marriages entered via cohabitation are said to be much worse than for those entering marriage directly, and some partnerships are 'fleeting and exploitative'.[57] Finally, couples and their families are disadvantaged by the ambiguous status of the relationship. Friends and kin need to know whether or when to acknowledge cohabitation as if it were a marriage. Parents, for example, need cues about whether they are really 'parents-in-law', or not.

Despite these concerns, *Something to Celebrate* recommends: 'The wisest and most practical way forward therefore may be for Christians both to hold fast to the centrality of marriage and at the same time to accept that cohabitation is, for many people, a step along the way towards that fuller and more complete commitment.'[58] Such an approach is said to have much in its favour. It is grounded in a corollary from the parable of the prodigal son.

---

[56] Ibid., p.113.   [57] Ibid., p.114.   [58] Ibid., p.115.

Jesus indicates by means of the parable that 'no one has grounds for boasting or self-righteousness in the way they live out their personal relationships. All relationships are marred by selfishness, greed and personal inadequacy', and need repentance and the renewing power of God. 'It is only in this spirit of humility, of acceptance and being accepted, that we can begin to consider properly the issue of cohabitation.' The report admits that the *relationship between the church and cohabitors* has lacked this spirit, and 'too often the Church has been censorious and judgemental in matters of personal ethics'. The relationship between the church and the people to whom it seeks to extend Christian teaching has to be addressed by both sides:

The beginning of a meeting of minds and hearts is only likely to occur if the Church is honest about its failure to embody the love of God in its teaching and practice of marriage and family life, and if people in search of loving relationships admit that if they wish to find true fulfilment they cannot go it alone.

The acceptance of cohabitation is based on three reasons. First, 'it is a way of responding sympathetically and realistically to the increasing number of people who are seeking a different form of partnership from that traditionally accepted'. Second, 'taking a "both-and" approach is a way of recognising that some forms of cohabitation are marriages already in all but name'.[59] Several theological fragments (although none is referenced or elaborated) are plied together in support of this judgment:

Theologically and morally, what makes a marriage is the freely given consent and commitment in public of both partners to live together for life. A wedding ceremony serves to solemnise and bless the commitment that the couple make to each other. The rite of marriage is a grace which each partner bestows upon the other. It is not something bestowed by an ordained minister or the Church. This being so, it is important to acknowledge that, in terms of the theology of marriage, cohabitation which involves a mutual, life-long, exclusive commitment may be a legitimate form of marriage, what might be called 'pre-ceremonial' or 'without ceremonial' marriage.

Third, cohabitation 'has to do with changes and developments in modern life'. These include the higher valuation placed on sexual

[59] Ibid., p.116.

intimacy, the influence of contraception, the 'shift in gender-role stereotypes' and feminism. These changes 'have gone hand in hand with a marked rise in the popularity of cohabitation, with marriage – whether for the first or second time – viewed as a still more serious commitment to be postponed until later and involving the raising of children'.[60]

The report concludes that the 'increasing popularity of cohabitation, among Christians and non-Christians' provides no reason for modifying the church's insistence on the priority of marriage.[61] Instead of condemning cohabitation 'it is an opportunity and a challenge to the Church to articulate its doctrine of marriage in ways so compelling, and to engage in a practice of marriage so life-enhancing, that the institution of marriage regains its centrality'. In celebrating marriage the Church must also affirm and support 'what in cohabiting relationships corresponds most with the Christian ideal'. By welcoming and listening to cohabitors, congregations will 'discover God's presence in their lives and in our own, at the same time as bearing witness to that sharing in God's love which is also available within marriage'.

Having praised the report for its sheer bravery in facing cohabitation and bringing recommendations to the church about it, it must be at once admitted that there are serious weaknesses in the treatment the problem received. While the working group does actually arrive at a recognizable 'betrothal solution', there are much clearer and stronger ways of presenting this solution which also do not appear to call traditional sticking points into question. The first question must be whether the new sexual ethic 'which embraces a dynamic view of sexual development' will affirm marriage as confidently as the present, or the past, sexual ethic. The report is ambiguous about this. The ambiguity is confirmed by the introduction of 'concerns'. The traditional sex-only-within-marriage norm is introduced in order to be questioned, and the identification of 'those who believe that all sexual intercourse outside marriage is wrong' as a group within the church among others who clearly hold different and non-traditional opinions is pretty obviously going to be seen as a marginalization of marriage and those Christian stalwarts who want to defend it.

[60] Ibid., pp.116–17.   [61] Ibid., p.118.

The 'concern' that cohabitation is a 'threat' to marriage is also poorly handled. If the several types of cohabitation are to be generalized together, then cohabitation *is* a threat to marriage, and the report would have won friends by saying so. But the report avoids the problem by comparing cohabitation with marriage. This involves the simple mistake of overlooking that when comparisons are made, like should be compared with like. But the two relationships are not alike: indeed, they may be different in kind (above, p.12, proposition 6). Why not say that premarital cohabitation begins the 'formal passage into a new social and legal status publicly acknowledged and confirmed', instead of comparing cohabitation *with* this formal passage? Why not acknowledge prenuptial cohabitation as the beginning of formal marriage?

Five years on, the remaining two 'concerns' about cohabitation actually loom larger, as chapter 1 has shown. But they were not dealt with back in 1995 when less about cohabitation was known. There is much evidence that cohabitation, if taken as a unitary phenomenon, is harmful. In fact none of the 'concerns' was adequately dealt with. They were described, and then ignored. Prenuptial and non-nuptial cohabitation is not distinguished. The explicit advocacy of betrothal could have been supported by vastly better theological resources (beginning with Mary and Joseph) than the appeal to the parable of the prodigal son. The parable does not deal with the difficulties. God's unbounded and unanticipated forgiveness for us when we wreck relationships does not answer the question at the root of these concerns. Is living together acceptable to God? Can living together be affirmed without weakening marriage? The tradition *can* answer these questions affirmatively when allowed to do so, without fudging or suspending them.

An appeal to the betrothal element of Christian marital traditions provides a much stronger argument for accepting some forms of cohabitation than the three reasons adopted in the report. The report rightly advocates that the Church of England should exercise a sympathetic and realistic ministry to cohabiting couples, but might this not also involve drawing tactful attention to some of the possible consequences of living together, and drawing the distinction between prenuptial and non-nuptial cohabitation in order to clarify and sharpen young intentions? Since the latter is generally bad for people, should not the church express regard for cohabitors by

pointing this out? The 'both-and' commendation of the two institutions perpetuates the fear that an additional institution alongside
marriage is being recognized, whereas the betrothal solution insists
that betrothal is the beginning of marriage, not an alternative to it.
If a second, albeit informal, institution is recognized, it is hard to see
how the charge that marriage is simultaneously being weakened,
can be countered.

It is right to claim that 'some forms of cohabitation are marriages
already in all but name', and to ask whether 'pre-ceremonial' marriage *may* be a valid form of marriage. Well, is it a valid form of
marriage, or not?

The argument seems to be that since consent to marry may be
made before the wedding, and since the couple are themselves
the ministers of the sacrament, neither the ceremony, nor the
ministry of the priest, is required for the marriage to be valid.
Undoubtedly this is historically and theologically right, and until
the Hardwicke Marriage Act of 1753, such 'marriages' would
have been accepted as contrary to canon law, but nonetheless
'valid'. (They would have required at least two witnesses to have
heard vows made in the present tense.) These marriages were not
'pre-ceremonial', for unlike cohabiting couples today who subsequently marry at a ceremony, these marriages generally avoided
ceremony (in earlier periods the church courts may have required
one). They were 'clandestine marriages'. Cohabitation is accommodated in *Something to Celebrate* by being compared with clandestine marriages of premodern and early modern times. This is a
helpful comparison. But the tradition also sanctions betrothal, and
betrothal would have helped this report to clinch the argument.
Betrothal is an event (far from private) with an available liturgy.
There is no doubt that betrothal may be viewed as the beginning
of marriage (chapters 4 and 5). It is not simply a prelude to marriage. Neither is it an alternative to marriage. It is an alternative
only to the complacent assumption that marriages begin with weddings. Betrothal, in other words, promises more than clandestine
marriage does.

The further 'changes and developments' in modern life are
welcomed with a misplaced enthusiasm. They are ambiguous. The
higher value placed on sexual intimacy may well be positive, but

it can lead to imbalance in a relationship; and the higher the expectation, the greater the disappointment when it is not realized. Contraception may be a positive influence, but it often fails, and when it fails outside marriage, the consequences may be disastrous for the children conceived. The belief that the presence of God will be discovered in the lives of cohabitors surely needs additional signification (e.g., in the qualities which most resemble good marriages?). The failure of cohabitation to turn into marriage in many cases is overlooked. Cohabitation is undoubtedly an opportunity for the churches everywhere to rediscover marriage. That part of the Christian heritage most germane to cohabitation is not merely clandestine marriage but betrothal. The working party was 'particularly asked' to deal with cohabitation and the church's response. It claims to have drawn on 'theological studies which examine cohabitation in the light of Scripture and the tradition of the Church'.[62] Unfortunately, for whatever reason, the contribution of each was hardly explored at all.

Marriage *(1999)*

The House of Bishops' teaching document, *Marriage*, addresses cohabitation in a light, confident tone. 'Those who approach marriage' face anxieties and challenges. 'The social and emotional steps by which couples come to enter marriage are often complicated, and some finally think about lifelong commitment only when they are already living together.' Cohabitation is acknowledged, but discouraged rather than condemned. 'This route of approaching marriage is exposed to uncertainties and tensions and is not to be recommended. But it was not uncommon in earlier periods of history, and the important thing is simply that the point of commitment should be reached.'[63]

There is a candid appendix, 'What does the Church have to say to a couple who are living together without being married?' These relationships are of many different kinds, one of which intends future marriage. Instead of offering written guidance, cohabitors are advised the Church would like to help them through the

---

[62] Ibid., p.109. [63] *Marriage*, p.11.

willingness of its ministers to talk and pray with them 'that God will show you his will for your future'.[64] And if they intend to marry, the church will smooth the passage into marriage without censure or fuss:

> But it may be, in fact, that you have resolved the question of your future between yourselves already, that you are quite certain of your lasting commitment to each other, and are living naturally together among your friends as husband and wife. Even so, the Church would encourage you to make the public stand that is implied in your way of life, expressing your promises to one another and praying together, as others pray with you for God's assistance.[65]

This teaching document provides a novel treatment of living together. Its growing prevalence is quietly noted. It is neither recommended nor forbidden, but discouraged. There is no discussion of the social circumstances that help to produce it. The bishops recognize the historical precedent of living together outside marriage, but do not develop or unravel possible comparisons between past and present. They also recognize that the 'point of commitment', presumably the irrevocable pledge formally expressed in marriage vows, can be reached earlier than the wedding. When this happens, objection to living together presumably ceases? There is no challenge to the *de facto* status of any couple who, not yet legally married, live together as husband and wife. Rather, they are gently encouraged to move toward formal marriage. The continuity between the two states is cleverly emphasized by the suggestion that marriage is already 'implied in your way of life'. The local congregation is waiting to express solidarity with the couple, with no hint of judgment. 'The worshipping community, which is ready to welcome you in celebrating and learning of God's love, is the proper supportive context for the personal relationship at the centre of your life to flourish.'[66]

The purpose of the document is 'to reaffirm the Church of England's teaching on marriage'. In doing this it also treats of the entry into, and the exit from, marriage. The document is very easily accessible, and given its intended audience it would be unfair to accuse it of failing to reach much historical or theological depth.

[64] Ibid., p.21.   [65] Ibid., p.22.   [66] Ibid.

It is fair to suggest, however, that a greater consciousness of the potentialities of the betrothal solution would have helped the bishops to affirm the continuity between the pre-ceremonial and post-ceremonial segments of a couple's life together. The understanding of marriage which emerges in the document actually embraces prenuptial cohabitation as long as the point of commitment is reached. A clear framework for setting out what is assumed in the document is needed (though not necessarily in the document itself).

Report on the Theology of Marriage *(Church of Scotland) (1994)*

Two further reports will be considered finally, one from Scotland, the other from South Africa. The Panel on Doctrine was instructed by the General Assembly of the Church of Scotland, together with other departments in that church, 'to undertake a review of the Church of Scotland's theology of marriage ... taking into account the increasing number of pastoral problems raised by broken marriages and changing social patterns'.[67] It reported in 1994. It expounded the theology of marriage thoroughly and sensitively. It 'reaffirm[ed] marriage as an institution in which the love of God exemplified in Christ is earthed in human relationship'. Marriage is 'a gift of God, one of the patterns of relationship offered by God for our human wellbeing because it is not good for us to be alone'.[68] It remains essential for the nurture of children and the good of society. 'The bonding of a man and woman which we understand as marriage therefore has vital implications for the wellbeing, indeed the very fabric, of society.'[69]

The Panel did not shirk its heavy responsibility of examining changing social patterns. These patterns include the falling numbers of people marrying, the rising number of people living together and divorcing, and the legal changes which have accompanied them.[70] The Panel takes seriously the fact that many church members are themselves living in relationships which traditional teaching cannot accommodate, and it commendably allows them

---

[67] Church of Scotland Panel on Doctrine, *Report on the Theology of Marriage* (1994), p.258.
[68] Ibid., pp.257, 265.   [69] Ibid., p.265.   [70] Ibid., pp.267, 272.

a voice. Lamenting 'the dwindling influence of the Church'[71] is dismissed as a form of disloyalty to *Christians* who are influenced by and even immersed in the new social patterns. '. . . Such a response would be simplistic and misleading, since it fails to take account of those committed Christians who choose, quite deliberately and in good faith, patterns of relationship other than traditional marriage.' This is a 'new situation', without precedent, for

It can no longer be assumed that those who enter into relationships other than marriage, even *Christians* who enter into such relationships, will accept the traditional evaluation of their lifestyle as deviant, morally wrong, or a matter for contrition, repentance and change. Their numbers make it quite unrealistic for the Church to treat them as rare exceptions to Christian standards, and the very prevalence of Christian lifestyles other than marriage opens up complex issues of pastoral care and discipline. It seems to us undeniable that a huge gulf has opened up between the Church's traditional teaching and the views of many younger church members.[72]

There is more than a hint of impatience with the Anglican statement *Issues in Human Sexuality*. By leaving a gap between 'pastoral discretion' and the reaffirmation of tradition, the possibility of hypocrisy may be hard to avoid.[73] Marriage is commended finally for the human well-being it promotes. 'We can only commend marriage if we show it to be capable of being a fruitful, nourishing and sustaining environment for those involved, since we believe that, like the Sabbath, marriage was "made for man".'[74] Marriage has evolved and the church is well rid of earlier forms of it which involved, for example, the subservience of women or 'the stay-at-home spouse'. It is unambiguously affirmed that 'marriage is the norm of man–woman sexual relationships',[75] but marriage is nonetheless skilfully extended to cover relationships other than marriage. A full chapter is devoted to 'Heterosexual Relationships other than Marriage', and this means (principally) cohabitation. 'Almost invariably' engaged couples have sex.[76] The church must resist the commercialization and trivialization of sex by a positive commendation of alternatives. There is a need 'to clarify above all that Christian moral energy in this area is fired by the insistence

[71] Ibid., p.267.   [72] Ibid., p.268.   [73] Ibid., p.270.
[74] Ibid., p.272.   [75] Ibid., p.271.   [76] Ibid., p.274.

that sex belongs in the context of shared and mutual giving, in which persons are committed to loving each other'.[77] This context, derived from marriage, is now shifted across to encompass prenuptial cohabitation, but without actually saying so explicitly. Whereas the virtue of chastity is destroyed by casual sex, '[i]t is less clear that it is threatened by the mutual self-giving of two people who love each other and who hope to make a life together'. Reasons given for subsuming cohabitation within marriage as an informal version of it are very similar to those adumbrated in *Something to Celebrate*:

It is important to recognise that it is the mutual willing commitment in love which constitutes the relationship, rather than its statutory recognition in the wedding ceremony. Nevertheless, the solemnisation of the marriage, whether or not sexually anticipated, is certainly important in terms of the social, public and ecclesiastical witness it offers to the intention of permanent faithful loving. But we must recognise that some of the taboo against even betrothed pre-marital sex was, until recently, the fear of pregnancy out of wedlock and its consequences.

Young unmarried people need to learn freedom and responsibility in relation to sexual intimacy, and the church must play its part in their growth to maturity. 'The central vision we wish to give young people is one of physical intimacy belonging in a relationship of committed loyalty which hopes and intends to be permanent.'[78] The church 'cannot relinquish its own ideal; yet it must also recognise the integrity and seriousness of commitment involved in many relationships which do not coincide with that ideal'. The recognition extends even as far as the fact that 'for many people the act of penetrative intercourse is part of a continuum of sexual intimacy, not an absolute watershed between acceptable and prohibited behaviour'.[79] The theological rationale for such recognition is that 'becoming one flesh' with another person 'is not, at its deepest, a matter of genital proximity, but of the deep long-term learning of mutual embodied cherishing of which penetrative intercourse is one element'.

The determination to stand by Christians whose relationships do not accord with traditional expectations is remarkable, a good

---

[77] Ibid., p.275.　　[78] Ibid., p.277.　　[79] Ibid., p.278.

Protestant example of the *sensus fidelium* which allows the experience of all faithful people to count. The willingness to embrace such Christians is a fine example of contemporaneity, but the price paid for doing so appears to be an ominous crack in the marital norm. Marriage is affirmed to be the norm; however, since it is but '*one*' of the patterns of relationship offered by God for our human well-being, '*an*' institution which earths God's love, the impression of the relativization of marriage is hard to avoid. The problem facing the working party can be simply put: is prenuptial cohabitation the beginning of marriage, or a rival institution which has to be accorded semi-official theological recognition because sexual relations expressing commitment take place inside it? The report falls between both positions. In fact it affirms both positions, but weakly, thereby satisfying proponents on neither side.

Since the Christian 'central vision' is not marriage but 'a relationship of committed loyalty which hopes and intends to be permanent', traditionalists will believe marriage is being further undermined. But if people who intend to proceed to a wedding ceremony are *already beginning marriage* (as the betrothal tradition asserts), then the central vision is already one of marriage and does not need to be accommodated as something different. Once again consent is thought to make the marriage (but it is called 'commitment') and its expression in the wedding service is highly desirable but optional. And once again the ground for legitimizing prenuptial cohabitation is not betrothal but clandestine marriage. There is mention of 'betrothed pre-marital sex' but this is undeveloped. It is also inaccurate, since 'pre-marital' assumes the marriage begins with the ceremony, not with the betrothal. The report has already conceded this by invoking the tradition of clandestine marriage in order to show that the marriage does *not* begin with the ceremony.

Before this report ever reached the General Assembly six members of the Panel had voted against sending it on, and appended their own trenchant criticism of their colleagues' efforts. Three of the nine counts of censure were that it 'fails sufficiently to represent the traditional view of Christian marriage ...'; it 'effectively drains away authority from the Scriptures'; and 'in its recommendations concerning same-sex relationships and pre-marital sex, [it] weakens the Church's ability to speak prophetically by implying that these forms of sexual relationships are *morally equivalent* to marriage, thereby weakening the normative status of marriage and diminishing the significance of the two-parent family'.[80] Once again speculation about the value of the recovery of betrothal to both sides in this heated conversation cannot be resisted. Traditionalists may not realize how embedded betrothal is in scripture and tradition, and if the revisionists had deployed it in making secure the connection between marriage and prenuptial cohabitation they might have avoided the accusation that they were introducing new sexual relationships and assigning them a legitimacy that the tradition cannot sanction.

The Church and Human Sexuality *(South Africa) (1995)*

Our final sexuality report is South African. The South African Anglican Theological Commission produced *The Church and Human Sexuality* in 1995. Once again the marital norm is strongly affirmed, the problem of cohabitation is admitted, and the betrothal solution is hinted at but not allowed to influence the treatment cohabitation receives. 'The church believes that the commitment entailed in sexual intimacy should find its full and proper expression in lifelong marriage.'[81] 'The traditional practice of engagement is strongly recommended as a way in which couples come to know each other.'[82] Echoing the language of the Church of England House of Bishops, marriage is said to be 'the ideal situation in which the couple can grow and realize their full personhood in mutual love, and so grow to maturity'. It is recommended that couples 'living together without being formally married should be freely offered pastoral care, among other things to help them recognize that the full expression of their sexuality is ideally to be found in lifelong union. The growth of real companionship and mutual trust also requires the covenant and promises of marriage. Such couples should be encouraged to be married with the blessing of the church and in accordance with the law of the land.'

[80] Ibid., p.285.
[81] South African Anglican Theological Commission, *The Church and Human Sexuality* (Marshalltown, South Africa, 1995), p.15.
[82] Ibid., p.18.

It is surprising that engagement is thought to be a 'traditional practice'. It turns out (below, p.202) to be a European practice exported to Africa, whereas the earlier European practice of betrothal actually turns out to be more congruent with African traditions of marriage. Cohabitors are not condemned but gently advised, for their own good, to seek the blessing of God and the church on their relationship by formalizing it. The betrothal solution would have added considerably to the analysis. Not only would a link have been made with biblical and traditional practice (instead of the link with non-traditional engagement): the willingness of the church to give its unreserved blessing to such premature unions would have been better explained. On this alternative view the marriages awaiting solemnization would have already begun.

The examination of denominational sexuality documents has shown the need for a systematic investigation and statement of the opportunities afforded by the biblical and premodern practice of betrothal. Betrothal assumes the marital norm. It has been shown that when the marital norm is weakened, or perceived to have been weakened, a fierce tussle ensues between different factions. Churches which have weakened the marital norm have paradoxically done so for sound evangelical and pastoral reasons. They have sought to reach, and to affirm in their congregations, members of sexual minorities who are excluded and alienated by the imposition of the marital norm as a rule. A recognition of the historically changing character of marriage and the opportunities it currently offers to embrace at least some cohabitors of heterosexual and homosexual orientation has not been taken up. Instead, marriage has been sidelined. Mainstream Protestant thought commits a triple whammy against lesbian and gay couples. Marriage is affirmed both as a norm and as a rule; it is sometimes used as a weapon ('heterosexual marriage'); and it perpetuates a discredited dogmatism by creating victims.

When the marital norm is affirmed in relation to heterosexual couples living together, the opportunity to rethink the entry into marriage in a manner suggested by the tradition of betrothal has not generally been taken. Sometimes the word 'betrothal' is used, indicating a lingering reminiscence of earlier methods of entry into marriage. The strident language of fornication is generally avoided, and the recognition that prenuptial cohabitation is in a different category from casual or promiscuous sex is often found. But the betrothal solution has not been rediscovered. There are references to clandestine marriage. Clandestine marriage is an important phenomenon in the voyage of rediscovery of betrothal, but its replication at the present time is likely to replicate many of the difficulties formerly associated with it. The solution offered by betrothal as the beginning of marriage beckons as both traditional and contemporary. We have reached the stage in the argument where delivery of the claims made for betrothal are becoming overdue. Its retrieval is the subject of part 2.

An exercise in retrieval: bringing back betrothal

CHAPTER 4

The Bible and betrothal

This chapter demonstrates that betrothal, as the customary method of entry into marriage, is embedded in the Bible. It is assumed by Jewish, Roman, and emerging Christian traditions. The separate cases of Mary the mother of Jesus (first section), Rebecca, Rachel, Zipporah and Sarah (second section) are examined. Roman marriage practices are described (third section). Betrothal is shown to be presupposed in the New Testament and its developing theologies of marriage (fourth section). Finally some remarks by Tertullian and two of the canons of the Synod of Elvira are taken as evidence of the incorporation of betrothal into Christian practice in the third and fourth centuries. Evidence from liturgy and law must await chapter 5.

THE BETROTHAL OF MARY AND JOSEPH

Mary the mother of Jesus was betrothed to Joseph when she became pregnant. In what sense, if any, was their relationship a marriage? The account of the birth of Jesus in the Gospel of Matthew takes us to the heart of this question. Mary was 'betrothed (*mnèsteutheisès*) to Joseph; before their marriage (*prin è suneltheîn*) she found she was going to have a child through the Holy Spirit' (Matt. 1:18). Mary was promised in marriage, and therefore by implication not yet married. Betrothal took place at a very early age, usually at twelve or twelve and a half.[1] The Authorized Version (AV) has 'was espoused to Joseph'. The language of espousal, spousals, espoused, etc., was still common in 1611. The Revised English Bible

---

[1] W.D. Davies and Dale C. Allison, *A Critical and Exegetical Commentary on The Gospel According to Saint Matthew*, 2 vols. (Edinburgh: T&T Clark, 1988), vol.I, p.199.

(REV) rendering 'before their marriage' translates an infinitive (*sunelthein*[2]) by a noun ('marriage') and so loses its verbal form. The AV translation ('before they came together') is preferable. Not only is 'came together' obviously a verb: it preserves the root meaning of the original ('go along with', 'meet', 'come together', 'assemble'). Matthew does not use the available term *gamos* ('marriage', 'wedding' or 'wedding feast' – although he uses it elsewhere[3]). If he had meant 'marriage', he could have used the appropriate noun. There is a sexual use of 'coming together', that of having sexual intercourse. Since Matthew's intention is to describe 'how the birth of Jesus Christ came about' (1:18) the sexual meaning is obvious. Mary and Joseph were betrothed, but they had not had sexual intercourse prior to the pregnancy with Jesus.

'Being a man of principle and at the same time wanting to save her from exposure, Joseph made up his mind to have the marriage contract quietly set aside' (1:19). Older translations are again to be preferred to the REV. The AV has, 'Then Joseph her husband, being a just *man*, [*Iòseph de ho anèr autès, dikaios òn*] and not willing to make her a publick example, was minded to put her away privily [*lathra apolusai autèn*].' 'Being a man of principle' avoids translating *anèr autès* as 'her husband'. (While *anèr* means 'man' and 'husband', the REV misses the genitive 'her'.) Immediately a question arises: is Joseph 'her man', i.e., 'hers' because he is her fiancé, or is he in law her 'husband' already on account of being betrothed to her?

Joseph is depicted as ignorant of the supernatural origin of Mary's child, and forgiving in his intention to have the marriage contract cancelled. She will be saved from prosecution for adultery and from full exposure to the rigour of the Deuteronomic law. The penalty for 'a virgin pledged in marriage to a man, and another man encounters her in the town and lies with her' was death by stoning for both of them (Deut. 22:23–4). There was apparently some relaxation of this terrible law.[4] A good argument that betrothal is the beginning of marriage is found in Joseph's intention to divorce her. The verb *apoluein* was certainly used of divorce. 'Marriage contract'

---

[2] *sunelthein* is the aorist infinitive of *sunerchomai*.   [3] Matt. 22:2f.; 25:10. And see John 2:1.

[4] See, e.g., Robert H. Gundry, *Matthew: A Commentary on His Literary and Theological Art* (Grand Rapids: Wm. B. Eerdmans, 1982), p.19.

rightly assumes the betrothal was legally binding. The angel dissuades Joseph from his intention with the words 'Joseph, son of David, do not be afraid to take Mary home with you to be your wife [*paralabein Marian tèn gunaika sou*]. It is through the Holy Spirit that she has conceived . . .' (1:20). The detail about taking Mary home (also at 1:22) suggests they were not living together, for this is what the angel urges. But this is again an unhelpful translation. There is no sound etymological reason for rendering *paralabein* as 'bring home': a literal meaning of this verb is 'to receive from another' or 'to take to oneself'. The marital meaning of the verb may derive from the practice of the bridegroom receiving his bride from her father or guardian. The AV 'take unto thee Mary thy wife' is archaic but accurate.

So 'Joseph took Mary home to be his wife, but had no intercourse with her until her son was born' (1:24–5). The narrative cannot bear the weight of the questions we might want to address to it. Is betrothal the prelude to marriage, or the beginning of marriage? Is Joseph Mary's husband, or her fiancé? Is Joseph's releasing of Mary from the betrothal contract the same thing as divorce? These are questions deriving from the concerns of this book. But there are prior (and more important) questions about the kind of literary source Matthew's prologue confronts us with and how that source might be read; about the theological and Christological concerns which shape the narrative and appear to subsume the historical detail; about the virgin birth tradition which Matthew and Luke alone record, and its relation to history; about its subsequent influence on the Church's understanding of sexuality; and about the impact of that understanding as it reflects back upon the virgin birth tradition. It will be necessary to deal with these questions only peripherally and attend merely to the literary fact that betrothal occurs at all in Matthew's birth narrative. The narrative requires a wider search of the Hebrew Bible, and of first-century betrothal customs. These customs will contextualize the narrative. We will then be in a better position to attend to the theological treatment which the marriage of Mary and Joseph receives in post-biblical periods.

The virgin birth tradition is unknown to Mark, Paul and John and may be the product of later reflection on the momentous event of the birth of Christ. It may be influenced by disdain for the act of sexual intercourse and by the belief that God the Son did not or could not enter the world in this way. It may truthfully reflect the convictions of Christians that the non-natural event of the divine incarnation could not have a wholly natural origin. If Joseph is not the father of Jesus, it is difficult to see how the genealogy of Matthew 1:1–17 works, since Joseph transmits the lineage of King David to Jesus. An earlier version of Luke's Gospel seems to want to dispel any assumption that Joseph was the father of Jesus ('. . .he was the son, *as people thought*, of Joseph son of Heli . . .': Luke 3:23, emphasis added). Matthew assumes the betrothal period was as binding as marriage, yet was without sexual experience. How far his assertion about Mary's virginity (assuming also his position to know) is driven by his Christology is impossible to say. We can, however, be confident that the assumption that betrothal periods at the time of Mary and Joseph did not include sexual intimacy owes more to an idealization of the facts than to the facts themselves.

The Halakhah describes the betrothal and nuptial events which together constitute marriage. There is a 'consecration' at the start of the betrothal. At the end of the betrothal period the nuptials occur and 'the husband brings his bride home or under the canopy'.[5] The marriage is sealed when the bride enters her husband's home (and that is probably why the REV translates *paralabein*, 'take home'). During the betrothal period, the daughter was neither totally under the authority of her father, nor yet controlled by her husband. The rabbis advocated that the length of betrothal should be a year.[6] According to Tal Ilan's detailed description of the custom, 'This period differed from the period that followed the nuptials only in that the betrothed couple were not permitted to have sexual intercourse; in order to insure this, the bride remained under the roof of her father.' And this custom 'explains Joseph's dilemma when, according to the Gospel of Matthew, he discovered that Mary, his betrothed, was pregnant, even though he had not yet married her'.[7]

[5] Tal Ilan, 'Premarital Cohabitation in Ancient Judea: The Evidence of the Babatha Archive and the Mishnah (*Ketubbot* 1.4)', *Harvard Theological Review* 86.3 (1993), 259.
[6] Davies and Allison, *Saint Matthew*, p.199.   [7] Ilan, 'Premarital Cohabitation', 259.

The REV translation of Matthew 1:19 assumes there was a 'marriage contract' which Joseph was minded to annul. This detail reflects the practice of contracts being completed at betrothal. Hillel the Elder produced a woman's betrothal contract written by her husband which said, 'When you enter my house you shall be my wife according to the law of Moses and Israel.'[8] However, there is evidence that in Judea prenuptial sexual practice (at least in the second century CE) was considerably more relaxed. A marriage contract from the Babatha archive in the Judean desert 'specifies that a couple had lived together for some time before the marriage contract was drawn up' and rabbinic sources confirm that '[s]ome men and women in Jewish society of second-century Palestine did indeed live together out of wedlock'. Indeed, continues Ilan, according to the Galileans and their rabbis 'Judeans were notorious in their premarital sexual license.'[9] A close reading of Talmudic texts leads Ilan to conclude that 'in Judea men and women continued to practice some sort of premarital cohabitation before the nuptials', and that 'premarital cohabitation was a local practice particular to and common in Judea'.[10] Adolf Harnack was aware that premarital sexual experience was common in Judea, and that is why he argued that Mary conceived by Joseph after the betrothal but before the wedding ceremony.[11]

The betrothal of Mary and Joseph as recorded by Matthew has led to an early encounter with a set of practices for entering marriage which differ from our own. Betrothal is as binding as marriage. In this sense they are married. It involves a marriage contract. It takes a divorce to break it. The betrothed couple do not live together or have sexual intercourse. In this sense their marriage lies in the future. The sign for sexual relations to commence is the groom's leading of the bride to the marital home and the nuptial celebrations. Much, perhaps all, of this can be found or assumed in Matthew's account, and corroborated independently. But Matthew's account is heavily influenced by theological considerations, and standard Jewish accounts of marital practice may also be driven by official views of what the rabbis believed ought to happen.

---

[8] Ibid., 260.   [9] Ibid., 247, 258.   [10] Ibid., 262.
[11] Davies and Allison, *Saint Matthew*, p.200, citing A. Harnack, *The Date of Acts and of the Synoptic Gospels* (London and New York: 1911), pp.149–50.

BETROTHAL IN THE HEBREW SCRIPTURES

The marriages of Isaac, Jacob, Moses and Tobias to Rebecca, Rachel, Zipporah and Sarah provide insights into early biblical marriage practice. There are similarities between the four narratives which have prompted the suggestion of a 'biblical betrothal type-scene'. The similarities include '*mutatis mutandis*, the encounter of the prospective groom and bride by a well, the act of drawing water, the swift communication of the encounter to the bride's family, followed by a festive meal and a betrothal agreement'.[12] There is much to discover here about ancient betrothal practice, and also little to emulate since all four of the betrothed women are treated as chattels at the disposal of men and given no say in the decision to give them away. There is a chilling ring to the phrases 'getting a wife', and 'taking a wife' (Gen. 24:38, 40). We are far from the settled assumption that marriage is a matter for two consenting individuals. The servant of Abraham is to choose a wife for his son Isaac. This is a task that can be delegated by his father to a servant. He sees Rebecca, 'very beautiful and a virgin guiltless of intercourse with any man' (Gen. 24:16), at the well. He petitions Rebecca's father (Bethuel) and brother (Laban) who answer, 'Here is Rebecca; take her and go. She shall be the wife of your master's son, as the LORD has decreed' (Gen. 24:51).[13]

Jacob sees Rachel at a well (Gen. 29:9). She was 'beautiful in face and figure, and Jacob had fallen in love with her' (17–18). Jacob works for seven years on Rachel's father's farm, and his labour is payment for Rachel (18–21). After seven years Jacob petitions Rachel's father, Laban, for Rachel – '"I have served my time. Give me my wife that I may lie with her"' (21). The presumption is that Rachel is Jacob's wife, and that they have not yet slept together. But Jacob is instead given Rachel's elder sister Leah. A wedding feast is held (which lasted seven days), and Jacob sleeps with his new bride. He agrees to work another seven years for Rachel, upon which 'Laban gave Jacob his daughter Rachel to be his wife' (28).

---

[12] Esther Fuchs, 'Structure, Ideology and Politics in the Biblical Betrothal Type-Scene', in Athalya Brenner (ed.), *A Feminist Companion to Genesis* (Sheffield: Sheffield Academic Press, 1993), p.274.

[13] Rebecca, unlike Rachel and Zipporah, is at least allowed to speak in the narrative. When she is asked (Gen. 24:58) whether she will go with the servant, the decision is not between going or staying, but between going there and then, or going a few days later.

Moses was sitting 'by a well one day' (Exod. 2:15) as Zipporah and her sisters were drawing water for their father's sheep, when other shepherds drove them off. When Reuel their father hears of the incident, Moses is invited for a meal (20). 'So it came about that Moses agreed to stay with the man, and he gave Moses his daughter Zipporah in marriage' (21).

These stories are certain to grate with gender-aware readers who may need to struggle particularly hard to discern the providential hand of God in the affairs of the ancestors of the Jewish and Christian traditions. But they corroborate what we know about the entry into marriage prior to the time of Christ. 'The betrothal type-scene, from the bride's perspective, is merely her transposition from her father's custody to her husband's custody . . .' She is 'characterized as a prized object whose acquisition exacts a price from the bridegroom'.[14] The bride's father may dispose of his daughter. There may be a bride price. There is an agreement between the groom (or his representative) and the bride's father, which is part of a binding betrothal and can last seven years. The transition (clearly marked in the treacherous marriage of Jacob to Leah) to full marriage is marked by sexual relations and by a wedding feast. The consent that makes the marriage is between men, and the constraints of monogamy belong far into the future. There is no hint (at least in these narratives) of any ceremony or invocation of blessing.

There are allusions to the wedding ceremony in the later Hebrew Bible. The bride wears jewels and the bridegroom a 'garland' (Isa. 49: 18; 61: 10). The Book of Tobit, a novella or Diasporan romance, written to inspire faith in God and in human endeavour,[15] describes in detail the practice of betrothal and its relation to marriage. It is patterned on the betrothal stories just discussed. Tobias is on his way to recover money owed to his father, when the angel Raphael tells him,

'We must stay tonight with Raguel, who is a relative of yours. He has a daughter named Sarah, but no other children, neither sons nor daughters. You as her next of kin have the right to marry her and inherit her father's

---

[14] Fuchs, 'Structure', p.279.
[15] Carey A. Moore, 'The Book of Tobit', in Bruce M. Metzger and Michael D. Coogan (eds.), *The Oxford Companion to the Bible* (New York: Oxford University Press, 1993), p.747.

property. The girl is sensible, brave, and very beautiful indeed, and her
father is an honourable man.' He went on: 'It is your right to marry her.
Be guided by me, my friend; I shall speak to her father this very night and
ask him to promise us the girl as your bride, and on our return from Rages
we shall celebrate her marriage. I know that Raguel cannot withhold her
from you or betroth her to another without incurring the death penalty
according to the decree in the book of Moses; and he is aware that his
daughter belongs by right to you rather than to any other man. Now be
guided by me, my friend; we shall talk about the girl tonight and betroth
her to you, and when we return from Rages we shall take her back with
us to your home.' (Tobit 6:10–13)

Another beautiful woman is about to be given to a man she does
not know without being consulted. Tobias (it turns out) is her
cousin, and because she is an only child, he is entitled (on one
interpretation of Numbers 27:8–11) to marry her and share her
inheritance. Her father alone has the power to give her away, and
because of the inheritance law he cannot refuse. The angel has in
mind an immediate betrothal, then a marriage celebration at their
joint homecoming. The promises are to be made by the bride's father. The legal point is one of ownership. Tobias has an irrefutable
claim.

    Later that evening Raguel is petitioned urgently to give his
daughter to Tobias. In Sarah's absence he does so with the words:

'I give her to you in accordance with the decree in the book of Moses, and
Heaven itself has decreed that she shall be yours. Take your kinswoman;
from now on you belong to her and she to you, from today she is yours
for ever. May all go well with you both this night, my son; may the Lord
of heaven grant you mercy and peace.' (7:12)

This saying may belong to a formal betrothal ceremony for in the
Vulgate it appears in 'a proper liturgical form'.[16] The benediction
pronounced on their first night in bed is timely – Sarah has married
seven times before and each of her husbands was killed by a demon
on their wedding night! After Sarah is at last fetched, her father
(in the absence of her mother) 'took her by the hand and gave
her to Tobias with these words: "Receive my daughter as your
wedded wife in accordance with the law, the decree written in the

---

[16] Kenneth Stevenson, *To Join Together: The Rite of Marriage* (New York: Pueblo Publishing
    Company, 1987), p.12.

book of Moses; keep her and take her safely home to your father. And may the God of heaven grant you prosperity and peace"' (7:13).

These sayings probably reflect liturgical and social practice at the time of their writing (*c.* 225–175 BCE). They influence later Judaism and probably Christianity. Custody of the woman is handed over from one man to another. In contemporary Christian wedding liturgies provision still exists for the bride's father to 'give away' his daughter. That this is a betrothal is clear from the contract that is prepared after the giving away. Raguel then 'sent for her mother and told her to fetch a roll of papyrus, and he wrote out and put this seal on a marriage contract giving Sarah to Tobias as his wife according to this decree' (7:14). This apparently contradicts the rabbinic *halakah* on marriage, since the groom writes the contract, not the bride's father.[17] The signing is followed by celebration, and the wedding night. The demon is distracted by the smell of a fish's liver and heart burning on incense and disappears. Tobias says a further (liturgical?) prayer (8:5–7), and the narrative includes several further prayers of blessing (8:15–17; 9:6; 11:14, 17).

The Book of Tobit influences Talmudic Judaism, and while the Talmud is composed in the third century CE, it reflects earlier practice. This is why it interests Christians as much as Jews.[18] It may come as a surprise to Christians to learn that only in the Talmudic period was non-marital sex discouraged. While Christians have noted the polygamy of the patriarchs, David's adultery with Bathsheba and Solomon's many wives, their reading of the Hebrew scriptures may have been influenced by the different standards of the New Testament, so that they may find difficult Rabbi Gold's asseverations that 'the written Torah never forbids sex outside the context of marriage, with the exception of adultery and incest. On the contrary, the Torah seems to assume that it is a natural part of life.'[19] 'The Bible is natural and unembarrassed about the sexual activities of its major personalities.' Judaism regards virginity as a 'tragedy'.[20] Virginity is a matter of economics. 'In rabbinic

---

[17] Moore, 'The Book of Tobit', pp.746–7. [18] Stevenson, *To Join Together*, p.13.
[19] Rabbi Michael Gold, *Does God Belong in the Bedroom?* (Philadelphia: Jewish Publication Society, 1992), p.60.
[20] Ibid., pp.61, 62.

law, a woman's virginity has certain financial consequences at the time of marriage. If the bride is a virgin, the *ketubbah* paid by the husband is two hundred *zuz*; if she is not a virgin, it is one hundred *zuz*.[21] Gold candidly admits betrothed couples had sex. 'A man's virginity is never discussed. An unmarried woman who chooses to have sex with an unmarried man and is willing to live with the financial consequences *has not broken any explicit law of the Torah*. In fact, in Judah *the established custom was for betrothed couples to have sexual relations before marriage*.'[22]

The rabbinic move against non-marital sex had several unacceptable consequences, one of which, replicated in Christianity, was insistence upon child marriage (below, p.148). This was the most obvious way of proscribing premarital sex and rendering virginity at marriage more likely. For the rabbis of the Talmud a father was expected to arrange a marriage for his daughter while she was still a *na'arah*, a young maiden between twelve and twelve and a half years old. This is still the practice of ultra-Orthodox Jews.[23] Another consequence was the segregation of the sexes. As Rabbi Gold explains, betrothal was too simple, for, as the Mishnah taught, 'A woman is acquired [as a wife] in three ways ... By money, by a document, and by sexual intercourse.'[24] Having sex with a woman, *at all*, was thought to have established marital intent. Not until the Middle Ages were betrothal and marriage brought together in a single ceremony.[25] In earlier times a year elapsed between the two stages. Once betrothal is scrapped as a separate stage, 'premarital' sex can be defined more clearly. Even then the keeping of a concubine was not forbidden. 'The Torah never explicitly forbids nonmarital sex. In fact, it permits the taking of a concubine, a woman who has an exclusive relationship with a man without kiddushin or ketubbah [hallowing or contract], the basic necessities of marriage. In other words, *it is parallel to our modern living together without benefit of clergy*.'[26]

---

[21] Ibid., p.62 (citing *Ketubbot*, 1.2).   [22] Ibid., p.62 (citing *Ketubbot*, 1.5)(emphases added).
[23] Ibid., p.63.   [24] Ibid. (citing *Kiddushin*, 1.1).   [25] Stevenson, *To Join Together*, p.15.
[26] Gold, *Does God Belong in the Bedroom?*, p.66 (emphasis added). And see David C. Gross and Esther R. Gross, *Under the Wedding Canopy: Love and Marriage in Judaism* (New York: Hippocrene Books, 1996), pp.26–7.

The Song of Songs has an important place in any biblical understanding of sexual love. This cycle of love-songs is 'a celebration of
romantic and sexual bliss between man and woman'.[27] However,
it is commonly assumed by scholars, on the basis of the language
found in the Song, that the lovers were *betrothed*.[28] Even conservative scholars take this view. One of them, Tom Gledhill, concedes
that 'it makes sense to assume that the lovers are a betrothed couple', and explains important differences between betrothal in the
ancient world and engagement in modernity:

Betrothal was the point of no return, and the future of the couple was irrevocably sealed. Their marriage had been arranged; they were not isolated
individuals who had casually crossed paths and happened to have fallen
in love. Members of their larger family units had brought them together,
and when all the negotiations between the families had been finalized and
the bride-price agreed and paid, then the couple were considered to be
officially betrothed. All that remained was for the wedding to take place
and the union to be consummated.[29]

Gledhill thinks 'it is not inappropriate to view the Song as the
joyous, tentative explorations of love of the betrothed couple, cul-
minating in their marriage and full sexual union in 5:1'.[30] This
verse undoubtedly assumes uninhibited love-making:

> *Consummation*
>
> I have entered in, my precious bride,
> I have taken possession of my garden,
> the home of ancient promise.
> I have tasted her milk.
> I have gathered her honey.
> I have tasted the wine from her grapes.
> O delightful delirium,
> O intimate union,
> a fusion of love.

[27] For an exhaustive treatment of the contested accounts of the meaning and message of
the Song, see Greg W. Parsons, 'Guidelines for Understanding and Utilizing the Song of
Songs', *Bibliotheca Sacra* 156, no.624 (October–December 1999), 399–422.

[28] Ibid., 412, note 99.

[29] Tom Gledhill, *The Message of the Song of Songs: The Lyrics of Love* (Leicester: Inter-Varsity
Press, 1994), p.27.

[30] Ibid., p.28.

Affirmation

Feast, O lovers,
drink your fill,
from all restraints set free.
Let passions pent, their floodgates vent,
and cast yourselves with joyful glee
upon the tide of love.[31]

It may be assuming too much to expect the lovers were 'awaiting' the consummation of their marriage. There is nothing 'tentative' about the celebration of sexual love prior to 5:1. It is probably prurient to press too closely the question when full love-making occurred, and since the text is a collection of edited songs, it cannot in any case be read as continuous narrative. The text resists chronological questions inviting answers with 'before' and 'after', for marriage is not a single event, and the period between betrothal and marriage ceremony is very much a period of 'in-between' when chastity between the couple was not seriously expected.

BETROTHAL IN THE ROMAN EMPIRE

The Jewish practice of betrothal was paralleled by a similar practice throughout the Roman empire, and this is a further reason why Christians adopted it. It was embedded in Roman law and custom. One historian writing at the end of the nineteenth century emphasized the continuity between established Roman, and innovative Christian, marital practice. 'The Christian Church for many centuries simply accepted and conformed to the Roman law and Roman customs so far as was compatible with Christian views, commonly confirming the unions by religious benedictions.'[32] A century later, this view is emphatically confirmed by Judith Evans Grubbs who, having reviewed recent relevant classical scholarship, says, 'The arranged marriage preceded by betrothal seems to have been customary among Christians in the Empire, as it was among

---

[31] Song of Songs 5:1, as translated by Gledhill, *Message of the Song of Songs*, p.75.
[32] Oscar D. Watkins, *Holy Matrimony: A Treatise on the Divine Laws of Marriage* (New York: Macmillan, 1895), p.78.

non-Christians.'[33] As we shall see (below, p.161) at the beginning of the second millennium Roman influence does not wane but rather enjoys a revival. Roman law stipulated that consent, and only consent, was the defining feature of legally valid marriages.[34] The traditional Roman view of marriage, as expressed by the lawyer Modestinus in the early third century, was 'the joining of a male and female and a partnership (*consortium*) of all of life, a sharing of divine and human law'.[35]

Living together as husband and wife constituted marriage, *de facto*, under Roman law. 'No marriage relied basically on any particular ceremony for its validity. Cohabitation of eligible partners, accompanied by "marital intention and regard", constituted marriage.'[36] If you lived together 'as' man and wife, 'man and wife you were'.[37] Your marriage was *iustum matrimonium*.[38] Philip Lyndon Reynolds emphasizes that Roman marriage is founded on 'continuous accord', not on 'contractual agreement'.[39] However, betrothal was generally celebrated, especially among the upper classes. The male head (*paterfamilias*) of each family entered protracted negotiations, each 'anxious to determine the suitability of the potential son-in-law or daughter-in-law, and to secure the best possible terms for their own family'.[40] The minimum ages of marriage were 12 for women and 14 for men: the actual average age of marriage was 15–18 for women, 12–15 for women from aristocratic families, and 25–30 for men.[41] There were two kinds of marriage available under Roman law, marriage with *manus* and marriage without *manus*. The *manus* was the husband's 'hand', and meant his full control over his wife: marriage

---

33 Judith Evans Grubbs, '"Pagan" and "Christian" Marriage: The State of the Question', *Journal of Early Christian Studies* 2.3 (1994), 388. And see James A. Brundage, *Law, Sex, and Christian Society in Medieval Europe* (Chicago and London: University of Chicago Press, 1987), pp.33–8.

34 Watkins, *Holy Matrimony*, p.78.

35 Grubbs, '"Pagan" and "Christian" Marriage', 363 (citing *The Digest of Justinian*, 23.2.1).

36 Beryl Rawson, 'The Roman Family', in Beryl Rawson (ed.), *The Family in Ancient Rome: New Perspectives* (London and Sydney: Croom Helm, 1986), p.20.

37 J.A. Crook, *Law and Life of Rome* (London: Thames and Hudson, 1967), p.101; Rawson, 'The Roman Family', p.20.

38 Grubbs, '"Pagan" and "Christian" Marriage', 365.

39 Philip Lyndon Reynolds, *Marriage in the Western Church: The Christianization of Marriage During the Patristic and Early Medieval Periods* (Leiden: E.J. Brill, 1994), p.35.

40 Grubbs, '"Pagan" and "Christian" Marriage', 363.   41 Ibid.

without *manus* allowed the wife more independence over her affairs. As a token of this independence she would spend a minimum of three nights every year away from the matrimonial home.[42]

Details are complicated by the retention of elements of the ways of entry into marriage with *manus* in ceremonies of entry into marriage without *manus*, and it can be assumed that Christian practice was based on the latter.[43] Even though none of these ceremonies was essential to marriage, and the rites for each type of marriage varied according to time and place, for the sake of clarity they are best distinguished. The most common of the three ways of entry into marriage with *manus* was by the *confarreatio*. Watkins calls this

the most ancient, the most honoured, and the most religious form of marriage. The contract had to be made in the presence of ten witnesses. It was accompanied by a religious ceremony in which a sheep was sacrificed and its skin spread over two chairs upon which the bride and bridegroom sat down with heads covered. The marriage was then ratified by the pronouncement of a solemn formula or prayer. Another sacrifice followed and a further religious ceremony in which the *panis farreus* was employed. This was a cake made of *far* with the *mola salsa* prepared by the Vestal Virgins.[44]

The eating of wedding cake has survived from this Roman custom, and it appears that Christians adopted the *confarreatio* and substituted their own prayers and rites instead of the pagan ones.[45] The other two ways of beginning marriage with *manus* were by *co-emptio* (bride-purchase, sometimes from slavery) and *usus*, the *de facto* recognition of a marriage if the man and wife had lived together for a year.

Entry into marriage without *manus* was through betrothal, followed later by ceremony. Betrothal was accomplished at the *sponsalia*, defined by the jurist Florentinus as 'the recital and promise

[42] Watkins, *Holy Matrimony*, pp.80–2.   [43] Ibid., p.82.   [44] Ibid., pp.80–1.
[45] T.A. Lacey, *Marriage in Church and State* (London: Robert Scott, 1912), p.47. Watkins is
    doubtful it was adopted by Christians (*Holy Matrimony*, p.81), not least because it was
    falling out of use at the time of the expansion of the Church. He believes Christians
    adopted *sponsalia* celebrations instead, but as he admits clear lines of demarcation between
    ceremonies cannot be drawn.

of future nuptials'.[46] The *sponsalia* would take place at the house of the bride's father. A contract would be signed (on *tabulae legitimae*) by the couple which would contain details of the financial settlement between the families and marriage partners. There would be as many as ten witnesses.[47] Wedding presents (*arrhae*) belonged to this earlier ceremony which would also include a kiss, the placing of an iron ring (*annulus pronubus*) on the bride's finger, and the joining of hands. An omen or auspices would also be sought from seers, and this would be the only part of the ceremony to incite Christian objection. The wedding day would begin with the adorning of the bride followed by her procession to her husband's house. The bride would wear a veil (the *flammeum*) and she would be crowned with a floral wreath. This became, and remains, a feature of Orthodox weddings. It would be possible to marry with two ceremonies, or one, or none. In Christian rites, a bishop or priest would pronounce a blessing, at the betrothal and the nuptials ('double benediction'[48]). In later periods the blessing would take place in church, accompanied by the eucharist (which replaced the pagan sacrifice and the eating of the *panis farreus*), and in the churches of the East, the priestly blessing became the defining meaning and moment of the marriage ceremony.

Betrothal, as a preliminary stage in the passage to marriage, was practised in Judaism, and the betrothal of Mary and Joseph is the best biblical example of it. It was extensively practised throughout the Roman empire. It is difficult to say when explicitly Christian rites of betrothal and marriage began, since there is no direct evidence (but see pp.143–4). Kenneth Stevenson concludes 'that there *was* a marriage rite, that it consisted of an adapted version of Jewish practice, and that it persisted at least in those parts of the early Christian world where Jews had gone before and were still influential on the new religion'.[49] He thinks 'early Christians knew a sequence of betrothal and marriage, together with negotiation and contract, and that the marriage rite took place at home with a lengthy blessing over the couple'. The practice of betrothal is also required to make sense of marriage in the New Testament.

---

[46] Watkins, *Holy Matrimony*, p.83, citing Florentinus, *Dig.* 23, tit.1, s.1.
[47] As recorded by Ambrose, *De laps. virg. 5*; see Watkins, *Holy Matrimony*, p.88.
[48] Watkins, *Holy Matrimony*, p.90.   [49] Stevenson, *To Join Together*, p.18.

BETROTHAL MYSTICISM IN THE NEW TESTAMENT

There is little in the New Testament directly about marriage. Paul discourages it (1 Cor. 7:25–40) and so does the Gospel of Luke (20:34–6). Christians broadly continued Jewish practice and were later open to the adoption and adaptation of Roman marital customs. The paucity of reference to marriage is exacerbated by the loss to contemporary understanding of betrothal which is assumed by the biblical text. The Christian theology of marriage is found principally in a single text (Eph. 5:21–33). An examination of part of this narrative will lead to an exploration of the possible meanings of other marital metaphors in the New Testament (e.g., Christ as Bridegroom, the gathered Kingdom of God as a wedding feast).

The author of the Letter to the Ephesians, as is well known, uses a 'household code' found elsewhere in the New Testament, and subjects it to profound theological and Christological reflection.[50] The author is the first known Christian to make the connection between the love of husbands for their wives (this love is emphatically not reciprocal) and the love of Christ for the Church. As he elaborates this basic analogy reference is made to the preparations for a marriage ceremony. 'Husbands, love your wives, as Christ loved the church and gave himself up for it, to consecrate and cleanse it by water and word, so that he might present the church to himself all glorious, with no stain or wrinkle or anything of the sort, but holy and without blemish' (5:25–7). The references to consecration and cleansing probably allude to a series of revolting and compressed images used by Ezekiel in his depiction of the faithlessness of the southern kingdom of Israel. The nation is compared with an abandoned baby girl who 'was thrown out on the bare ground in your own filth on the day you were born' (Ezek. 16:5). The Lord rescues and tends this baby but also decrees she should live unwashed in

---

[50] See my *Marriage after Modernity: Christian Marriage in Postmodern Times* (Sheffield and New York: Sheffield Academic Press and New York University Press, 1999), pp.75–7, 87–95. The intractable sexism of the passage must first be acknowledged and eliminated before the full potential of the text for undergirding egalitarian marriage can be tapped. For a different but equally positive way of dealing with this difficulty, see Don S. Browning, Bonnie J. Miller-McLemore, Pamela D. Couture, K. Brynolf Lyon and Robert M. Franklin, *From Culture Wars to Common Ground: Religion and the American Family Debate* (Louisville: Westminster/ John Knox Press, 1997), pp.143–7.

her own blood (16:6). As the girl passes through puberty the Lord becomes betrothed to her.

I came by again and saw that you were ripe for love. I spread the skirt of my robe over you and covered your naked body. I plighted my troth and entered into a covenant with you, says the Lord GOD, and you became mine. Then I bathed you with water to wash off the blood; I anointed you with oil. (16:8–9)

A description follows of the betrothed's robes, girdle, linen, crown and sumptuous living as a queen. 'Your beauty was famed throughout the world; it was perfect because of the splendour I bestowed on you' (16:14).

There appear to be close allusions to Ezekiel in the Ephesian text. The Church is the new Israel. God makes a new covenant, with the Church. When God made a covenant with Judah, God washed the birth-blood of his newly betrothed bride off her body, anointed her with oil, and dressed her as a queen. God makes a new covenant by the shedding of Christ's blood (Eph. 1:7; 2:13). The Church too is washed by the water of baptism (later exegetes would link this verse with the flowing of blood and water from the side of Christ (John 19:34)) administered with the baptismal formula ('and word').[51] Christ in the Ephesian meditation is both bridegroom and presenter of the bride, or 'bridal page'.[52] In Ezekiel God administers the bridal bath, and prepares and dresses the body of his betrothed for the wedding. God is the beautician in attendance.[53] In Ephesians, Christ administers the bridal bath and makes the bride ready. She too has to be washed and the stains of sin removed. Christ is 'the beautician'.[54] In Ezekiel God bestows the bride's beauty on her. In Ephesians it is through Christ's action that the body of the Church is perfected, without stain, wrinkle or blemish. As presenter of the bride he gets her ready for the wedding, 'all glorious'. As the bridegroom he prepares *himself* to become one flesh with her (Eph. 5:31; Gen. 2:24).

---

[51] Ernest Best, *A Critical and Exegetical Commentary on Ephesians* (Edinburgh: T&T Clark, 1998), pp.543–4.
[52] Edward Schillebeeckx, *Marriage: Secular Reality and Saving Mystery*, 2 vols. (London: Sheed and Ward, 1965), vol.1, p.162.
[53] See Walther Eichrodt, *Ezekiel: A Commentary* (London: SCM Press, 1970), p.206.
[54] Best, *Ephesians*, p.546.

It is clear that only a perfected body can copulate with Christ. Now Christ and the Church are one body. The Church, all cleansed and glorious, *is* his body. How is the Church his body? It is the 'great mystery' (5:32) which is also the great mystery of becoming one flesh in marriage. That the Church *is* both the body of Christ as well as a separate body from Christ, as the object of his sacrificial love, is very clear from the text. On the human level, 'in loving his wife a man loves himself. For no one ever hated his own body; on the contrary, he keeps it nourished and warm, and that is how Christ treats the church' (5:29). Treating one's partner as one would treat oneself, the argument runs, is something all married people ought to do, and it is something Christ does with his partner, the Church. But Christ does not simply and prudently love his spouse's body as his own, he 'gave himself up for it' so that it could become his spouse at all. Christian husbands are to love their wives, not just because in doing so they love themselves. The self-giving of Christ for his mystical bride, the Church, is the example that all Christian husbands must emulate.

In Ezekiel and in Ephesians there are cases of covenant-union, and in each case the bride of God is betrothed. While the bride is prepared for the wedding in Ezekiel, there is no mention of the wedding itself. Rather, the bride uses her bridal clothes and beauty to entice 'every passer-by' to have sex with her (Ezek. 16:15). In Ephesians the role of Christ as presenter of the bride should not be eclipsed by the more familiar role of bridegroom. His role as presenter or beautician is also to make the Church ready for what is still in the future. Reference to sexual union later in the passage should not be allowed to obscure the eschatological sense in which the marriage ceremony and feast stands as symbol for the future union of all people and things in and with God.

In another New Testament letter the church is presented to Christ as his betrothed bride. Paul tells the Corinthians, 'I am jealous for you, with the jealousy of God; for I betrothed you to Christ, thinking to present you as a chaste virgin to her true and only husband. Now I am afraid that, as the serpent in his cunning seduced Eve, your thoughts may be corrupted and you may lose your single-hearted devotion to Christ' (2 Cor. 11:2–3). There is no exegetical theology of marriage here as there is in Ephesians. Rather, the marital metaphor gives Paul the material for a sharp rebuke. He imagines himself to be the presenter of the bride to Christ the bridegroom. The bride is not the whole Church, as in Ephesians, but the local Corinthian church. Paul is their spiritual 'father' because they owe their Christian faith to him. However, Paul fears he may be unable to present the church as Christ's virgin bride to Christ, because the church has listened to 'some newcomer' who 'proclaims another Jesus', or because it has received 'a spirit different from the Spirit already given to you' (2 Cor. 11:4). As one commentator observes, 'The presentation to Christ will presumably take place at his coming. In the meantime, during the period of the engagement, it is the duty of the Corinthians to keep themselves completely loyal to the one to whom they are to be united – within Paul's metaphor, to preserve their virgin status.'[55]

Paul's depiction of the Corinthians as the bride of Christ is best understood today as granting further licence to the churches to use the nuptial metaphor in respect of their self-understanding and mission. Christians have made promises to Christ and he has made promises to them. Their destiny is final union with Christ, and Christ's betrothal pledge is his sacrifice of himself for everyone. The Christian faith, then, is an experience of deepening love and escalating hope for the promised eschatological consummation, and the 'moments' of this faith are expressed in the experience of being betrothed. A further question to arise from the nuptial analogy of Ephesians 5 is whether the analogy between bridegroom and bride, and between Christ and the Church, is able to operate in each direction. An analogy of this kind might be assumed to *begin* with a human, finite comparison which is then extended in order to illustrate some aspect of the relation between God and humankind. In that case, the direction is from below upwards, or *anabatic*, and the love of husband for wife is the primary analogical term for speaking of Christ's love for the Church. The intriguing possibility exists that the direction of the analogy is also from above, downwards, or *katabatic*. If so, then the primary term is Christ's love for the Church. The one-flesh union which is human

55 C.K. Barrett, *A Commentary on the Second Epistle to the Corinthians* (London: Adam and Charles Black, 1973), p.272. And see Best, *Ephesians*, p.545.

marriage is secondary. The primary reality is the one-flesh union
between Christ and the Church which is achieved in the self-gift
of Christ in his sacrificial death. On this view the greater reality is
the 'great mystery' or 'paschal mystery' of the union of God with
humankind in the passionate love of Christ's passion. The vocation
of marriage is that of living the paschal mystery with one's spouse.
This *is* marriage on a Christian understanding, and preparation
for it is preparing oneself to love one's partner as Christ loved and
loves the Church.

The understanding of Christ's love for the Church as itself the
primary divine reality which is shared with all people but uniquely
with faithful married partners is a regular feature of Catholic and
Orthodox thought. Ultimately, the intelligibility of such talk depends on the legitimacy of the analogy working katabatically. Pope
John Paul II, for example, teaches:

> The communion between God and his people finds its definitive fulfill-
> ment in Jesus Christ, the bridegroom who loves and gives himself as the
> savior of humanity, uniting it to himself as his body. He reveals the orig-
> inal truth of marriage . . . This revelation reaches its definitive fullness in
> the gift of love which the word of God makes to humanity in assuming a
> human nature, and in the sacrifice which Jesus Christ makes of himself
> on the cross for his bride, the church ... The Spirit which the Lord pours
> forth gives a new heart, and renders man and woman capable of loving
> one another as Christ has loved us. Conjugal love reaches that fullness to
> which it is interiorly ordained, conjugal charity, which is the proper and
> specific way in which the spouses participate in and are called to live the
> very charity of Christ, who gave himself on the cross.[56]

I think that nuptial katabatic imagery, whereby the divine self-
giving for the whole creation is modelled as marriage, is theologically legitimate but should be used only with caution. It makes
self-giving the essence of marriage, and therein lies its profound
truth and greatest danger. If there are unequal power-relations
within marriage, self-giving is readily converted into exploitation.
Katabatic marital theology can also alienate unmarried people by
assuming marriage to be normative. When it is used to convey the
sense that Christ is the bridegroom to individual men and women,

---

[56] Pope John Paul II, *Familiaris Consortio* (Vatican City: Vatican Press, 1981), ch.13, 'Jesus
Christ, Bridegroom of the Church, and the Sacrament of Matrimony'.

married or single, who are individually 'wedded' to Christ, nuptial imagery is forced beyond itself and can legitimize an unhealthy disembodied mysticism. Another difficulty with the katabatic analogy is that it assumes that the relationship between Christ and the Church is one solely of conjugality. But as we have seen, it is also one of betrothal, with the nuptials postponed until the time of the end. In this respect Catholic thought may be seen to have lost contact with earlier traditions (below, p.247).

There is a further betrothal narrative in the New Testament which has not received adequate attention. It provides an additional warrant for a katabatic theology of betrothal. It is likely that the lengthy story of Jesus at the well with the Samaritan woman (John 4:1–42) is to be understood as a betrothal story because it relies on the literary conventions found in the betrothals of Rebecca, Rachel and Zipporah. The first clue that there is a marital meaning to the story is contained in the preceding testimony of John the Baptist, who describes his ancillary role in preparing for the ministry of Jesus in a series of marital metaphors. John explains he is the 'forerunner' of Jesus and compares his relationship to Jesus with the relationship of the 'bridegroom's friend' or 'bridal page'[57] to the bridegroom. 'It is the bridegroom who marries the bride. The bridegroom's friend, who stands by and listens to him, is overjoyed at hearing the bridegroom's voice' (John 3:29). There is no doubt: Christ is the bridegroom. But who is the bride?

We have already had reason to consider betrothal narratives in the Hebrew scriptures as a distinctive type-scene (above, p.124). Another theologian plausibly extends the conventions of these scenes to cover the narrative between Jesus and the woman at the well, explaining that while John 4 'is not a betrothal type-scene as such ... it is clear that it plays on the betrothal conventions, sometimes reversing them, sometimes reshaping them for the sake of the Gospel's christology'.[58] While there are variations, the conventions are:

1. The hero travels to a foreign land far away.
2. The hero stops at a well.

---

[57] Schillebeeckx, *Marriage*, p.162.
[58] James G. Williams, 'The Beautiful and the Barren: Conventions in Biblical Type-Scenes', *Journal for the Study of the Old Testament* 17 (June 1980), 113.

3. A maiden comes to the well.
4. Hero does something for the maiden, showing superhuman strength or ability.
5. The maiden hurries home and reports what has occurred.
6. The stranger is invited into the household of the maiden.
7. Hero marries maiden-at-the-well. (He will eventually take her back to his native land.)[59]

If it can be accepted that these conventions derive plausibly from the betrothal stories themselves and that John both knows and deploys them in the present narrative, the theological consequences are remarkable. Jesus, too, travels to a foreign land, Samaria. He too stops at a well, Jacob's well. A woman comes to the well. Unlike Rebecca and Rachel who are strikingly attractive and virginal, the Samaritan woman has had five husbands and a live-in lover. Jesus, like Abraham's servant, asks her for a drink. Abraham's servant gives gifts to Rebecca (Gen. 24:22) and her family (24:53); Jacob single-handedly removes 'a huge stone' from a well so Rachel and her sheep can drink (Gen. 29:2, 8–10). Jesus has 'living water' to offer the woman (John 4:10). Just as Rebecca 'ran to her mother's house' (Gen. 24:28), Rachel 'ran and told her father' (Gen. 29:12), and the seven daughters of Reuel returned to him (Exod. 2:18), so the Samaritan woman 'left her water-jar and went off to the town, where she said to the people, "Come and see a man who has told me everything I ever did. Could this be the Messiah?"' (John 4:29) Abraham's servant, Jacob and Moses all stay in the homes of the betrothed women's fathers: 'when these Samaritans came to him they pressed him to stay with them; and he stayed two days' (John 4:40).

John has used the betrothal conventions, which would have been 'a source of delight' both to him 'and to allegorically or typologically inclined teachers',[60] for his own profound theological purposes. When he departs from them, he does so in order to make pointed contrasts with what is already familiar. It is Jesus, not the woman, who has water to offer, and even Samaritans are welcome to drink it. Even the final convention, that of marriage, is not exactly neglected, just adjusted. Jesus does not marry the woman but union

59 Ibid., 109.   60 Ibid., 114.

with him is possible, even for a Samaritan with a chaotic love-life. The use of 'We know' (*oidamen*: 'we ... know that this is indeed the Christ, the Saviour of the world' – AV) at 4:42 suggests union with Christ, which, along with indwelling, is a wider theme of John's Gospel.

While the allegorical details of this story may appear to have taken us some distance from the topic of betrothal mysticism, it may be plausibly suggested that the very gift of salvation is to be understood as the self-gift of marriage. It provides a katabatic theology of betrothal in which God takes the initiative of self-giving to all humanity in a relationship of infinite love that is finitely lived out in the loving commitments that make marriage. Christ is the bridegroom. There are no worries about virginal status here. The woman who appears in the guise of his betrothed at the well is immoral, and aware that Jews regard her racial origin as inferior (4:9). Unlike the brides of Ezekiel and Ephesians who have to be prepared by the beautician in order to be made ready for the nuptial ceremonies, this woman does not conform to type. Such is the depth of the love of God for humanity that no-one is excluded on grounds of religion, sex or race. Christ in offering them living water offers himself. Like all the other encounters that began at a well and led to betrothal and the union of marriage, the encounter with Christ the bridegroom leads to a union of faith and knowledge which has its counterparts in betrothed love.

Schillebeeckx confirms that the meanings of marriage in the New Testament are principally to be found in the expectation of consummation rather than in consummation itself. He says, 'In the New Testament marriage is used first of all as a means of revealing the eschatological or heavenly glorification in which Christians, together with Christ, are to celebrate the eternal wedding-feast with God.'[61] This is right but even Schillebeeckx may underplay the eschatological dimension he finds there. Betrothal adds an edge to the eschatological consummation. There is an eagerness and anticipation about the coming future because pledges have already been made. This gives a deeper meaning to the joy of the wedding-feast (and to the crime of turning down an invitation to it

---

[61] Schillebeeckx, *Marriage*, p.159.

(Matt. 22:1–10)). Just as Christ is the one who makes ready the bride in Ephesians, so the eschaton is a final making ready of the betrothed: '"Hallelujah! The Lord our God, sovereign over all, has entered on his reign! Let us rejoice and shout for joy and pay homage to him, for the wedding day of the Lamb has come! His bride has made herself ready, and she has been given fine linen, shining and clean, to wear"' (Rev. 19:7–8). The new Jerusalem comes 'down out of heaven from God, made ready like a bride adorned for her husband' (Rev. 21:2).

It is possible to link three levels of anticipation amidst the freeplay of these bridal metaphors at the anabatic level. At the first level betrothal anticipates the living together of marriage. At the second level the celebration of marriage anticipates the heavenly banquet when the final victory over evil is celebrated. At the third level the Church itself bears fragmentary witness in its (particularly eucharistic) life to the final reconciliation of all things in God. Walter Kasper speaks for several Catholic and Orthodox theologians when he observes:

The Church always continues to be a sacramental sign and instrument and a symbolic anticipation of the gathering together and reconciliation of mankind at the end of time and the establishment of peace among the nations. The festive mood at a wedding is a symbol of the joy and the fulfilment of human hopes that will be present at the end of time (see Mark 2:19ff; Matt. 22:1–14; 25:1–13 etc.). It is therefore not simply necessary from the human point of view alone to celebrate the wedding as festively as possible, it is also important to mark the occasion in this way as a hopeful anticipation and celebration in advance of the feast at the end of time.[62]

All these levels are anabatic in that they are rooted in human anticipation. But they have their origin in the unfathomable and katabatic love of God for all things through Christ which is God's gift and not simply the grounded experience of deep human yearning. Betrothal and marriage are what they are in Christianity not simply because they are pre-Christian social conventions, but because the love of God made known in Christ is the paschal mystery which is also a union of one flesh.

[62] Walter Kasper, *Theology of Christian Marriage* (New York: Seabury Press, 1980), pp.42–3.

BETROTHAL IN EARLY CHRISTIAN HISTORY

Betrothal, then, is embedded in the Bible. Since betrothal was a common means of entering marriage for Jews and Romans too, it is not surprising that it was also adopted by Christians, as Christian rites and ceremonies became established. According to David Petras, the twofold pre-Christian rite had 'two important moments', the handing over of the bride from her father or guardian to the husband, and the leading in procession of the bride to her new home. The rite of betrothal, or 'solemn pledge', took the place of the handing over of the bride and the crowning took the place of the entrance to the new home.[63] Marriage ceremonies took place originally at home, the bridal chamber was blessed, and the crowns remained in the house for eight days before being removed with a blessing and a prayer. Whereas the exchange of rings once symbolized the transactions specified in the marriage contract, the rings were soon spiritualized into a sign of commitment. In the West, they became 'signs of eternity or the unity of hearts, from the ancient notion that a vein led from the fourth finger directly to the heart'.[64]

The writings of Tertullian (*c.* 160–*c.* 225) provide good evidence of betrothal. He opposed the practice of drifting into marriage by living together or by marrying secretly or privately, options, as we have seen, for citizens under Roman law. He argues in *On Modesty* that clandestine betrothal and marriage cannot escape the charge of fornication and adultery. 'Accordingly, among *us*, secret connections as well – connections, that is, not first professed in presence of the Church – run the risk of being judged akin to adultery and fornication.' It is clear that Christians *did* enter marriage this way, for Tertullian adds, 'Nor must we let them, if thereafter woven together by the covering of marriage, elude the charge.'[65] In his treatise *To His Wife* he observes that it is rare to find a rich bachelor in 'the house of God', and commends the 'Gentile' practice of women marrying husbands poorer than themselves. This practice is fine among Christians, he thinks, because a Christian husband

[63] David M. Petras, 'The Liturgical Theology of Marriage', *Diakonia* 16.3 (1981), 228.
[64] Ibid., 228–9.
[65] Tertullian, *On Modesty*, 4. Text in A. Roberts and J. Donaldson (eds.), *The Ante-Nicene Fathers*, 10 vols. (Grand Rapids: Eerdmans, 1951), vol.IV, p.77.

poorer than his bride makes up his financial deficit with spiritual
riches. As he develops this slightly trivial point (that a husband who
is 'rich in God' brings more to a marriage than one who is only
rich in possessions), he makes remarks which assume betrothal and
liturgical practice:

Let her be on an equality with him, on earth, who in the heavens will
perhaps not be so. Is there need for doubt, and inquiry, and repeated
deliberation, whether he whom God has entrusted with His own property
is fit for dotal endowments? Whence are we to find (words) enough fully
to tell the happiness of that marriage which the Church cements, and
the oblation confirms, and the benediction signs and seals; (which) angels
carry back the news of (to heaven), (which) the Father holds for ratified?
For even on earth children do not rightly and lawfully wed without their
father's consent.

Since God has entrusted the bridegroom with the gift of his
bride, there is no reason why the bridegroom should not also profit
from the wealth she brings into the marriage when the details are
arranged. This is the betrothal phase, and what Tertullian says next
clearly refers to the wedding or *nuptials*. The church 'cements' what
is already joined together at betrothal. The eucharist replaces the
animal sacrifice of pagan Rome, and the blessing marks the point
when the marriage assumes a permanent bond between the couple.
The wedding must be public ('no stealthy signing' Tertullian says
later), and the consent of the earthly fathers and the heavenly Father
is required.

The practice of betrothal is clear from another of Tertullian's
works, *On the Veiling of Virgins*, and although the argument he pursues is, by present standards, shamefully demeaning to women, it
will be described for the light it throws on ancient practice. Com-
menting on the details of Paul's teaching about the need for women
to keep their heads covered in church (1 Cor. 11:1–16), Tertullian
teaches that *all* virgins must wear veils, only to qualify this ruling by
exempting children. This ruling places him in difficulty. When is
a child no longer a child? His answer causes him to introduce two
concepts of 'virgin'. In one a virgin is someone who has not had
sexual intercourse. In the other, a virgin ceases to be a virgin, not
when she has sexual intercourse with a man, but when her body
behaves and looks like a woman's. Tertullian has had to distinguish

between girls and women and he does so by reference to puberty and how young women look. With this second concept 'a virgin ceases to be a virgin from the time that it becomes possible for her *not* to be one'.[66] Using the metaphor of fruit ripe for plucking, he says a virgin 'ceases to be a virgin when she is perceived to be ripe'. A woman is no longer innocent as soon as men start noticing and desiring her, and for that reason she must wear a veil. An *a fortiori* argument is now aimed at betrothed women. If all women that men start to notice should wear veils, how much more should betrothed women do so, also? And at this juncture Tertullian invokes the example of Rebecca (above, p.124), unwittingly confirming for future generations some details about betrothal:

> And the *betrothed* indeed have the example of Rebecca, who, when she was being conducted – herself still unknown – to an unknown betrothed, as soon as she learned that he whom she had sighted from afar was the man, awaited not the grasp of the hand, nor the meeting of the kiss, nor the interchange of salutation; but confessing what she had felt – namely, that she had been (already) wedded in spirit – denied herself to be a *virgin* by then and there veiling herself.

Rebecca 'took her veil and covered herself' (Gen. 24:65) as soon as Isaac became known to her. Tertullian is impressed that she did not wait for a ceremony in order to understand that she was already 'wedded in spirit'. The details of the ceremony include the joining of hands, the kiss between the couple, and probably the exchange of rings and pledges.

There are still other insights to be gleaned about marital entry from this balefully androcentric text. Betrothed Christian brides-to-be are to wear veils until the nuptials. Rebecca's example shows 'that marriage likewise, as fornication is, is transacted by gaze and mind'. This is exactly the kind of thinking condemned by feminists as 'the male gaze'. The desire of young men for young women is fuelled by how women appear to them, and Christian parents should take advantage of this and show off their daughters to make sure they get proposals of marriage. On the other hand, betrothed women are already wedded in spirit and so should not be exciting

---

[66] Tertullian, *On the Veiling of Virgins*, ch.11. Text in Roberts and Donaldson, *The Ante-Nicene Fathers*, p.34 (translators' emphases).

male attention. Parents of unbetrothed daughters should marry them off, without worrying about lack of money or being excessively choosey about the right partner ('straitened means or scrupulosity'). They are married already to Christ, and their parents should be finding them a second husband, as soon as puberty is reached ('her "shame" everywhere clothing itself, the months paying their tributes; and do you deny her to be a *woman* whom you assert to be undergoing *womanly* experiences?'). Veiling, Tertullian tells these parents, can wait: 'If the contact of a *man* makes a *woman*, let there be no covering except after actual experience of marriage' (i.e., betrothal).[67]

Another *a fortiori* argument ensues which tells us more about betrothal. Among the 'heathen' brides are led veiled to their husbands. How much more then, thinks Tertullian, should Christian brides also wear veils:

Nay, but even among the heathens (the betrothed) are led *veiled* to the husband. But if it is at *betrothal* that they are veiled, because (then) both in body and in spirit they have mingled with a male, through the kiss and the right hands, through which means they first in spirit unsealed their modesty, through the common pledge of conscience whereby they mutually plighted their whole confusion; how much more will time veil them?

Betrothal, for heathens and Christians alike, occurs at a ceremony whose components symbolize the joining of two lives. The kiss and the joining of hands are given sexual meanings which anticipate the full 'mixing together' ('confusion') of each other both in sexual intercourse and in a common life. They promise each to the other, and this is the reason for the veiling of the bride-to-be, whose betrothed state, like that of the mother of Jesus, has binding force. The elliptical reference to the veiling by time refers to the urgency of marrying early, i.e., ideally, at twelve and fourteen years. Daughters are also 'wedded' to 'mother Nature' and 'father Time' who will ensure that if parents do not marry their daughters early, 'the girls themselves decide the match' for themselves by having premarital sex.[68] The heathen are commended for marrying girls at twelve and boys at fourteen. They rightly understand puberty

---

[67] Ibid. (translators' emphases).   [68] Grubbs, '"Pagan" and "Christian" Marriage', 402.

to consist 'in years, not in espousals or nuptials', and this, explains Tertullian, is mere 'obedience to the law of nature'. Christians, by a further *a fortiori* argument, are urged to adopt this law for themselves since the laws of nature are the laws of the Christians' God. 'By *us*', he complains, 'not even natural *laws* are observed; as if the God of nature were some other than ours!'[69]

Tertullian gives a further meaning to the veil worn by betrothed women. It represents the internal veil they already wear.

Recognise the *woman*, ay, recognise the *wedded woman*, by the testimonies both of body and of spirit, which she experiences both in conscience and in flesh. These are the earlier tablets of *natural* espousals and nuptials. Impose a veil externally upon her who has (already) a covering internally. Let her whose lower parts are not bare have her upper likewise covered.[70]

The betrothed woman is a married woman, and the different elements of the betrothal ceremony (the kisses, the pledges, the joining of hands) amply indicate her newly conferred status. The coming together of the couple, even before the joint ceremonies of spousals and nuptials, reveals earlier phases, the 'natural espousals and nuptials', the counterparts to the betrothal liturgy in the couple's life. The bride-to-be is pledged to her husband alone. A veil may be placed over her desires for any other man and over her desirability to any other man.

So Tertullian's rule on the veiling of young women confirms much about the entry into marriage described already in this chapter. He offers a poor, prejudiced argument. What begins as a rule about young women wearing veils turns out to be an exhortation *not* to wear them until betrothal, in the hope that men will be paradoxically attracted to unveiled pubescent girls as prospective suitors. Tertullian's insistence that as soon as a girl reaches puberty and becomes sexually attractive to men she is no longer a virgin is a dubious extension of the term 'virgin', perhaps dumping on to women responsibility for the guilty desires they arouse in men, which the veil is supposed to inhibit. One might also want to know whether, if virginity in one of its senses is inevitably lost at puberty,

[69] Tertullian, *On the Veiling of Virgins*, ch.11. Text in Roberts and Donaldson, *The Ante-Nicene Fathers*, p.34 (translators' emphases).
[70] Ibid., ch.12, p.35 (translators' emphases).

there remains any value attached to the normative meaning of that term. But we learn much about how at least one Christian community practised the entry into marriage. There are elements in the domestic, but also religious, ceremony which symbolize the growing unity of the couple and their pledging of themselves to each other. Tertullian clearly thinks betrothal is the beginning of marriage. Betrothed women are married women, reserved for their husbands. The betrothal also includes the contract which specifies the financial and domestic details of the marriage, written on 'tablets'.

Perhaps the most remarkable detail to etch itself on the late modern mind is the age at which marriage is to begin. An attempt to have penetrative sex with a girl of twelve is still regarded as a very serious offence in most western countries, punishable by imprisonment. Not so in earlier years. Twelve and fourteen remained the legal minimum ages for the nuptials for most of the history of Christendom with betrothals recognized from the age of seven, provided they were confirmed later. Tertullian clearly thought that the contracting of marriage at the age of puberty was a law of nature and so a law of God. This must be one of countless cases where what appears to be grounded in the 'natural' order of things turns out retrospectively to have more to do with social custom than with any natural circumstance which conveniently turns out to require obedience. Since it was a Jewish and a Roman practice to marry very early (by our standards) it is not surprising that Christians adopted it. Christians, along with Stoics, had an eye on avoiding the disaster of premarital sex. Marriage, at, or just before, puberty was a principal means of ensuring it.

Two of the canons passed at the Synod of Elvira in Spain some time between 305 and 314 deal with betrothal. About half of the 81 canons passed at the Synod were about sexual matters, and as Samuel Laeuchli explains, the Synod adopted an attitude to sex and sexuality which by earlier Christian standards was both strict and repressive. 'The clerics of Spain forced themselves to live a life without sexual intercourse. Yet, those same clerics dealt with women all the time in the business of the church. The resulting repressed sexuality caused by the prohibition of any normal sexual outlet led to the clerics' constant desire to punish the women with whom they came in contact.'[71] Two of the canons deal explicitly with premarital sex and the surprise is that the matter is leniently dealt with. Canon 14 stipulated:

Virgins who have not preserved their virginity, if they marry those who violated them and keep them as husband, they must be reconciled without penance after a year since they have broken only the nuptials. If, however, they have been intimate with other men – becoming guilty of real sexual offense – they ought to be admitted to communion only after five years, having fulfilled the required penance.[72]

Girls having sex before marriage are punished by a year's abstention from communion without the need for penance, provided they marry their sexual partner. This was not regarded seriously. 'Real sexual offence', i.e., serial sex with more than one partner outside marriage, renders them 'fornicators' (*moechatae*) which deserves much more severe penalties.

Canon 54 stipulates:

If parents break the faith of a betrothal agreement (*fides sponsaliorum*), they shall abstain [from communion] for three years. However, if either the *sponsus* or the *sponsa* has been caught in a serious offense (*crimen*), the parents will be excused. If it was a sin (*vitium*) between the couple and they have polluted themselves, the former decision shall stand.[73]

It is clear that parents arrange their children's marriages, for some of them culpably default on the betrothals they arrange. Conditional but unfulfilled promises which involve, e.g., the provision of a dowry will cause the nuptials to be cancelled, thereby precipitating the betrothed into the cancellation of a proleptic marital state. The *crimen* is probably having sex with someone else, an offence serious enough to justify the cancellation of the marriage. If they have had sex with each other, 'they are committed to the match and it would be wrong for the parents of either party to try to break it off'.[74] Of both canons Grubbs writes:

[71] Samuel Laeuchli, *Power and Sexuality: The Emergence of Canon Law at the Synod of Elvira* (Philadelphia: Temple University Press, 1972), p.97.
[72] Ibid., p.128.
[73] Judith Evans Grubbs' translation, in Grubbs, '"Pagan" and "Christian" Marriage', 401.
[74] Ibid., 402.

It is clear that premarital sex, unlike extra-marital sex, is pardoned if the lovers get married: indeed it was thought that sexual relations between unmarried people created a bond which was not to be broken by marriage to someone else. The bond of betrothal is important, but a fiancé(e) whose betrothed has been unfaithful is not under obligation to marry him or her.[75]

The canons are remarkable for their leniency towards betrothed couples. Perhaps, though, even Grubbs projects a contemporary distinction between premarital and marital sex which is somewhat alien to the canons' own appreciation of the matter. The reason why premarital sex is pardonable is because it is not premarital. The marital relation has already begun with betrothal.

Betrothal, then, is grounded in the Bible. The biblical theology of marriage assumes it. Jews and Romans, whose moralities are sharply contrasted (Rom. 1:18–32), both practised it, and it is incorporated in the developing practice of the early church. Evidence from liturgy and canon law is considered in the next chapter.

[75] Ibid.

CHAPTER 5

Evidence from liturgy and law

Chapter 4 has shown that betrothal was central to the earliest theology of Christian marriage. In the present chapter the process of 'retrieving' betrothal continues apace. If betrothal really was central to the Christian experience of marriage, then one would expect evidence of it to be found in surviving liturgies. Such evidence exists, and is described in the first half of the chapter. When canon law began to develop at the turn of the second millennium, crucial questions about the meaning of marriage, and about how it was contracted, began to be debated. The answers given then remain profoundly influential, even today. Aquinas' forgotten reflections on betrothal are discussed, and the chapter closes with an examination of the work of the seventeenth-century English lawyer Henry Swinburne, *A Treatise of Spousals or Matrimonial Contracts*. This work closely follows Aquinas and is included here because it brings betrothal into the modern period and demonstrates a valuable continuity with pre-Reformation traditions of marriage. What happened to betrothal in the Reformation and modern periods must await chapter 6. While in the midst of the present historical section, it is appropriate to encourage ourselves by thinking of the rewards that may be won. Confronted with the widespread phenomenon of prenuptial cohabitation and the problem of responding appropriately to it from within the Christian faith and tradition, patient excavation is yielding a view of marriage and marriage formation that is strange and unlikely and which still has the power, when it comes fully into view, of aiding and helping to shape the Christian *praxis* of the future.

BETROTHAL IN THE WEST

The importance of Tertullian as a source for early Christian marriage practice has just been discussed (above, p.143). In the West, unlike the East, there is almost no surviving evidence of marriage liturgies until the twelfth century, when the new emphasis on consent as the essence of marriage began to make a marked impact on liturgical form. At the end of the fourth century, betrothal and marriage were separate occasions. Both took place in the home, and at least for the nuptials there was a formal liturgy. By the eleventh century, betrothal and marriage were telescoped into a single ceremony. As the Western Church grew stronger in Northern Europe it sought to exercise control over marriage, and an obvious way of doing this was to insist (with dubious success) on marriages being performed in church. This single trend was itself sufficient to cause the centuries-old practice of betrothal to diminish in significance. Its eventual incorporation in the marriage rite, *as a single rite*, became almost inevitable (below, p.164). Much earlier, in the sixth century, Justinian attempted to make betrothal promises binding, 'and this resulted in the gradual narrowing of the gap in time between betrothal and marriage, so that from the eighth century the two grew close together, and from the tenth they tended to follow immediately upon each other'.[1] But the surviving Visigothic rites from this period retain the traditional threefold structure. Two rites are preparatory to the final marriage rite and nuptial mass. These are the blessing of the pledges (betrothal) and the blessing of the bedchamber.[2] These rites, however, almost certainly reflect much older practice.

It is safe to say that by the sixth century two types of wedding ritual are discernible, one based in Gaul, the other in Italy. The differences between them reflect a growing *theological* difference about the meaning of marriage which was still unresolved six centuries later. In Gaul, the ritual always seems to have included the nuptial blessing of the couple as they lay in bed. The blessing obviously recognizes and sacralizes sexual relations between the couple. In

---

[1] Kenneth Stevenson, *To Join Together: The Rite of Marriage* (New York: Pueblo Publishing Company, 1987), p.76.
[2] Ibid., p.29.

Italy the couple was blessed at the time of the exchange of consent, which was likely to have been at the church door, or even inside the building. As Brundage notes, 'Thus the symbolism of the Italian rites centered upon consent and the Church's role in marriage, while French wedding symbolism stressed consummation and treated the nuptial ceremony as primarily a domestic affair.'[3]

Older practice is also preserved by the poems written in France between *c.* 1175 and 1290, known as the *Romans D'Aventure*. Many of these describe weddings and mention betrothals. Since the *Romans* belong to the gentry and nobility of feudal society, it should not be assumed that they reflect common practice. Weddings usually occurred in a church; the ceremony was conducted by a priest; it included mass; and it took place between 6 and 9 a.m. The rest of the day was given over to feasting and merrymaking. Banquets were held in the evening, and the wedding entertainment commonly included bear baiting. Late into the night the bride would be 'conducted to the nuptial chamber, where she was prepared by her lady attendants to receive her groom. Then occurred the benediction of the priest, who sprinkled with holy water the nuptial couch.'[4] Not until the following day were the wedding gifts presented, and at the same time gifts of food were given to the church to distribute to the poor of the parish.

The blessing of the bed, or *benedictio thalami*, was common practice during the early Middle Ages throughout the Church, East and West. By the ninth century it had almost disappeared in the West, only to be reinstated again in the twelfth century. As Brundage explains, the 'belief that sex played a central role in the very formation of marriage helps to explain the reappearance of the marriage bed as a marital symbol'. Manuscript paintings of the period 'also began to depict the marriage bed to symbolize matrimony itself'.[5] The bridal couple, and their bridal bed, would be blessed and sprinkled with holy water. There are six examples of these ceremonies in the *Romans D'Aventure*. In four of these the priest blesses

---

3 James A. Brundage, *Law, Sex, and Christian Society in Medieval Europe* (Chicago and London: University of Chicago Press, 1987), p.88.

4 F.L. Critchlow, 'On the Forms of Betrothal and Wedding Ceremonies in the Old-French *Romans D'Aventure*', *Modern Philology* 2 (1904–5), 525. Critchlow's essay, nearly a century old, has proved a most valuable source.

5 Brundage, *Law, Sex, and Christian Society*, p.279.

the couple as they lie together in bed; in the other two, the bride is ushered into the nuptial chamber by her relatives or her attendants and blessed by the priest before the bridegroom appears at the chamber door. The bed-blessing did not survive in the West, and in two of the *Romans D'Aventure* the substitute for the *benedictio thalami*, adopted later as a more refined form of procedure, is in evidence. This is the use of the *abrifol* or covering which is brought over the couple as they stand before the priest.[6] It is not surprising that a Church which grew increasingly wary of sexual intercourse even within marriage 'refined', i.e., abolished, the bed-blessing procedure. Kenneth Stevenson, with a view to regaining contact with a lost generation of young marrieds, observes how the ancient practice ritualized sexuality 'in a most wholesome manner'. Such a blessing, whether as 'part of a sequence of church rites ending there or part of a full service celebrated in a domestic context, can have far more force in ritualizing reality, namely, that the couple indeed do make love when they are left alone together and that this lovemaking is part of the natural instincts and affections implanted in us by God'.[7]

Our interest lies principally in the events preceding the wedding day. The picture that emerges at the beginning of the second millennium is one where betrothal and marriage appear as the secular and sacred elements of marriage respectively. 'The *sponsalia* were the secular and the *matrimonium* the spiritual phases of mediaeval marriage; the former had to do more strictly with the civil, the latter with the church authorities.'[8] By the beginning of the twelfth century in Western Europe the Roman Catholic Church was intervening in the regulation and legal control of marriage with little resistance from the secular powers. Its growing prestige enabled it to absorb 'parts of the *sponsalia* ceremony into the sphere of the *matrimonium* formalities with the purpose of imbuing the whole marriage celebration with a religious spirit and of ridding that ceremony of any taint of barter which profane tradition had always attached to nuptials both in Latin and Teutonic history'. The betrothal had always taken place when agreements between the families of bride and groom were finalized, and these inevitably involved haggling

[6] Critchlow, 'On the Forms of Betrothal', 531–2.
[7] Stevenson, *To Join Together*, p.175.   [8] Critchlow, 'On the Forms of Betrothal', 499.

about dowry and property. In Germany this was 'bride-purchase' or *Kaufehe*, and it was followed by a public transfer of the bride from the head of the bride's family to the head of the family of the groom.[9] We may surmise that, as the influence of the Church in Northern Europe grew, the Church was prepared quietly to withdraw its insistence on betrothal. It did this liturgically by transferring from the *spousals* to the *nuptials* the promises once reserved for the spousals only. But the changes did not accord fully with changes in early canon law (below, p.164). When the defining element of marriage is defined as consent, pressure to define consent led to the resurgence of a much older distinction, consent in the future (*de futuro*), verbalized in the future tense, and consent performatively in the present (*de praesenti*), verbalized in the present tense. While liturgical emphasis on betrothal was waning, its emphasis in canon law was assuming greater importance.

The *Romans D'Aventure* confirm that by the middle of the thirteenth century, the relative importance of betrothal vis-à-vis marriage had become reversed. 'The influence of the church has prevailed to such an extent in the ceremonies of marriage that *sponsalia* and *matrimonium* have been changed about in importance as compared with their position at the period of the Frankish immigrations.' English language usage carries this reversal even today, though the changes that brought it about are almost entirely forgotten. The word 'wedding' derives 'from the *weds*, pledges or securities, that passed between the bridegroom and the parents, or the guardians, of the bride'. As Critchlow, writing almost a century ago, explains, 'We now give the name betrothal to the wedding of our forefathers, having transferred the older name and greater importance of the *desponsatio et dotatio* to the *traditio et sanctificatio* or the giving away.'[10] The first pair of these Latin terms refers to the financial agreements preceding the marriage: the second pair to the 'handing over' or 'giving away' of the bride followed by the blessing. 'The giving away represented the final completion of the marriage after the necessary arrangements had been concluded, and upon this conclusion . . . a priest was to be present in order to sanctify the legal union with the blessing of the Church.'

[9] Brundage, *Law, Sex, and Christian Society*, p.128.
[10] Critchlow, 'On the Forms of Betrothal', 499, note 4.

It is suggested that the decline in importance of the betrothal ceremony is evidence for a small degree of early emancipation of women. Since marriage rested officially on consent, no marriage could be contracted without the free consent of both parties. There were, however, obvious means of coercion open to parents to ensure that the match their children contracted was the match their parents wanted. If betrothal is now on its way to becoming a purely secular ceremony, then the church is not seen to be blessing what may in part have been (at least in Northern Europe) a vulgar trading in saleable marital goods. We sense first the loss of religious significance of the *spousals* as it accommodates the bartering practices of the newer nations of Christendom. As it became more secular the economic meaning, which was always part of it, came to predominate, and this became a further reason for religious withdrawal. By the time of the *Romans D'Aventure* 'woman is no longer a mere subject of barter, as she once had been'. She 'has emerged from the lowly condition where she was looked upon as a chattel in marriage transactions and has acquired a fair amount of independence'.[11]

Betrothal ceremonies did not occur in church, and a ring was always given to the bride at betrothal. In the *Romans d'Aventure* a priest was present only for the very rich.

There was no law which demanded a priest to preside at betrothals. All that was necessary to validity of promise to marry was, from of old, that the bride should be present with her relatives at the ceremony of betrothal; further, the consent of both man and woman was obligatory and the contract, if broken, subjected either to a fine or compensation.[12]

LITURGIES IN THE EAST

The evidence for betrothal in Eastern rites is much more abundant (and I shall rely in this section on Kenneth Stevenson's admirable presentation of it in his *To Join Together: The Rite of Marriage*). All extant rites bring betrothal and marriage together in a single ceremony, or ceremonies which take place very close in time to one another, but they were originally separate and must be understood

---

[11] Ibid., 501.   [12] Ibid., 510.

as temporally distanced from one another. The betrothal rite 'is not a legal-sounding form of consent; it is a liturgy in its own right, which prays for the couple as they offer their resolve to God'. Every single rite from the surviving Armenian-Syrian cluster of rites, says Stevenson,

> employs a special symbolism at betrothal, as if there were a need to make this rite significant in the lives of ordinary men and women. Thus, betrothed Armenian couples exchange crosses; the Syrian orthodox priest goes to the home of each partner to act as a sort of intermediary; the Maronites include an anointing of the couple (which they probably took from the Copts); and the East Syrians make a curious mixture of water, ash, and wine in a chalice (the *henana*) for the couple to drink, to symbolize the dying of the old relationship in order to come to life in the new.[13]

The Armenian rite included the blessing of jewellery followed by 'the blessing of robes, with more readings preceded by hymns and censing; and the rite of joining of the right hands, which starts at home and moves from there to church and which involves the giving of consent at the church door'.[14]

The similar Syrian rite has four main parts, and again the priest acts as an intermediary and as the spokesperson for the whole community. The first part is the betrothal ceremony, followed by the joining of right hands, then the blessing of the rings and the blessing of the crowns. Stevenson comments on the first phase: 'The priest goes to the home of the bridegroom, then to that of the bride, and offers the ring to the bride. The ring (if accepted) is blessed and then placed on her finger. The blessing is elaborate in comparison with any Western formula.'[15] As in the *Romans d'Aventure* a ring is always given to the bride at betrothal, a custom that goes back to pre-Christian times. The Maronites and Copts anoint the foreheads of the bride and groom at betrothal. While the imagery of anointing suggests royal and messianic images, Stevenson reminds us that the reading from Mark's Gospel of the story of the anointing of Jesus by 'a woman' in the house of Simon the leper (14:3–6) introduces a different sequence of thought: '[O]il is not a symbol of the kingdom, but rather a preparation for a change of state: marriage is a dying

[13] Stevenson, *To Join Together*, pp.57–8.   [14] Ibid., p.59.   [15] Ibid., p.62.

to the old (separate) relationship in order to live to the new (united) one.'[16]

A hymn in the East-Syrian marriage rite makes explicit reference to Christ as the divine spouse, a striking example of biblical betrothal mysticism (above, chapter 4, fourth section). If the Church is betrothed to Christ, Christ is betrothed to the Church, and this prayer assumes the relation between each is well understood as betrothal. The prayer, moreover, wonderfully plants the couple's joining in the embracing dynamic of the Christ–Church relationship:-

> O Christ, adorned spouse, whose betrothal has given us a
>   type,
> complete the foundation and the building, and their [the
>   couple's] laudable work;
> sanctify their marriage and their bed;
> and dismiss their sins and offenses;
> and make them a temple for you and bestow on their mar-
>   riage chamber your light;
> and may their odor be as a roseshoot in paradise,
> and as a garden full of smells,
> and as a myrtle tree may be for your praise.
> May they be a bastion for our orthodox band and a house
>   of refuge.[17]

In modern Coptic texts, betrothal is retained, but unusually, 'the couple are veiled at the end of the betrothal service'. As Stevenson explains: 'This is yet one more symbol of the passage character of the entire scheme. The couple have been standing in separate parts of the church, at the head of the men's and women's side, respectively. Only now do they come together in church. The veil conceals them and also unites and blinds [*sic*] them.'[18] One of the prayers in the betrothal part of the ceremony contains the words, 'Now, therefore, our Master, we ask you to make your servants worthy through the nature of the sign of your word in the yoke of betrothal, so that an indivisible love may be in them toward one another in each of them being joined firmly to the other.' In the Ethiopic rite, the priest cuts locks of hair from each of the couple's

---

[16] Ibid., p.66.   [17] Cited by Stevenson, ibid., p.69.   [18] Ibid., p.73.

heads and places them on the other's, 'one more curious custom, symbolizing in one more way the union of the couple'.[19]

The earliest surviving prayers in the Byzantine rite are contained in an eighth-century manuscript, which some scholars think reflects even older usage, possibly going back to the fifth century. The manuscript contains a Byzantine rite of betrothal (the *Arrhas*) and the marriage rite (called 'crowning'). While expanded, this rite is still used in Byzantine churches today. A recent (and official) service book of the Orthodox Church in the United States contains the same two rites merged into one. The anticipatory character of the prayers, even before the betrothal takes place, is striking:

'For these servants of God *(N.)* and *(N.)* who here pledge themselves to one another, and for their safekeeping, let us pray to the Lord.' ['Lord, have mercy']

'That the Lord will send down upon them perfect and peaceful love, guarding them in oneness of mind and steadfast faith, let us pray to the Lord.'

'That he will vouchsafe to them a blameless life, granting them an honorable marriage and a household above reproach, let us pray to the Lord.'[20]

More prayers are said, one of them linking the couple with the most detailed betrothal story in the Bible, that of Isaac and Rebecca:

'Everlasting God, those who were divided You brought into oneness, setting for them an unbreakable bond of love: You blessed Isaac and Rebecca and made them heirs to Your promise.

Bless these Your servants *(N.)* and *(N.)* guiding them into every good work.

For You are a merciful and loving God, and to You we give the glory, Father, Son and Holy Spirit, now and always and forever and ever.'

A further prayer now links the betrothed status of the Church with the new status of the couple:

'Lord God, You chose the Church out of the Gentile world and made Her Your betrothed. Will you bless this betrothal, uniting and preserving these Your servants in peace and oneness of mind.'[21]

---

[19] Ibid., pp.74–5.
[20] *Sacraments and Services, Book One* (Northridge, Calif.: Narthex Press, 1995), pp.43–4.
[21] Ibid., p.46.

The priest now betrothes (or declares betrothed) the couple by the part of the service called 'The Placing of the Rings'. He makes the sign of the cross, three times, on the foreheads of the bride and groom, and repeats three times:

'The servant of God (*N.*) is betrothed [*arrabònizetai*] to the handmaid of God (*N.*) in the Name of the Father and of the Son and of the Holy Spirit. Amen.'

'The handmaid of God (*N.*) is betrothed [*arrabònizetai*] to the servant of God (*N.*) in the Name of the Father and of the Son and of the Holy Spirit. Amen.'

A magnificent prayer, translated into a modern idiom and absorbing inclusive language, invoking God's blessing on the betrothal is said next:

'Lord our God, when the servant of the Patriarch Abraham was sent into Mesopotamia to seek a wife for his master Isaac, You walked with him; and through the meeting at the well You revealed to him that he should engage Rebecca. Will You now, Lord, bless the betrothal of Your servants (*N.*) and (*N.*) and confirm the word they have given. Establish them in that sacred oneness that rests in You. For in the beginning You made them man and woman, and it is by You that woman is joined to man, to support one another and to perpetuate humankind. As You sent forth Your truth to Your inheritance, making Your covenant with Your servants, our fathers, Your chosen ones in every generation, look on these Your servants (*N.*) and (*N.*) and ground their betrothal firmly in faith and oneness of mind, in truth and in love. For You, Lord, have made Your will clear: that a pledge should be given and confirmed by every means.'[22]

This contemporary North American rite is based on and developed from very early Christian marriage traditions, and preserves betrothal in a way that Protestant and Roman Catholic liturgies do not. Prayers for the couple prior to betrothal, the blessing of the betrothal, the declaration and enactment of the betrothal all reinforce the sense of betrothal as an event within a sequence, with more to come. It is an 'important step' in the couple's life, one which 'puts a seal of church recognition on the intentions and mutual feelings of the bride and the groom, cements their mutual pledge with the church blessing and prayers and reaffirms them in the importance

---

[22] Ibid., p.47.

of God's help in their future life together'.[23] The link between the couple's betrothal and the betrothal between Christ and the Church sets the real-life event of the couple within the context that makes total sense of it. Just as the people of God long for the final consummation of all time and history in Christ, so the couple long for their consummation in one another through their union. These are ancient meanings too rich to be permanently excluded from Western rites. A very strong argument exists, not just for the reintroduction of a betrothal rite for Western Christians, but for its reintroduction at a convenient and separate time prior to the wedding ceremony and nuptials.

CANON LAW

The Church began to develop canon law at the start of the second millennium.[24] What defined marriage? There was already a diversity of customs and views about this question, and the attention it received in ancient universities occurred at about the same time that there was a revival of interest in Roman law. Not surprisingly an ancient Roman solution was adopted: the essence of marriage was *consent*. As Brooke summarizes,

Working on ancient and traditional foundations, the popes and the canonists hammered out a definition something like this: when a man and woman freely and legitimately promised to marry – when they made no conditions, but said in the presence of witnesses that they took each other as husband and wife – then there could be no turning back; only annulment could part them.[25]

However, this solution was arrived at only slowly, and was equally slow in its reception. It gave rise to further problems, in particular the role of sex in marriage. What was consent, and to what was consent being given (below, p.221)? What constituted the beginning of marriage? Even in some Protestant churches, where marriage is

[23] Gennady Nefedov, 'The Sacrament of Matrimony: The Betrothal Service', *Journal of the Moscow Patriarchate* 9–10 (1989), 75.

[24] For the background to this development, see Brundage, *Law, Sex, and Christian Society*, pp.176–87.

[25] Christopher Brooke, *The Medieval Idea of Marriage* (Oxford: Clarendon Press, 1989), p.137.

not generally regarded as a sacrament, the custom has grown of speaking of marriage informally as a sacrament, because it involves the special mediation of God's blessing or grace. In this case, the key question is, what makes it special?

These questions arise from the definition of marriage as consent, but the decision to treat marriage in this way must be seen in the light of the pressing problems of widespread concubinage (both clerical and lay) and the equally widespread practice of informal or clandestine marriage. While always irregular, these practices or their equivalents are common today and the varying attitude of the Church towards them in different periods is highly instructive for a contemporary pastoral theology. The Church had a long history of toleration of concubinage. A man with a wife *and* a concubine could not expect to escape censure, but the informal unions of men with concubines were generally tolerated. Indeed by the fourth and fifth centuries, a period of growing sexual restriction, the argument that the Church should recognize concubinage as a variant form of marriage was often heard. When the First Council of Toledo (397–400) ruled on the matter, unmarried men with concubines were not to be refused communion. A reason for this decision was probably that concubinage was already so common among Christians that the Church was unable to excommunicate them all even if it had wished to. Even in the twelfth century when strict reforms were being implemented and the power of the Church in Europe had never been stronger, concubinage among the laity was not forbidden.[26]

Because the Church wished to vest control of marriage (and much else) from feudal states and secular powers to itself, it sought to impose a uniform ecclesiastical marriage law in place of local custom. It sought also to prevent marriages within the prohibited degrees. Entry into marriage, therefore, also had to be controlled, and since vast numbers of marriages were informally or secretly conducted, and so not controlled at all, the Church desired to move against them. However, the definition of marriage as the exchange of consent in the present tense actually impeded the task of eliminating informal marriage, since verifiable consent needed

---

[26] Brundage, *Law, Sex, and Christian Society*, pp.99–102, 206.

only witnesses, not ceremonies. Gratian was the first writer to write a complete textbook of canon law (*c.* 1140) and it is clear that he regarded clandestine marriages as valid. Gratian found the revival of the ancient Roman concept of *maritalis affectio* congenial: it is the quality of the personal relationship which confirms a marriage as a marriage, and if a marriage was entered into by free consent, then the marriage was valid. While it might be regretted that the Church had not solemnized and blessed the union, the union was valid, and indissoluble, in law.

Gratian's understanding of marriage is important for other reasons which take us directly to the role of betrothal in marriage-making. Gratian tries to bring into harmony two contrasting theories about marriage formation: one emphasized consent, the other sexual intercourse. According to the French solution, advocated by Peter Lombard and others, consent *alone* is necessary for a valid marriage. A strong influence behind this view is the understanding of the 'marriage' of Mary the Mother of God with Joseph as a perfect marriage. That Mary had sex with Joseph was unthinkable.[27] The French solution famously distinguishes between two types of consent, future (*de futuro*) and present (*de praesenti*). The promise to marry *in the future* is a real promise, and constitutes betrothal. The exchange of consent *per verba de praesenti* is valid, sacramental, indissoluble marriage (*matrimonium ratum*) whether or not it is followed by sexual intercourse. On this view, consummation, understood as sexual intercourse, is simply unnecessary.

Gratian also rejected the theory that *maritalis affectio* and sexual intercourse were sufficient for marriage. His ingenious *via media* allows that free consent in either tense, accompanied by *maritalis affectio*, is a real beginning of marriage (as the Latin terms *matrimonium initiatum* or *coniugium initiatum* indicate). This is the betrothal period. Only by sexual intercourse is marriage perfected (*matrimonium perfectum*). Indeed, without sex it is not a valid marriage. Brundage comments that 'Gratian considered marriage came into being, not as the result of a single action, but rather as a two-stage process.'[28] This conclusion was particularly difficult for the French school

---

[27] Oscar D. Watkins, *Holy Matrimony: A Treatise on the Divine Laws of Marriage* (New York: Macmillan, 1895), pp.120–4.
[28] Brundage, *Law, Sex, and Christian Society*, p.235.

to accept. Even if consent is given in the future tense, no further consent is required once the couple have sexual intercourse, since *de facto* their promises are fulfilled. An unconsummated marriage is no marriage and can therefore be annulled. The French view, that consent makes the marriage, *concensus facit matrimonium*, prevailed, while the failure to consummate the marriage sexually constituted a ground for annulment. A consequence of this controversy was that the betrothal vows or 'contract of espousal' were always distinguished from the marriage vows by being said *per verba de futuro*, while the marriage vows or 'nuptial contract' were always said *per verba de praesenti*. Lacey holds that this development was also responsible for the telescoping of spousals and nuptials. 'It became general to simplify matters by doing away with the interval of time between espousals and nuptials, and the contract of espousal was effected at the church-door, immediately before the benediction.'[29]

There remains a fragment of the old betrothal vows even in the present-day marriage services in many Protestant denominations. An example is the recent (2000) *Common Worship* Marriage Service of the Church of England. The bride and bridegroom are each asked two questions. These are: to the bridegroom, '*N*, will you take *N* to be your wife? Will you love her, comfort her, honour her and protect her, and, forsaking all others, be faithful to her as long as you both shall live?'; and, to the bride, '*N*, will you take *N* to be your husband? Will you love him, comfort him, honour him and protect him, and, forsaking all others, be faithful to him as long as you both shall live?'[30] Each declares 'I will.' The congregation is invited to promise to 'support and uphold' the couple. After the collect, readings, the sermon, and perhaps a hymn, the couple make their vows. Their parents are invited to indicate that 'you will entrust your son and daughter to one another as they come to be married'. Then in words of the present tense each of them performatively 'takes' the other by saying: 'I, *N*, take you, *N*, to be my wife/husband, to have and to hold from this day forward; for better, for worse, for richer, for poorer, in sickness and in health, to

[29] T.A. Lacey, *Marriage in Church and State* (London: Robert Scott, 1912), p.48.
[30] Text in Stephen Lake, *Using Common Worship: Marriage* (London: Church House Publishing/Praxis, 2000), pp.45, 49.

love and to cherish, till death us do part; according to God's holy law. In the presence of God I make this vow.'

It may be doubted whether many clergy or marrying couples are aware that the future tense of the question and the future tense of the response 'I will' is a tangible relic of the first millennium, when the vows, or *weds*, or *troths* were exchanged by the be*troth*ed in anticipation of their nuptial ceremony some time in the future. The future and present tenses correspond to the *verba de futuro* and *de praesenti* of another age. *Common Worship* follows *The Alternative Service Book* (1980) and the 1662 *Book of Common Prayer* in requiring responses first in the future, and then in the present, tense. (It differs from the 1980 version by creating distance between the two sets of responses.) Lacey explains that the requirement that the nuptial contract be said in the present tense 'was met in many Churches by an addition to the older form of espousal'. Behind the *Book of Common Prayer* wording lies the future tense question in the early Sarum manual, 'Wilt thou have this woman to thy wife?' (with variations in the question put to the woman), and the answer (of both), 'I will.' He thinks 'it can hardly be doubted that we see here a survival from a time when the promise of espousal was held to be sufficiently ratified, even after a considerable time, by the nuptial ceremony following'.[31]

Medieval influence over contemporary marriage is great, but many elements of this influence are forgotten. 'It must often have been the case', argues Brooke, 'that a couple once firmly betrothed, who had given their mutual consent, were reckoned free to cohabit; and this the Church, while preferring and promoting more open, formal, and visible ceremonies, felt bound to respect.'[32] Living together prior to the nuptials is no new development. In the high Middle Ages betrothal was widely practised, and some penitential writings even forbade women to marry men to whom they had not been first betrothed.[33] But the growing legislation on marriage was matched by a determination to evade its constraints. By the fifteenth century, only 'a pious few' waited for the nuptials before they had sex: 'many more couples probably consummated their marriages

---

[31] Lacey, *Marriage in Church and State*, pp.48–9.
[32] Brooke, *The Medieval Idea of Marriage*, p.130.
[33] Brundage, *Law, Sex, and Christian Society*, p.163.

in advance of any formal ceremony'.[34] Clandestine marriage and concubinage continued to be common throughout Europe, even among the clergy, and conditional marriages (i.e., spousals with conditions) continued to vex the legislators. Each of these must be briefly described.

In the first place an unintended consequence of Pope Alexander III's compromise over marriage may actually have made clandestine marriages *easier* to contract. Alexander had ruled that the essence of marriage was consent in the present tense: consent in the future tense was betrothal. In his later period (*c.* 1176) he ruled that betrothal followed by sexual intercourse made a valid marriage. He also ruled that clandestine marriages were anathema and that witnesses must hear the vows. But this did not stop clandestine marriages happening. A secret marriage was still a valid marriage because it complied with the supreme condition for its initiation, viz., consent. And many people preferred their marriages to be contracted quietly. If they were already living together or having sex, a forthcoming public ceremony would draw attention to the irregularity of their situation. To some extent Alexander's compromise covered the irregularity by assuming they were *de facto* married. But there was a further consequence of clandestine marriage perceived by many to be an advantage – if the marriage didn't work, a 'divorce' could be agreed as clandestinely as the marriage had been.[35] There seems little doubt that the very arrangements which were intended to regulate the entry into marriage encouraged couples to undertake what a different generation has called 'trial-marriages'. In the next century 'the records of the Cérisy court make it clear that at least in Normandy couples treated betrothal as a trial marriage and normally slept together once they had exchanged future consent'.[36] 'Similar customs were common elsewhere in Europe', adds Brundage, 'and while some thirteenth-century English synods legislated against these practices it is not clear that they succeeded in suppressing them.'

Concubinage is often associated with informal marriage, but there were important differences between them, even in the Middle Ages. For an informal marriage to be valid, consent had to be

---

[34] Ibid., p.504.   [35] Ibid., p.336, and see pp.333–6.   [36] Ibid., pp.436–7.

exchanged, albeit secretly or in a semi-public context. The main identifying characteristic of concubinage was the existence of *maritalis affectio*, an old Roman idea which referred to the existential quality of the relationship instead of its formal or legal properties. The early decretists were generally inclined to treat concubinage as if it were clandestine marriage, provided that neither party was married, and that the relationship was enduring and potentially permanent. It was assumed that masters had sexual relations with female servants – these the Church condemned as fornication, or concubinage without *maritalis affectio*. But concubinage was not initially classified under the rubric of fornication. Huguccio, Sicard of Cremona and the author of the *Summa Parisiensis* all proposed to treat concubinage with *maritalis affectio* as informal marriage.[37] But clerical concubinage and fornication continued and in the fourteenth century may even have increased, for at that time 'priests seem to have lived with their female companions almost as openly and as often as had their 11th-century predecessors'.[38] Still later (1562) the representative of the Duke of Bavaria reported to a sitting of the Council of Trent that ninety-six or ninety-seven Bavarian priests out of a hundred had concubines or clandestine wives.[39]

The Church of the twelfth century, when confronted by the irregularity of clandestine marriage, sought to 'regularize' it by accepting it as a valid form of marriage. By the fourteenth century the Church sought to suppress it, declaring it a serious sin. The earlier, more permissive, attitude appears to have more to commend it. The reason for the more liberal attitude appears to be the determination to regard as many relationships as possible as marriage. 'The law seems to have assumed an unstated premiss that it was important to define as many relationships as possible as marriages.'[40] If this premiss is expressed in terms already used (above, pp.53–61), we may say the Church *affirmed the marital norm* while seeking to extend it inclusively both to those who were living together without ceremony and to those in enduring relationships of concubinage.

A similar trend, from regularization to coercion, has been discovered by a particular study of the marriage laws of medieval

---

[37] Ibid., pp.297–9, and see pp.444–7.   [38] Ibid., p.474.
[39] See ibid., p.568, and the references there.
[40] Ibid., p.362 (speaking of the aftermath of the Fourth Lateran Council).

England. Michael Sheehan's original work on the earliest diocesan
statutes yields conclusions both about people's entry into marriage
over time, and, related to this, about the English dioceses' tolerant
attitudes to couples beginning sexual experience, which were later
sharpened. Sheehan thinks that at the Council of Westminster
(1220), where 'no distinction of the stages of the marriage was made,
the term *matrimonium* may well have been intended to apply to the
whole process that brought about the union of the couple'.[41] Several
of the English dioceses had to face the problem of couples enjoying
sexual intimacy, being free to marry, but postponing, perhaps in-
definitely, the solemnization of their union. The solution adopted
was to require such couples to take an oath which was very similar
to the formal betrothal vows. The vow was: 'I swear that if I have
further carnal knowledge of you, I will have you as my wife if holy
church allows.'[42] The couple were not condemned for fornication
but required to marry or refrain from sex. However, says Sheehan,
what began as legislation which required from couples the conditional promise of marriage, should they continue sexual liaison,
quickly became the means for assuming that, if they had sex, they
would, *de facto*, be regarded as presumptively married (*matrimonium
presumptum*). Sexual intercourse is changed from the event which
requires marriage to the event that brings it about.

Sheehan's analysis of *matrimonium* as a process of several stages
is similar to that of Beatrice Gottlieb who examined 800 cases of
clandestine marriage in the dioceses of Troyes and Châlons-sur-
Marne between 1455 and 1494, and found 'a long, elaborate, and
public procedure in the making of most marriages', which in many
cases included informal betrothal as a prelude to, or in place of,
formal betrothal.[43] But the historical trend, continuing through the
Reformation, defines marriage ever more exclusively. Concubinage
is condemned. Betrothal vows come to have no legal, moral or

[41] Michael M. Sheehan, CSB, 'Marriage Theory and Practice in the Conciliar Legislation
and Diocesan Statutes of Medieval England', *Medieval Studies* 40 (1978), 446–8.
[42] 'Iuro quod si te decetero cognovero carnaliter, habebo te in uxorem meam si sancta
ecclesia permittit.' The wording is in *1 London 3*, ascribed to Roger Niger, Bishop of
London (1229–41). See Sheehan, 'Marriage Theory and Practice', 447.
[43] Beatrice Gottlieb, 'The Meaning of Clandestine Marriage', in Robert Wheaton and
Tamara K. Hareven (eds.), *Family and Sexuality in French History* (Philadelphia: University
of Pennsylvania Press, 1980), p.72.

religious authority, marriages begin with weddings, additional criteria for the validity of marriages are invented (marriages must be inside a church and conducted by a priest, and so on). The twelfth and thirteenth centuries remind us that there are gentler ways of affirming the marital norm which may yet assist the contemporary churches in wrestling with comparable problems.

AQUINAS AND SWINBURNE ON BETROTHAL

Aquinas' reflections on betrothal provide a fascinating glimpse into thirteenth-century controversy, yet his teaching on the matter is much less influential on future doctrinal development than almost anything else he wrote. In one place he is preoccupied with the question 'did a true marriage exist between the Lord's mother and Joseph?'[44] We have already had occasion to note (above, p.119) that, if Matthew's account is factually accurate, the couple were midway between the spousals and nuptials. Whether they were married depends upon a prior view of when marriage begins. Aquinas and his contemporaries could not have allowed that the Mother of God had undergone the inevitable impurities of sexual intercourse, even with her lawful spouse. However, the adoption of the consent theory of marriage allowed them to be considered married since sexual intercourse was inessential to the marriage. Indeed, the 'marriage' of Mary and Joseph was a major influence on the consent theory. What the consent theory did not do was explain how Jesus was born before the nuptials had taken place. So the question whether the marriage was 'a true marriage' remained.

Aquinas proceeds by stipulating crucial definitions and distinctions. A marriage is a true marriage when it 'attains its perfection' (*suam perfectionem attingit*) or 'completion'. He means not that the marriage was qualitatively perfect (although he may have believed this) but that 'their marriage fulfilled enough of the natural requirements to be called a true marriage'.[45] Aquinas holds there are two sorts of requirements for a marriage to be true or complete. 'The first kind is the form which gives the specific character. The second

[44] Thomas Aquinas, *Summa Theologiae*, 61 vols. (London: Blackfriars, 1964), vol.LI, 'Our Lady' (3a.29.2), p.65.
[45] See the Blackfriars edition, p.65, note [a].

is through the operation by which, in some way, the thing achieves its purpose.' Aquinas calls the 'form' or definition of marriage 'an inseparable union of souls in which husband and wife are pledged in an unbreakable bond of mutual love (*fides*)'. The second requirement of a true marriage is that it must conform to marriage's true purpose, namely, 'the birth and training of children'. Aquinas admits that sexual intercourse is needed for children to be born but does not concede that this detail invalidates the marriage from being perfect, for the marriage of Mary and Joseph was one where children were brought up and trained. So according to the two criteria Aquinas sets for *all* marriages this marriage was, and was not, perfect. It was perfect because each 'consented to the marital bond'. Doubt creeps in with regard to the second criterion. There was no sex in the marriage but it 'did enjoy the other kind of completion, regarding the training of children'. So the lack of sexual union does not compromise the marital union. Since the bond and the children are there, the marriage is perfect but different from other marriages in that Mary is the Mother of God and Jesus is conceived by the Holy Spirit.

There are lessons to be learned here from Aquinas' way of treating the matter and from the conclusions he drew. There is doubt, as he acknowledges, whether the marriage passes the second criterion, but there is also doubt (which he does not acknowledge) whether it passes the first. Few Christians today would deny that sexual union contributes positively to the total union which is the bond of marriage, yet this perfect marriage appears to lack an essential ingredient. Aquinas covers the point partially by saying that both of them 'consented to the marital bond but not expressly to union except under the condition that it be pleasing to God' (and it never was). I press the question whether Aquinas thought the marriage was a proper marriage because of what that might tell us about thirteenth-century presuppositions about marriage and the means of entering it. While allowing that the union of Mary and Joseph is unique in all Christian tradition (and so ungeneralizable), Aquinas *does* compare it with other marriages in order to answer his own question. And this comparison is instructive for at least two reasons. First, Aquinas concludes Mary and Joseph were married. However, their marriage is brought into being without a wedding or nuptial ceremony. But these unconventional arrangements are not allowed to interfere with the marriage's validity. Second, the 'inseparable union of souls' which is the form of all marriages is able to be contracted by means of betrothal, requiring nothing else. So Aquinas' treatment of the marriage of Mary and Joseph opens up intriguing possibilities for us. The very grounds on which it is asserted that Mary and Joseph were truly married also allow it to be asserted that all marriages which begin with betrothals and proceed without ceremony are valid marriages. These same grounds also admit the conclusion that the marital bond or inseparable union of souls is established without recourse to formal matrimony. Betrothal is a real *matrimonium initiatum*. The Church of course has backed away from both conclusions. But the work of retrieval brings to the surface earlier solutions which have the strange power of commending themselves to a different age which sits ever more loosely with the marital conventions of modernity.

In a supplement to the *Summa Theologica* Aquinas raised three rhetorical questions about betrothal: whether it is a promise of future marriage? Whether a child can be betrothed as young as seven? And whether betrothals can be dissolved? The answer to the first question is that '[c]onsent to conjugal union if expressed in words of the future does not make a marriage, but a promise of marriage; and this promise is called *a betrothal from plighting one's troth*'.[46] The promise can be made 'absolutely' or 'conditionally'. An absolute promise to marry may be made by saying 'I will take thee for my wife', by giving a pledge 'such as money and the like', by giving a betrothal ring and/or by taking an oath. There are honourable and dishonourable conditions which may attach to betrothal promises. An example of an honourable condition is parental consent: examples of dishonourable conditions are to remain childless or to consent to theft. Conditional promises of marriage can nonetheless be cancelled.[47] Failure to honour the promise of marriage constitutes a mortal sin, but Aquinas sides with those who do not require betrothed couples who no longer wish to proceed to the nuptials, to

[46] Thomas Aquinas, *Summa Theologica, Part 3 (Supp.)* (Qq. xxxiv–lxviii) (New York: Benziger Bros, 1922), p.96 (q.43 art.1).
[47] On conditional marriages, see Brundage, *Law, Sex, and Christian Society*, pp.277f.

do so, 'because compulsory marriages are wont to have evil results'. A betrothed person has a 'spouse' because the espousals have been contracted. Spousals are promises. At betrothal the promise of marriage is made: at the nuptials there is another promise made – 'the marriage act'.

Promises of marriage can be exchanged at the age of seven (or just before).[48] Following Aristotle Aquinas affirms the 'three degrees of reason', each of which is linked to the first three seven-year periods of a young life. In the first period, avers Aquinas, 'a person neither understands by himself nor is able to learn from another'. Towards the end of this period learning becomes possible and so a child is sent to school. Towards the end of the second period, a person is able to understand what making a promise means because he or she 'begins to be fit to make certain promises for the future'. Reason develops slowly 'in proportion as the movement and fluctuation of the humours is calmed'. By the end of the second period reason is developed enough for anyone to arbitrate in 'matters concerning his person', and only at the end of the third period is one sufficiently wise in the ways of the world to dispose of property. So promises of marriage can be made as early as seven and ratified later when the will has become firmer. Since procreation is a necessary end of marriage, a couple may not marry until they are capable of having children. Aristotle remains the guide in such matters. Girls can have babies when they are twelve; boys can be fathers at fourteen. So these are the minimum ages of marriage (and, indeed, following Tertullian (above, p.146), the recommended ages as well).

Aquinas allows the dissolution of betrothal in many cases.[49] He gives eight examples. If a spouse enters the religious life, or is deserted, or becomes ill, or is prevented by a prohibited affinity, the betrothal is *de facto* dissolved. Mutual consent also dissolves the agreement, so does having sex with someone else (because it would be difficult to trust one's partner again). A betrothal is voided by marrying someone else (provided the words used are in the present tense) and by the discovery that a betrothed person was under age (!) when the promises were made. Much of this teaching strikes us as

[48] *Summa Theologica, Part 3 (Supp.)*, (Benziger edn), pp.98–102 (q.43 art.2).
[49] *Summa Theologica, Part 3 (Supp.)*, (Benziger edn), pp.102–5 (q.43 art.3).

plain strange. What salient features of it remain, if any, for us to appropriate in reconstructing betrothal for a different age?

In this passage, far away from the consideration of the marriage of Mary and Joseph, betrothal is not the beginning of marriage, not *matrimonium initiatum*, but a promise of marriage. It is hard to reconcile what is said here with the assumption that when Mary and Joseph were betrothed they had already entered the form of matrimony, their pledges having already constituted an unbreakable bond of mutual love. That betrothal is a promise of marriage strongly suggests that the marriage, like the tense of the betrothal vows, is still in the future. One might still say that the relationship is already a beginning of marriage, since no promise to marry one's partner should and perhaps would be made without some prospect of its lifelong ideal being realized. However, Aquinas says different things about betrothal. What he says indicates that it was widely practised and that the meanings attached to it were not uniform.

His remarks about the minimum ages for betrothal and marriage are more likely to shock than to edify the late modern mind. Do we commend him for his positive child-centred assumptions which allow 'minors' supreme control over their marital destinies? Or chide him for assuming (along with everyone else in his age) that readiness for puberty and readiness for sexual experience were the same thing? Neither, of course. He belongs to an age with so many different assumptions from ours that contact with it is sometimes impossible for us. His assumptions about readiness for betrothal belong with others which are equally questionable. Aristotle does not have the last word about when and how children learn, nor about maturation, nor about the acquisition of powers of thought, or knowledge or wisdom, or the distinction between self-knowledge and knowledge of the external world. Where freedom of choice is more highly prized, and life expectancy considerably greater seven centuries on, we are likely to take the choice of a marriage partner much more earnestly than did Aquinas, and the choice *whether* to marry at all is a prior matter for many people. There are biologistic assumptions too about what marriage is which over-influence the argument.

Not all people married at these ages, nor were they all betrothed as young children. Nevertheless the contrast between the medieval and the late modern periods is probably most marked at this point. Since the average age of first marriages for men is now nearly thirty and for women nearly twenty-seven, this aspect of marriage is probably unprecedented in Christendom. Here is a clear case of discontinuity within the tradition which, if recognized and explored positively, can become a potent force for innovation. The belief that sexual experience is inevitable, and inevitable at an early age, is expressed in these assumptions. It is also strongly held by Luther.

The idea of a conditional betrothal is easier to accept. Any promise in the future tense is conditional at least to the extent that conditions which cannot be predicted will be necessary for the promise to be carried out. I cannot fulfil my promise to take my friend to the station if my car won't start. But Aquinas also recognizes that relationships can go wrong, that people sometimes regret making promises and the kinder course of action is not to insist on their being bound to them if greater harm is likely to result. Betrothal provides for mistakes, for failures of adjustment and adaptation, which are better made before unconditional, permanent promises are made. In this respect Aquinas is a person of our own time.

Henry Swinburne's *A Treatise of Spousals or Matrimonial Contracts* is a very different work. Swinburne was no theologian, but an ecclesiastical lawyer. He wrote the work in 1686, in England. Since his work occurs after the Reformation, it is strictly out of place in the present chapter. It is included here because, even after the drastic changes to marriage in the Reformation and Counter-Reformation, English law continued to recognize the medieval ways of entry into marriage. Swinburne's work is a reminder of remarkable continuity in an age of upheaval. Even if the practices he described were already becoming obsolete, and in many cases were to cease to receive legal recognition in 1753, his book is remarkably detailed evidence for marital practice that has now been abandoned. As we shall see, both English law and Swinburne's understanding of it are heavily influenced, either directly by Aquinas, or less directly, by the broader understanding of marriage in the late medieval and early modern periods.

Swinburne reminds his seventeenth-century readers that '*In ancient Times* Spoufals *did regularly precede Marriage ... And in fome places the Woman, after thefe* Spoufals, *prefently cohabited with the Man, but continued unknown till the Marriage-day.*'[50] He apparently thought it necessary also to remind them that the *Book of Common Prayer* had conflated the spousals and nuptials:

In our Publick Office of Marriage, Spoufals *and* Matrimony *are united, and performed in one continued Act; When the Minifter demands,* Wilt thou have this Woman to thy wedded Wife, *etc. And the Man anfwers,* I will, *and fo the Woman vice verfa, there's a* Specimen *of* Spoufals de futuro. *When the Man repeats the Words,* J.N. take thee N. to my wedded Wife, *etc. and fo the Woman* vice verfa, *there's the form of* Spoufals de praefenti, *which in Subftance are perfect* Matrimony, *(as I faid before) though not as to all Legal Effects. When the Minifter adds his Benediction, and pronounces them to be Man and Wife, then 'tis a perfect* Marriage *to all constructions and purpofes in Law.*[51]

The passage is full of terms which were already falling into disuse. 'Matrimony' refers to the wedding liturgy: the celebration of the marriage at the 'nuptials' is more presupposed than omitted. The priestly blessing is necessary to complete the marriage in the sight of God and English law. Spousals, Swinburne tells us, translates the Latin *Sponsalia*, which 'being properly underftood, doth only fignifie Promifes of future Marriage' of 'the Parties betroathed'.[52] The spousals are not yet marriage. While English lawyers were already using 'Efpoufals' and 'Marriage' as synonyms, only after the 'Solemnization' of the marriage did they 'repute the affianced Couple for one Perfon'.[53] 'Efpoufed', 'affianced' or 'betroathed' couples are promised to each other as the terms *Sponfus* and *Sponfa* (deriving, as Swinburne tells us, from *spondeo*, to promise) have always indicated. The history of the terms reveals earlier times when the promises to marry were made by the parents, not the parties. The passive voice, 'promised' or 'having been promised', indicates that the parties were promised *by their parents* – parental promises constituted the betrothal. Swinburne clearly approves of

[50] Henry Swinburne, *A Treatise of Spousals or Matrimonial Contracts,* 2nd edn (London, 1711) (author's emphasis). The archaic spelling and emphases are retained in all quotations.
[51] Ibid., Introduction (unpaginated).   [52] Ibid., p.1.   [53] Ibid., p.2 (and see also p.3).

the earlier practice, contrasting it with 'the wicked Examples of curfed Children in thefe days'[54] who attempt to marry without their parents' consent.

Spousals 'are a mutual Promife of future Marriage, being duly made between thofe Perfons, to whom it is lawful'. Spousals, like marriages, are based on the consent of the couple to marry in the future ('it is the Confent alone of the Parties whereby this Knot is tied'). The consent need not be made by means of words. Letters, exchanges of gifts, tokens or signs will suffice.[55] One of the partners does not even need to be present.[56] But Swinburne was aware of the practice, in his day, of contracting spousals in the *present* tense. Could this practice be reconciled with earlier practice? Yes, he thought. The exchange of vows in the present tense *is marriage*, yet 'marriage' has more than one meaning. The plural *Nuptiae*, or Marriages, may refer both to the vows in the present tense (the 'substance' of marriage), and, to 'the Rites and Ceremonies obferved at the Celebration of Matrimony only'.[57] Swinburne acknowledged, as Aquinas had done, that some betrothal promises were provisional. He distinguished between '*pure* and *fimple*', and '*conditional*' spousals (the sole example of a condition is the consent of the father). There was no problem about 'Private or Clandeftine Spoufals'. They could be 'private' or 'publick': however, a strong sense of 'private' was intended – *no* witnesses were required.

Swinburne also acknowledged grave problems with future tense promises, or promises to promise. These problems were to lead to the abolition of all legal recognition of promises to marry within the next century. Swinburne, however, defended betrothal promises. It may be helpful to suggest that the problems were logical, legal, theological, and practical. The *logical* problem was the lack of any performative utterance in the present tense to bind the promise-giver to the promise made. Conditional promises were allowed, but does not the future tense itself impose conditions on the promises because the future is unpredictable and circumstances change? The legal problems were considerable. Even public promises to marry were sometimes difficult to verify; private promises as Swinburne defined them were impossible to check. Enforcement was also

[54] Ibid., p.3.   [55] Ibid., pp.5, 6, 7.   [56] Ibid., p.154.   [57] Ibid., p.9.

difficult. If the couple came to hate each other, no good would come of requiring them to marry, as Aquinas noted and Swinburne later admits. The theological problem was whether betrothal was a beginning of marriage or a promise of marriage (Swinburne was adamant that it was the latter). And one of the practical problems was the ease of withdrawal from what was expected to be a binding obligation.

Against the odds Swinburne attempted a defence of future tense espousals, and did not think that the more recent practice of present tense espousals followed by a ceremony was superior to older precedents. Noting that the distinction between spousals *de futuro* and *de praesenti* was 'moft commonly received throughout all Chriftendom, and which all the Confiftories in *England* do ftill retain', he concedes that espoused persons are not married – they are merely espoused. Why retain spousals at all then? The situation is compared with that of a landowner who promises to sell some land at a future time. It is

as when a man doth promife, that he will fell his Land, the Land is not thereby fold in deed, but promifed to be fold afterwards; fo while the Parties do promife only, that they will take, or will marry; they do not thereby prefently take or marry: But deferring the accomplifhment of that promife, until another, the Knot in the mean time is not fo furely tied, but that it may be loofed, whiles the matter is in fufpenfe and unperfect.[58]

Swinburne's answer reveals a soft metaphorical understanding of the social value of betrothal, unlike the usual dispassionate legal tone. The knot is tied, but not so securely that it cannot be loosed. There is a legitimate uncertainty regarding the future. Their future together has not been finally settled (it is in suspense). It is not yet complete ('unperfect'). Termination ought to be a possibility, albeit a regrettable one. But vows in the present tense, whether made at the spousals or at the solemnization, are indissoluble because they partake of the 'substance' of matrimony (i.e., consent).

There is a further outcome of Swinburne's handling of the present/future distinction which he thought threw new light on the marital status of the parents of Jesus. Swinburne's age was

[58] Ibid., p.13.

one where espousals in the *present* tense were becoming common, and this form of espousal, he declares, was the one the parents of Jesus exchanged. Espousal in the present tense requires 'a prefent and perfect Confent' which does not require either 'Publick Solemnization' or 'Carnal Copulation' for its further legitimacy. In other words, consummation adds nothing to the marriage. As Swinburne explains, 'Such a Wife was the bleffed Virgin *Mary*, that is to fay, betroathed to *Jofeph*, but neither folemnly married with him, nor fecretly known by him, at the Conception of Chrift; and yet neverthelefs termed Wife in the Holy Scriptures.' The Bible concurs with civil and canon law in giving 'to Women betroathed only, or affianced, the Name and Title of *Wife*, because in truth the man and woman, thus perfectly affured, by words of *prefent time*, are Husband and Wife before God and his Church.'[59]

Betrothals may be contracted, from or just before the age of seven, but they must be confirmed later. Otherwise they are void. However, a kiss, an embrace, or living together in the same house, may be sufficient to confirm the contract,[60] even though 'thefe Amorous Actions of *Kiffings, Gifts, etc.* are often practifed as Preambles and Allurements rather to accomplifh the accomplifh-ment of unlawful Lufts, and to quench the Flames of Youthful Defires, than to tye the indiffoluble Knot of chaft Wedlock, or to undergo the perpetual Burthen of fo weighty a Charge.' 'Carnal Knowledge' confirms consent.[61]

Swinburne continues the line we have met in Tertullian and Aquinas of advocating very early marriages. What may be new are the supporting reasons he advances. First, at the ages of fourteen and twelve the parties know what they are doing. 'At thefe years the Man and the Woman are ... prefumed to be of difcretion, and able to difcern betwixt good and evil ...' Second, at these ages they are old enough for sexual experience and, indeed, ready for it. They 'have Natural and Corporal Ability to perform the duty of Marriage'. Third, at these ages they are like budding flowers and ripe fruit and should be treated as such. They are 'termed Puberes, as it were Plants, now fending forth Buds and Flowers, apparent Teftimonies of inward Sap, and immediate Meffengers

59 Ibid., p.14.   60 Ibid., pp.20–2.   61 Ibid., pp.42, 121, 224.

of approaching Fruit'. Fourth, at the ages of fourteen and twelve God has wisely given them the freedom to procreate, and the use of this gift ought not to be postponed. 'This Liberty is to be denied to none, whom otherwife the Almighty hath naturally difpofed and enabled to encreafe and multiply.' Fifth, sexual desire can be tamed by being expressed early so that it causes no problem in later life. 'The little Sparks are to be extinguifhed at the very firft, leaft afterwards they mount to an unquenchable Flame.' Finally, God has designed a remedy against lust which ought not to be denied to young people who are in fact only fourteen and twelve years old. 'To thefe Persons, albeit very young, the Remedy againft Luft is not to be denied.' Those people who are 'ftinged with Carnal Appetite' must not be denied 'the bleffed and Sovereign Remedy againft this Poifon, invented by Divine Philofophy'.[62]

How may an espousal contract be terminated? The answer is that as a rule it may *not* be terminated, but to the rule there are plenty of exceptions. First the rule: 'The Parties which have contracted Spoufals together, are bound by the *Laws Ecclefiaftical* of this Realm, to perform their promife, and to celebrate Matrimony together accordingly.' Now the exceptions. Top of the list is mutual agreement to dissolve the contract 'left a worfe thing happen unto them'. Once they have had sex, they *de facto* exchange consent in the present tense and so cannot dissolve what is indissoluble. If the promise to marry is by or on a certain day, and that day passes, the contract is void but the defaulting party is punishable. Other conditions include desertion or absence for at least two years, or the failure to fulfil a condition (e.g., to provide an agreed financial contribution to the forthcoming marriage). Having sex with someone else voids the spousal promise, but only if the 'Innocent Party' chooses. Heresy (i.e., 'Spiritual Fornication'), or a newly acquired disease or deformity, are included in the exceptions. Neither should the marriage be proceeded with 'when fome deadly enmity and unquenchable *hatred* is fprung up between the Parties affianced'. The other exceptions are, a new or newly discovered affinity within the prohibited degrees, cruelty, marriage with another, and, the final catch-all phrase, 'whenfoever there is juft and reafonable Caufe'.[63]

---

[62] Ibid., pp.47–8.   [63] Ibid., pp.236–9.

The strangeness of Swinburne's work shows its value in the attempt to recover a lost way of thinking. Swinburne had to remind his own readers of the earlier tradition of betrothal and to explain that the Prayer Book had conflated two separate events into a single liturgy. He clearly felt obliged to deal with a new situation, viz., the practice of making the spousal vows in the present tense (below, pp.175–9), and in effect bringing the marriage ceremony forward to coincide with what was still called the spousals or *sponsalia*. Protestantism did not shake the settled view that the essence of marriage is consent. Swinburne's separation of consent from consummation allowed him to accord full marital status to the allegedly sexless marriage of Mary and Joseph. But present tense espousals were unknown in the time of Jesus.

Swinburne insists that spousals are not marriages but he is unconvincing. He follows the tradition that eventually sided against Gratian's view that the spousals are a genuine beginning of marriage. The knot-tying metaphor also suggests otherwise. While a landowner who promises to sell his land does not sell his land by promising but by selling, a betrothed couple who tie the knot, tie the knot. They *do* something and they refrain from doing something. What they refrain from doing is tying the knot so tightly it is untiable. He might equally well have said that the marriage had begun, but that its first phase was provisional ('in suspense and unperfect').

Swinburne's advocacy of very early marriage provides a drastic discontinuity between early modernity and the present time. How is this discontinuity to be explained? Perhaps Swinburne was simply exercising consistency? He knew that one of the justifications for marriage in the Prayer Book service for the Solemnization of Matrimony was that '[i]t was ordained for a remedy against sin, and to avoid fornication'. Since the temptation towards sexual sins arises at puberty, the God-given remedy against them, he may have thought, could and should be invoked. But other explanations (albeit partial) may be at hand. We have already noted the anxiety (that led Tertullian to advocate the veil) that the young might indulge in promiscuity. Marriage at puberty was, according to one particular mindset, a powerful defence against this. A more likely explanation lies in the anxieties of Swinburne's own class that sons and daughters should not be too readily propelled, especially by the tragedy of 'falling in love', into financially disadvantageous matches. Marrying very early in life, but in accord with parental permission, was thought to avoid many dangers, including that of dealing with repressed desire. Early satisfaction prevents repression.

It will be helpful to recall Swinburne's treatment of sexual desire when reflecting theologically on the widening gap between puberty and the average age of first marriage (below, pp.248, 265). Our next task is the completion of the historical section, indicating what happened to betrothal during and after the Reformation.

CHAPTER 6

Whatever happened to betrothal?

This, the final chapter of the historical section of the book, traces the demise of the understanding and practice of betrothal from the Reformation to the present time. It completes the attempt to sketch a lack, to account for an absence, and thereby to retrieve from the past an understanding of the beginnings of Christian marriage vital to its future. The legacy of Luther and Calvin is examined (first section) followed by the Council of Trent (second section) and, in England and Wales, the legacy of the 1753 Hardwicke Marriage Act (third section). The final section explores the 'rigidification' of marriage without betrothal, and, in the twentieth century, the loss of meaning, even of engagement.

THE REFORMATION AND ITS LEGACY

The difficulties of the Missouri Synod of the Lutheran Church in the USA over the practice of engagement have already been described (above, pp.78–83). These Lutherans were trying to make sense of scripture, of their own tradition, and of social practices believed to be at variance with both. But their own tradition was also a source of confusion, for if Luther had successfully brought about a break with much medieval marital theology and practice, his successors had to cope with the consequences of the changes he himself advocated. These must now be explored more fully.

A very strong influence on Luther was the sense of widespread promiscuity fuelled by clandestine marriages. While Protestants doubtless propagandized these problems in order to justify the break with Rome,[1] they considered 'the marriage of minors without their parents' consent or knowledge', and 'the pandemic sexual promiscuity and discord' to be 'the two worst violations of the natural social order'.[2] When they looked for reasons for these disorders, they blamed the current state of canon law, which allowed marriages to be entered into too easily. They also attacked what they saw as the corrupt administration of dispensations allowing people to marry within the maze of prohibited degrees. Luther brandished the ecclesiastical authorities as '[sellers] of vulvas and genitals – merchandise indeed most worthy of such merchants, grown altogether filthy and obscene through greed and godlessness'.[3]

Luther's proposals for remedying the situation struck at the heart of the canonical distinction between spousals and nuptials, betrothal and marriage, vows *de futuro* and vows *de praesenti*. His belief that this twofold distinction lay at the root of much promiscuity is indicated by his coarse, impatient remark,

> ... what a coarse rabble there is in the world. Loose fellows are wandering around through the land from one place to the other, and wherever one of them sees a wench that takes his fancy he starts getting hot and right away he tries to see how he can get her, goes ahead and gets engaged again, and thus wants to forget and abandon the first engagement that he entered into elsewhere with another woman.[4]

Luther's solution, albeit diffidently proffered ('Whoever wishes to or can comply, let him do so; whoever will not or cannot, let him refrain'), was based in part on abolishing the distinction between future tense and present tense vows. This was to have the effect of abolishing the distinction between the events at which each set of vows was made. In other words, the betrothal becomes the marriage. Surprisingly, Luther's strongest argument for the change was

---

[1] The issue of polemicism with regard to sexual misconduct, and its justification, is superbly handled in Joel F. Harrington, *Reordering Marriage and Society in Reformation Germany* (Cambridge: Cambridge University Press, 1995).

[2] Ibid., p.28.

[3] Martin Luther, *Babylonian Captivity*, in *Luther's Works*, Jaroslav Pelikan and Helmut Lehman (eds.), American edition, 55 vols. (Philadelphia: Fortress Press, 1955–), cited in ibid., p.32.

[4] Martin Luther, *On Marriage Matters*, in Robert Schultz (ed.), *Luther's Works*, American edition, vol.XLVI (Philadelphia: Fortress Press, 1967), p.293.

linguistic: when a prospective husband said in the German language, 'I will have you as a wife', this would have been understood at the time as a *present tense* avowal, not a promise to marry in the future, and Luther affirms what he understood as the *common language meaning* of the vows against the tensed distinction preserved in the Latin (the future tense *accipiam te* and the present tense *accipio te*). This distinction was, of course, accepted in canon law, and presupposed by betrothal practice. In *On Marriage Matters* he savages what he calls 'the scoundrelly game',[5] whose linguistic rules relied on this tensed distinction, accusing the church authorities of deliberate pretence and deception in operating it:

The words, 'I will have you as a wife,' or, 'I will take you, I will have you,' 'you shall be mine,' and the like[6] they have generally called future verbs and pretended that the man should say, '*accipio te in uxorem*,' 'I take you to be my wife,' and the wife should likewise say, 'I take you to be my husband.' They have not seen or noticed that this is not the custom in speaking German when one is speaking in the present, for in German one says in the present, 'I will have you,' '*ego volo te habere*'; this is present tense, not future. Thus no German is speaking of a future betrothal when he says, 'I will have you' or 'take you,' for one does not say, 'I am going to have you,' as they juggle with *accipiam te*. On the other hand, *accipio te* really means in German, 'I will take you' or 'have you' and is understood to be present, that the man now is saying 'yes' in these words and giving his consent to the bargain.[7]

An obvious corollary of Luther's 'advice' was that betrothal vows, although uttered grammatically in the future tense, were understood to be uttered performatively in the present tense. In other words betrothal vows became marriage vows. Conditional betrothals continued to be allowed, provided the conditions were

---

[5] Witte's translation of 'ein lauter Narrenspiel'. See John Witte, Jr., *From Sacrament to Contract: Marriage, Religion and Law in the Western Tradition* (Louisville: Westminster/John Knox Press, 1997), p.57.

[6] 'Ich will Dich zum Weibe haben', 'Ich will Dich nehmen; Ich will Dich haben; Du sollst mein sein'.

[7] Luther, *On Marriage Matters*, p.274. For insightful comment on this passage, see Harrington, *Reordering Marriage*, p.30; Witte, *From Sacrament to Contract*, pp.56–7; and Pamela Biel, 'Let the Fiancées Beware: Luther, the Lawyers and Betrothal in Sixteenth-Century Saxony', in Bruce Gordon (ed.), *Protestant History and Identity in Sixteenth-Century Europe*, 2 vols. (Aldershot and Vermont: Scolar Press and Ashgate Publishing, 1996), vol.II, *The Later Reformation*, pp.125–6.

specified at the time. For example one might say 'I will marry you if you contribute 100 guilders to our household'.[8] Nonetheless, the legitimacy of clearly labelled conditional promises did nothing to mitigate the logical and social force of the new proposal. Since betrothal promises are promises of marriage, and not of future marriage, 'Let the Fiancées Beware'.[9] Betrothal promises are indissoluble. There is no escape from them. A sexual relation with someone other than one's betrothed falls under the category of adultery against him or her. A further service of marriage *after* public betrothal is rendered legally superfluous since it could add nothing to what had already been promised. As Biel notes, Luther's understanding of betrothal 'made marriage, or at least the formal, public and ecclesiastical ceremony of matrimony, appear irrelevant'.[10]

Luther also insisted that parental permission be required before either church or state recognized a marriage between minors. This too was seen as a modification of earlier canon law which required only the consent of the parties for validity. This was a highly popular change in the German states. But Germany was not prepared for the consequences of the virtual abolition of betrothal and the telescoping of two sets of events and promises into one. And Lutheran theologians struggled to find an intermediate position between the new orthodoxy and well-established customs. For example Martin Chemnitz (1522–86) reckoned to find two kinds of betrothal in the Bible, corresponding to present and future vows, and he concluded that 'futuristic betrothals', while not legally binding, were theologically and socially permissible.[11] Melchior Kling (in 1553) also distinguished between two types of betrothal, distinguishing them by the consents given at each. If the consent given was sworn, it was indissoluble and therefore marriage: but if it was unsworn (e.g., made with a gift instead of a vow in the presence of witnesses) it was less binding than marital consent and the vows were dissoluble for

---

[8] Biel, 'Let the Fiancées Beware', p.127.

[9] The title of Biel's essay which draws the full conclusions of the change and the legal chaos it created.

[10] Biel, 'Let the Fiancées Beware', p.128.

[11] Martin Chemnitz, *Loci theologici*, III (1690), p.197, cited in Paul B. Hansen, Oscar E. Feucht, Fred Kramer and Erwin L. Lueker, *Engagement and Marriage: A Sociological, Historical, and Theological Investigation of Engagement and Marriage* (St. Louis: Concordia Publishing House, 1959), p.78.

good cause.[12] J.A. Quenstedt (1617–85) spoke of betrothal 'as an antecedent cause, preparing and disposing for marriage, since it was a promise of future marriage'.[13] John Gerhard (1582–1637), like Kling before him, distinguished between two types of consent, one given at betrothal, thereby reinstating it, the other being the consent given at marriage.

While these and other attempts were made to restore betrothal within a revised framework of marriage, betrothal ceased to have legal force or to retain any sense of being a beginning of marriage. What happens among Lutherans can be described as *the replacement of betrothal by engagement*. Whereas in earlier times, the betrothal was a precursor to the nuptials, the precursor to a Lutheran wedding was a period during which the necessary consents could be obtained. The number of persons giving consent was increased from two to seven, i.e., the couple, both sets of parents or guardians, and often the pastor conducting the wedding service.[14] Since engagement fulfils a different function, it seems appropriate to delineate it by means of a different concept. The Protestant Reformation, according to Pamela Biel, 'changed the place of betrothal in the usual procedure of getting married. It made engagements necessary, public and invalid *without the permission of the parents*. In the course of these changes engagement became *a way to keep order* in the community.'[15]

The fate of betrothal in Calvin's Geneva after the Marriage Ordinance of 1545 has been fully described by John Witte.[16] The same transition, from betrothal to engagement, is not hard to discern. There is no ecclesiastical ceremony, more a declaration of intent. Betrothals have to be unconditional; secret betrothals are automatically void, with the parties and their accomplices facing the threat of imprisonment. Paternal consent for minors was required (twenty for men, eighteen for women), but undue paternal pressure on children to marry was also susceptible to a jail sentence. What

[12] Melchior Kling, *Matrimonalium Causarum Tractatus, Methodico ordine scriptus* (Frankfurt, 1553), fol.1ᵛ, fo.3ʳ, cited in Biel, 'Let the Fiancées Beware', p.129.

[13] Cited in Hansen, et al., *Engagement and Marriage*, p.82.

[14] Biel, 'Let the Fiancées Beware', p.140.

[15] Ibid., pp.140–1.   [16] Witte, *From Sacrament to Contract*, pp.83–5, 91.

happened at betrothal was registration with a civil magistrate who publicized the forthcoming marriage and issued the couple with a marriage certificate which would then be filed with a local church. Banns would be called, thereby inviting objection from both civil and ecclesiastical authorities. The publicization of the intention to marry secured 'the consent of the broader state and church community'.[17] Assuming no objection it was required that a wedding follow within three to six weeks of betrothal. Living together and sexual consummation of the marriage were forbidden, with imprisonment facing guilty parties. Pregnant brides were spared prison but 'required to do public confession' and 'on the day of the wedding had to wear a veil signaling their sin of fornication'.[18]

The shift from the theological to the social significance of betrothal, found also in Lutheranism, is evident here also. Protestant determination to address the sin of fornication used the Ordinance to bring about 'the abbreviation and careful communal policing of the interim between betrothal and marriage'. This austere policing of the betrothal period did not survive long in other Reformed areas of Europe and the gradual liberalization of the judiciaries' decisions with regard to release from betrothal contracts in the next two centuries has been tracked by Jeffery Watt. The binding character of betrothal in the Reformed Church in France was so strong that a petition to a tribunal for release from a betrothal was treated as a petition for divorce. Yet as early as 1612 that same church decreed that betrothal was not legally binding at all,[19] and in Reformed Holland 'marriage betrothals, even those written and notarized, were not necessarily regarded as contractually binding; magistrates seemed reluctant to enforce them without the drastic element of sexual violation'.[20]

Watt examined the marriage records of Neuchâtel, a French-speaking principality that converted to the Reformed faith in the sixteenth century, from 1550 to 1800. He found that 'the courts often canceled marriage contracts based on one party's refusal to go through with the marriage, provided that that party

---

[17] Ibid., p.84. [18] Ibid., p.85.
[19] Jeffrey R. Watt, *The Making of Modern Marriage: Matrimonial Control and The Rise of Sentiment in Neuchâtel, 1550–1800* (Ithaca and London: Cornell University Press, 1992), pp.72–3.
[20] Ibid., p.73.

paid damages to the other'.[21] This liberalization coincides with a broader, uncontrollable phenomenon – the enormous increase in premarital pregnancies which occurred simultaneously in Britain and America. Between 1760 and 1790, the rate of premarital conceptions rose in the Neuchâtel area to over 50 per cent of first births, leading Watt to conclude that, 'in spite of the views of pastors and moralists, eighteenth-century Neuchâtelois condoned sexual relations between fiancés'.[22] The favoured explanation for this huge rise in premarital sex is the sudden extent of wage labour, leading to greater economic freedom, and greater expression given to romantic love. Older ways of becoming married were not forgotten; newer ways were merely grafted on to them. Engagements were probably still regarded as betrothals. They were probably still believed to signify the beginning of marriage and to confer sexual rights if accompanied by binding promises. While magistrates were increasingly willing to release engaged couples from commitments to marry, release was not extended to couples who had become pregnant. The industrial upheavals of the eighteenth century made the enforcement of sexual abstinence during the engagement period impossible.

What traces still remain of betrothal in Lutheran and Reformed churches at the present time? Almost none. Some evidence is found in the Lutheran reports already discussed, especially the Evangelical Lutheran Church in America in 1993 (above, p.87). But what was called 'the betrothal solution' was not on offer, even though there was recognition that a ceremony is not always required in the making of a marriage. The report *Body and Soul* for the Presbyterian Church of the USA was criticized, not for its neglect of betrothal, but for its neglect of marriage. At the other end of the Reformed spectrum Jeffery Ford rails against ministers who 'have blessed with the words of Christ couples who have already borne a bastard child or openly lived together before marriage', calling their practice 'sickening' and 'sacrilege'.[23] Each is equally extreme, and each is equally victim of theological memory loss. The 'betrothal solution' would have provided a helpful

[21] Ibid., p.207.   [22] Ibid., p.192.

[23] Jeffery E. Ford, *Love, Marriage and Sex in the Christian Tradition from Antiquity to Today* (San Francisco: International Scholars Publications, 1999), p.116.

perspective on beginning marriage both for liberal working parties sceptical of its benefits and fundamentalist ministers dealing with Christians eager to anticipate its benefits before the wedding ceremony.

THE COUNCIL OF TRENT AND ITS LEGACY

In the Roman Catholic Church, betrothal ceased to have any legal or theological significance after the Council of Trent in 1563. The Council, eager to distinguish Catholic teaching from that of the schismatic Protestants, while anxious to prevent the evil of clandestine marriage and the abuses and excesses that went with it, commanded (in the decree *Tametsi*, passed 150 in favour, 55 against)

that in the future, before a marriage is contracted, the proper pastor of the contracting parties shall publicly announce three times in the church, during the celebration of the mass on three successive festival days, between whom marriage is to be contracted; after which publications, if no legitimate impediment is revealed, the marriage may be proceeded with in the presence of the people, where the parish priest, after having questioned the man and the woman and heard their mutual consent, shall either say: 'I join you together in matrimony, in the name of the Father, and of the Son, and of the Holy Ghost,' or he may use other words, according to the accepted rite of each province.[24]

As a further measure against clandestine marriage,

those who shall attempt to contract marriage otherwise than in the presence of the parish priest or of another priest authorized by the parish priest or by the ordinary and in the presence of two or three witnesses, the holy council renders absolutely incapable of thus contracting marriage and declares such contracts invalid and null, as by the present decree it invalidates and annuls them.

Pastors were required to be vigilant 'lest young persons, whose period of life is marked by extreme indiscretion, should be deceived by a merely nominal marriage and foolishly rush into sinful love-unions'. They 'cannot too frequently remind them that there can be no true and valid marriage unless it be contracted in the presence of

[24] 'Decree concerning the Reform of Matrimony', chapter 1. Text in *The Canons and Decrees of the Council of Trent*, tr. H.J. Schroeder (Rockford, Ill.: Tan Books, 1978), pp.183–4.

the parish priest . . .'[25] The Council did not legislate for a valid form
of conducting betrothals but warned 'betrothed parties not to live
together in the same house until they have received the sacerdotal
blessing in the church'.[26]

Cephas Lerewonu has well described some of the consequences
of the *Tametsi* decree. First, betrothals 'were now outside what was
prescribed as a valid marriage union'. They had no legal significance and were rendered optional. Second, marrying couples
'could contract betrothals in any form they chose', just because they
had no validity, and official requests to provide a form for general
use were refused. Local and provincial councils 'continued to issue
legislation concerning betrothals' but since their purpose had been
undermined the efforts of the councils had little influence. Third,
barring exceptional circumstances 'betrothals and marriages are
invalid if they are not celebrated in a manner presided over by a
priest'. This was a major change, since the church had hitherto
regarded clandestine marriages as valid, even though they were
contrary to canon law. Fourth, 'a binding public form of celebration' was introduced as 'one of the conditions required for a valid
celebration of marriage'.[27]

The significance of these changes is greater than at first appears,
for they belong to a time when betrothal was taken for granted,
whereas a reader of *Tametsi* over 450 years later is unlikely to notice anything unusual. For the first time in the Catholic tradition,
the consent of two parties who are free to marry *is no longer enough*.
They must be married in church, and blessed by a priest in accordance with a required form. This adds much to the traditional
teaching and represents 'a radical departure from past teaching'.
The peculiar understanding of the ministry of the sacrament of
marriage, that the couple administer it to one another, is compromised. The blessing of the priest, as in the Orthodox churches,
becomes the *sine qua non* for the validity of the marriage. Lerewonu
concludes that as a result of *Tametsi* betrothal was 'apparently lost

---

[25] *The Roman Catechism*, or *The Catechism of the Council of Trent*, tr. John A. McHugh and
Charles J. Callan (Rockford, Ill.: Tan Books, 1982), p.353.
[26] *The Canons and Decrees of the Council of Trent*, p.184.
[27] Cephas N. Lerewonu, 'The Betrothal Commitment in the Making of Marriage', PhD
thesis, Katholieke Universiteit Leuven (1996), pp.135, 137–8.

to view', and marriage 'totally dissociated from any stage prior to it like betrothal'.[28]

Enforcement of the decree was slow and difficult. No attempt was made to enforce it in England. A meticulous examination of parish records in Ourense, north-west Spain, between 1550 and 1700 has shown that local populations continued to believe, as before, that betrothal was a beginning of marriage which licensed sexual activity. In this respect the responses of local populations under Catholicism and Calvinism were similar. 'Despite the injunctions of the Council of Trent, not all promises of marriage and sexual activity led to marriage, principally because local religious culture tolerated sexual activity between promised partners whether or not the promise was made in the presence of a priest.'[29] Eventually, as Witte notes, the decrees of the Council were accepted 'throughout the early modern Catholic world', i.e., in Italy, France, Spain, and Portugal, and eventually in their colonies in Latin America, Mexico, Florida, California, Louisiana, Quebec, and beyond.[30] In an attempt to further enforce them, Pope Pius X issued the decree *Ne Temere* in 1907. This was incorporated into the Code of Canon Law in 1917. But there is no reference to betrothal either in *Arcanum*, the 1880 encyclical of Pope Leo XIII, on Christian marriage, or in *Casti Connubii*, the 1930 encyclical of Pope Pius XI on chastity in marriage. An officially approved pre-Vatican II work was allowed to express regret 'that the former Catholic practice of solemn betrothal before a priest has largely lapsed'.[31] The Vatican II document *Gaudium et Spes* does, however, contain a solitary reference. 'On several occasions the Word of God invites the betrothed to nourish and foster their betrothal with chaste love, and likewise spouses their marriage. Many of our contemporaries, too, have a high regard for true love between husband and wife as manifested in the worthy customs of various times and peoples.'[32]

[28] Ibid., pp.165–6.
[29] Allyson M. Poska, 'When Love Goes Wrong: Getting Out of Marriage in Seventeenth-Century Spain', *Journal of Social History*, 29.3–4 (1996), 872.
[30] Witte, *From Sacrament to Contract*, p.41.
[31] R.F. Trevett, *The Church and Sex* (New York: Hawthorn Publishers, 1960), p.98.
[32] *Gaudium et Spes: Pastoral Constitution on the Church in the Modern World*, section 49. Text in e.g. Austin Flannery, OP (ed.), *Vatican Council II: the conciliar and post conciliar documents* (Grand Rapids: Wm. B. Eerdmans, 1981).

The reference belongs in a section entitled 'Married Love' where it appears in a combination of remarks about love. Love is made one of the purposes of married life. 'The intimate partnership of life and the love which constitutes the married state has been established by the creator and endowed by him with its own proper laws.'[33] Married love, and not merely marriage itself, is said to be universal, while taking different forms among different peoples at different times. The contrast between betrothed and married love probably contrasts love which has not yet reached full sexual expression with the 'eminently human love' which is marriage. Lerewonu sees in this minor reference the basis for a processive understanding of marriage – 'the conjugal union is developed and nurtured from the betrothed love . . . The betrothed love will be seen as the source from which a commitment is initiated between a man and a woman to continue in a marital state of life ...'[34] This may be true: it may also be true that no more than a contrast is intended between married and premarried love, thus yielding the warning that couples who have not been formally married are to abstain from sexual intercourse. Whatever sense is given to the reference, it is surprising to find it here at all.

The appetite for continuing reform of Roman Catholic teaching on sexuality and marriage was not quenched by the publication of *Humanae Vitae* in 1968. The 1980 Synod of Bishops, entitled 'On the Role of the Family', meeting in Rome, made many requests to the Pope,[35] including one for permission to reintroduce a betrothal ceremony. Amazingly, Proposition 13 (of 43 Propositions submitted) 'suggests that episcopal conferences introduce some form of betrothal ceremony (*quaetam forma sponsalium*) to enhance the premarital decision-making process'.[36] The reference to the episcopal conferences suggests that Rome allow local autonomy to introduce a *forma sponsalium* where there were pastoral grounds for doing so. African bishops were particularly supportive of this suggestion. Reference to the *sponsalia* is a clear allusion to earlier times and practice which belong to the Roman Catholic tradition. These

---

[33] *Gaudium et Spes*, section 48.   [34] Lerewonu, 'The Betrothal Commitment', p.13.

[35] Jan Grootaers and Joseph A. Selling, *The 1980 Synod of Bishops 'On the Role of the Family'* (Leuven: Leuven University Press, 1983), pp.292–3.

[36] Ibid., pp.271, 352.

two suggestions were 'important and even revolutionary'.[37] But the bishops did not get what they wanted. What they got was *Familiaris Consortio* which, despite its length, mentioned neither betrothal nor the request for a betrothal ceremony.

While developmental language is used in *Familiaris Consortio* (part 4 is entitled 'Stages of Pastoral Care of the Family'), and metaphors of process (development, growth, pilgrimage, journey, maturation, formation, etc.) are plentiful, it is clear that engagement is altogether a premarital stage, and marriage begins with the ceremony. The Pope says, 'After the preparation of engagement and the sacramental celebration of marriage, the couple begin their daily journey toward the progressive actuation of the values and duties of marriage itself.'[38] This seems to be a particularly unfortunate passage, not least because of the earlier emphasis on the need for urgent, focussed pastoral care exercised towards the engaged, and in particular for people who 'are in difficult or irregular situations'. The acknowledgment that the engaged might have begun their marriage could have added considerably to the nature of pastoral interventions. But engagement and marriage preparation form no part of the sacramental marriage itself. Engagement and the growth it expects and requires are distinct from the growth of marriage. The 'daily journey' only begins once the ceremony has, as it were, intervened upon the couple's lives. Here, and later in the *Catechism of the Catholic Church*, there is no trace of earlier formulations.

The 1983 changes to canon law confirm the redundancy of betrothal. Canons 1062.1 and 2 deal with the *sponsalia*. The first of these says: 'A promise of marriage (*matrimonii promissio*), whether unilateral or bilateral, known as engagement (*quam sponsalia vocant*), is regulated by particular law that the episcopal conference has enacted, with regard to customs and civil laws that may exist.'[39] The term *sponsalia*, used in the 1917 code, is retained, but a 'promise of marriage' is optional and has no legal or theological place in the constitution of the marriage. A promise of marriage is not

37 Ibid., p.271. And see Lerewonu, 'The Betrothal Commitment', pp.279–80.
38 Pope John Paul II, *Familiaris Consortio* (Apostolic Exhortation On the Family) (London: Catholic Truth Society, 1981), section 65.
39 Text from Ladislas Örsy, SJ, *Marriage in Canon Law* (Dublin and Leominster: Dominican Publications and Fowler Wright, 1986), p.70.

a beginning of marriage, but a promise to begin it in the future (which according to Canon 1062.2 cannot be compelled). Episcopal conferences were not given the powers to use betrothal ceremonies as the 1980 Synod had requested: they were merely to be allowed to continue to tolerate local anomalies which were incidental to the longstanding Tridentine understanding and practice. Lerewonu rightly observes that the *sponsalia* 'does not constitute part of legal marriage'. 'The future marriage is what is considered as the only legal and true marriage ... Betrothal and marriage thus do not appear to have any significant relationship as they are presented as two separate realities.'[40]

THE HARDWICKE MARRIAGE ACT AND ITS LEGACY

It took nearly 200 years after the Council of Trent before legislation depriving betrothal promises of legal force was passed in England. Only in 1753, by the passing of Lord Hardwicke's Marriage Act – 'An Act for the better preventing of clandestine marriages' – were the English and Welsh subjected to marriage legislation remarkably similar to that passed by the Council of Trent. The reasons for the 'extraordinary explosion of clandestine marriages between 1660 and 1753' have been described by Lawrence Stone. During the Civil War in England, the churches were forbidden to perform marriages. Banns were read but 'the couple were to present themselves to a JP [Justice of the Peace], who would perform a simple secular ceremony in a private house. All other forms of marriage were declared illegal, especially any performed by clergymen or in a church.'[41] After the Restoration the population was unwilling generally to resume church weddings. Other reasons include the breakdown in the eighteenth century of the controls on bundling (the custom which allowed an unmarried couple to occupy the same bed, often in the young woman's home with the full knowledge of her parents, and apparently without the couple undressing!)

[40] Lerewonu, 'The Betrothal Commitment', p.9.
[41] Lawrence Stone, *Uncertain Unions: Marriage in England 1660–1753* (Oxford: Oxford University Press, 1992), pp.30, 20. Stone defines a clandestine marriage as 'a ceremony conducted by a man who at least purported to be a clergyman (although often one not holding a cure) and which followed the ritual prescribed by the Book of Common Prayer' (p.22).

which coincided with a remarkable rise in prenuptial pregnancies. 'By the late 18th century consummation and conception *normally* preceded – and indeed precipitated – marriage, as shown by the fact that a third of all brides were pregnant on their wedding-day, and over half of all first births were conceived out of wedlock.' These marriages were popularly seen as 'marriages in the sight of God' and were 'clearly widely accepted among the lower sort in the eighteenth century as a moral justification for starting sexual relations, on the assumption, usually justified, that the man would marry the woman if and when she became pregnant'.[42]

We have already encountered Henry Swinburne's description of the legal provision for entry into marriage (above, p.175) and noted that some of this provision was already obsolete in 1686. However, since much of the population of Britain married informally (or not at all) before and after Hardwicke's Act, its impact must be set within the social context of Britain after the Reformation. The legal framework for entry into marriage via betrothal did not *require* couples intending marriage to enter it this way. It was permissible for them to proceed directly to the nuptials without the 'contracting' of a betrothal ceremony. Of the seventeenth century, David Cressy observes, 'Neither law nor religion required marriage contracts, and a huge number of couples dispensed with them, moving directly to church or bed.'[43] The 1549 Prayer Book contained evidence of the earlier ceremony which was now combined in a single liturgy of solemnization. Thomas Cranmer based the new liturgy on the old Sarum rite but made changes. For the first time the whole service took place in church. The prior ceremony of handfasting at the church door, indicative of separate occasions and separate liturgies of earlier times, was incorporated into the rite. An influential interpretation of this liturgical change stresses the determination of the new Protestant faith to control marriage and to remove any independence from official sanction that the old ceremony, *in facie ecclesiae*, at the church door but not inside the church, might provide:

In reality the marriage service had been an ecclesiastical matter for centuries, but the old practice of the handfasting taking place at the

---

[42] Ibid., p.17 (emphasis added).

[43] David Cressy, *Birth, Marriage and Death: Ritual, Religion, and the Life-Cycle in Tudor and Stuart England* (Oxford: Oxford University Press, 1997), pp.271, 336–9.

church door had been retained. In the old service, the couple did not enter the church until after the exchange of the ring and the prayers which followed. The Protestant service disposed of the old fiction and appropriated marriage from first to last for the church.[44]

The blessing of the ring was replaced by a prayer indicating that its significance lay in being a token of the vow made, and '[t]he new Prayer Book of 1552 made practically no changes in this service. References to the gold and silver token of spousals, given with the ring, were removed, and rubrics for signing with the cross at various points were deleted. In other respects the new service was the same as its predecessor.'[45]

While the unification of the liturgical enactment of marriage is completed at the Reformation, the old social customs and practices continued much as before, and it was the depth and persistence of the old ways, still fully legal (and exhaustively described by Swinburne), which led to the Hardwicke Act. The social transition 'from wooing to wiving'[46] could not be kaleidoscoped so easily. The lack of a betrothal ceremony led to demands to reintroduce one, and the moderate Puritan Richard Greenham refused to marry couples who had not first taken part in the betrothal ceremony he himself used.[47] There were several grounds for confusion about what made a valid marriage after the Reformation. The church was fiercely opposed to premarital sexual intercourse, yet the church itself had for centuries operated a system whereby the 'pleding' or promising of the couple to each other, followed by sexual intercourse, constituted, at least presumptively, marriage, with public celebration following later. According to Alan Macfarlane these 'two stages remained separate in essence until they were united into one occasion after the Reformation. Thus the modern Anglican wedding service includes both spousals and nuptials.'[48] But the concatenation of events liturgically did little to achieve social assent, and the belief, however convenient,

44 Eric Josef Carlson, *Marriage and the English Reformation* (Oxford, UK and Cambridge, Mass.: Blackwell, 1994), p.45.
45 Ibid., p.47.   46 Cressy's phrase, *Birth, Marriage and Death*, p.267.
47 Carlson, *Marriage and the English Reformation*, p.49.
48 Alan Macfarlane, *Marriage and Love in England: Modes of Reproduction 1300–1840* (Oxford: Blackwell, 1987), p.309 (citing Whitelock, *English Society*, 152; Howard, *Matrimonial Institutions*, i, 381).

that betrothal conferred on couples the right of cohabitation and sexual intercourse continued on well into the eighteenth century and beyond.[49]

The Act was motivated by several factors. There was anxiety about the continuation of clandestine marriages and the bypassing of the banns and licensing system. This anxiety principally belonged to the upper classes who had much to lose from unsuitable matches and bargains struck without parental consent. Marriages between families of landowners and merchants were particularly favoured, for, as R. Porter says, the 'alliance of a gentleman's son with a merchant's daughter, the landed embracing the loaded, was marriage à la mode'.[50] John Gillis introduces the politics of class-consciousness into his explanation of the legal changes, showing that '[f]rom the mid eighteenth century onwards sexual politics became increasingly bitter as the propertied classes attempted to impose their standards on the rest of society'.[51] Stephen Parker posits ideological reasons for the attack on 'the plurality of marriage forms' which existed in eighteenth-century England, contrasting them with the new rationalism typical of economics, politics and government. 'For that rationalism to take hold, the rulers' world view had to be embraced throughout the social order ... The rulers' *culture* must be accepted by a significant proportion of the population, as well as their political and economic institutions.'[52] The Act, according to a near contemporary source, was 'one of a series of measures intended to "bring about a general reformation of manners among the lower sort of people"'.[53] Informal marriages could no longer be tolerated and the Act, so it was hoped, would at last get rid of them.

---

[49] The literature supporting this judgment is extensive. See, e.g., Macfarlane, *Marriage and Love*, especially ch.13, 'Courtship and Wedding'; John Gillis, *For Better, For Worse: British Marriages, 1600 to the Present* (New York and Oxford: Oxford University Press, 1985).

[50] R. Porter, *English Society in the Eighteenth Century* (Harmondsworth: Penguin, 1982), p.66 (cited in Stephen Parker, *Informal Marriage, Cohabitation and the Law* (New York: St. Martin's Press, 1990), p.33).

[51] Gillis, *For Better, For Worse*, p.135.

[52] Parker, *Informal Marriage*, pp.27, 40 (author's emphasis).

[53] London *Packet*, No.807 (December 21–3, 1774), cited in Christopher Lasch, 'The Suppression Of Clandestine Marriage In England: The Marriage Act Of 1753', *Salmagundi* (1974), 105.

The Act decreed that '[a]ll marriages in any place other than in a church or public chapel, and without banns or licence, were to be "null and Void to all Intents and Purposes whatsoever"'.[54] Very detailed rules were specified for the publishing of banns or the granting of licences. Anyone performing a marriage ceremony outside of the provisions of the Act was to be transported to America and to remain there for fourteen years. More detailed rules specified the precise keeping of registers. The officiant, marrying parties and at least two witnesses were required to sign. 'Any person intentionally taking part in any irregularities concerning the register, the publication of banns or the issue of a licence "shall be guilty of a Felony, and shall suffer Death as a Felon, without Benefit of Clergy".'

The Act forbade clandestine marriages (its principal purpose) and robbed betrothals of any legal force (breach of promise suits, however, filed by jilted lovers continued to reach the courts). The opportunity simply to live together informally, or to marry informally in accordance with local custom, was not lost, even though such informal unions had no legal recognition. As Gillis notes, 'The Hardwicke Marriage Act of 1753 terminated the old rights of betrothal and clandestine marriage, but their disappearance did not deter a large part of the population from making marriages in their own way, regardless of the laws of church and state.' Poorer people could not afford the wedding fees or the cost of the ostentatious weddings increasingly set before them as a norm. Working-class people, whose major assets lay in their children, sometimes avoided formal marriage or waited until the bride-to-be was well pregnant, thereby 'proving' the wisdom of the match.[55] Several authors speak of enormous regional variation in conformity to the Act, with Wales being particularly unmoved by it. In Scotland (where the Act did not apply) the tradition of 'common law' or 'presumptive' marriage persists to this day. British legislation after the end of the First World War recognized that many deceased soldiers' widows were to be denied the widows' pension on the ground that their marriages were

---

54 Parker, *Informal Marriage*, p.29. I have relied on Parker's account for the main provisions of the Act (see pp.29–30).
55 Gillis, *For Better, For Worse*, p.127.

unrecognized in law. Legislation was extended to cover 'unmarried wives'.[56]

The practice of engagement has, of course, continued up to the present time. It is a semi-private matter which has no legal standing. No engaged couples think themselves beginning marriage: nor do their churches (if they have any), nor does society. Since divorce is readily available 'if things don't work out' the liminal period between singleness and marriage (below, chapter 8, third section) is less important, since marriage is no longer indissoluble. The theological meaning of marriage now assumes, in contradistinction to most of Christian history, that marriages begin with weddings. The liturgical reduction of events within a process to a single event which begins a process, has become also a theological reduction of the gradual entry into marriage to a single event notable principally for the exchange of consent (to make it legal) and the priestly blessing (to make it Christian and controlled by the Church).

Anglican theology is generally silent about betrothal. The report *Marriage and the Church's Task* in 1978 defined 'marriage' as 'both the wedding ceremony' and the '"state of holy matrimony"', which was begun on the wedding day.[57] It never occurred to the report writers, attempting self-conscious precision in their working definition of marriage, that it might have been possible for marriages to begin before their solemnization. A further report to the General Synod in 1988, *An Honourable Estate*, made a serious and honest attempt to draw on the historical and theological background to the church's marital practice,[58] but its terms of reference did not permit it to make the kind of historically grounded proposal for recognizing the diverse beginnings of marriage suggested in this book. Bishop

[56] Parker, *Informal Marriage*, p.28. But the legislation was further amended in 1927 in order to remove unmarried wives from the list (Parker, p.40).

[57] *Marriage and the Church's Task: The Report of the General Synod Marriage Commission* (The Lichfield Report, London: CIO Publishing, 1978), p.16 (section 39).

[58] Report of a Working Party established by the Standing Committee of the General Synod of the Church of England (GS801), *An Honourable Estate: The doctrine of Marriage according to English law and the obligation of the Church to marry all parishioners who are not divorced* (London: Church House Publishing, 1988), esp. ch.2. The authors recognize that in the sixteenth century, 'the espousal or betrothal followed by consummation was as much a marriage in the eyes of the [church] courts as any subsequent ceremony' (p.20, para.60), and they endorse Lawrence Stone's judgment that 'before the mid-eighteenth century ... marriage could be entered by a "bewildering variety of ways"' (p.21, para.60).

John Spong mounted a solitary argument for introducing a liturgical form of betrothal ceremonies in 1988, proclaiming that it was 'an
idea whose time has come'.[59] However, the argument was carelessly
formulated and too easily detachable from marriage.[60] We have
already noted the fate of another report, *Something to Celebrate*
(above, p.101), and the thoughtful appendix to the Bishops' teaching document, *Marriage*. These prepare for 'the betrothal solution',
but centuries of neglect, aided and abetted by the Hardwicke
Marriage Act, have made that solution very difficult to achieve.

In Scotland, the Kirk banned formal betrothal ceremonies in
1575. Until as late as 1940 'regular' and 'irregular' marriages were
alike recognized. Regular marriages were performed by clergy
(though not necessarily in church); irregular marriages were performed by couples themselves. These marriages were disapproved
of, and the Reformers considered them sinful; but no-one considered them unlawful. T.C. Smout explains that an irregular marriage
'has always been valid' in Scottish law, because 'the Scots held to
the blindingly simple doctrine' that if any couple capable of legal
marriage 'both freely expressed this wish and freely accepted each
other in marriage, they were married. Consent made a marriage –
not the clergy, nor the civil official – but the consent of two people
wishing to marry.'[61] We have seen that this 'blindingly simple doctrine' was once held by the whole of the Western Church. Smout
speaks for the wider church when he accounts for irregular marriages by observing, 'In the Middle Ages, as later (in fact as late
as 1 July 1940) intercourse subsequent on a proven handfasting,
alias promise of marriage *per verba de futuro*, amounted to proof of
marriage in law.'[62]

Scottish law was unaffected either by the Council of Trent or
the Hardwicke Marriage Act. In fact we find in this Protestant Reformed country retention of an important element of undisturbed

[59] John Shelby Spong, *Living in Sin? A Bishop Rethinks Human Sexuality* (San Francisco: Harper
and Row, 1988). Chapter 12 is entitled 'Betrothal: An Idea Whose Time Has Come'.

[60] For a thorough critical analysis see my *Marriage after Modernity: Christian Marriage in
Postmodern Times* (Sheffield and New York: Sheffield Academic Press and New York
University Press, 1999), pp.124–7.

[61] T.C. Smout, 'Scottish Marriage, Regular and Irregular, 1500–1940', in R.B. Outhwaite
(ed.), *Marriage and Society: Studies in the Social History of Marriage* (London: Europa, 1981),
p.206.

[62] Ibid., p.211.

and unrevised medieval doctrine – *concensus facit matrimonium*. The Reformers took power in Scotland in 1560. They rejected the Tridentine solution to the problem of clandestine marriage, not least on the ground that it detracted from the centrality of the consent of the parties to the making of marriage. Why then did they move against betrothal? Smout explains that betrothed couples who had gone through a handfasting ceremony and made promises *de futuro* increasingly failed to attend a second ceremony of solemnization. In this regard they again followed common medieval practice – betrothal followed by sexual intercourse equals marriage, but, in the sixteenth century, 'sex after betrothal was considered as fornication, even though it was clearly very commonly practised'.[63] While Luther's sympathies lay with collapsing the two ceremonies into the betrothal ceremony (thereby changing its meaning), the Scottish solution was to collapse them into the solemnization. Formal betrothal ceremonies ceased to have legal force, but informally they continued much as before. An attempt was made to reduce the number of 'premarital' pregnancies by requiring caution money from couples who had requested the reading of the banns. The money would be refunded if no 'untimely pregnancy' occurred. There can be little doubt that the toleration of 'irregular marriages' in Scotland until the mid-twentieth century is a preservation of informed medieval practice.

`TRIDENTINISM´ AND `ENGAGEMENT DRIFT´

Much of Protestantism has never known betrothal. Its historical roots lie in the last quarter of the history of Christianity, the quarter which has seen betrothal fall out of use. Despite the biblical evidence for the practice, there has been little attempt to emulate it, and arguments about marriage are more likely to have been about purging the ceremony of traces of popery, defending the value of marriage after its desacramentalization at the Reformation, ensuring the possibility of divorce, or, in Britain, objecting to the imposition of the rite of an Established Church. The demise of betrothal was not queried.

[63] Ibid., p.212.

Since the demise of betrothal coincides with the missionary expansion of Christendom in modernity, European Christians exported a European solution to the problem about marriage-entry to territories where there was no such problem. The missionaries themselves problematized marriage-entry by seeking to impose tidy European practices on populations who did not need (or understand) them. A telling example is the Hardwicke Marriage Act. Since there was no problem of clandestine marriage in Africa, and the Hardwicke Act was designed for the better prevention of clandestine marriage, Hardwicke-style laws and the ecclesiastical ceremonies that go with them might have been thought to have little application in Africa, yet this is precisely what Anglican missionaries attempted. 'When Anglican missionaries came to Africa in the mid-nineteenth century, they had a century of what was in effect "Tridentinism" behind them and nearly automatically applied the same rule there: for a Christian recognized marriage must be in church.'[64]

A report by Adrian Hastings (commissioned by Anglican archbishops meeting in Lusaka in 1970) showed that pre-Reformation marriage practice would have suited the missionaries, and the needs of their new converts, better than the Reformed marriage system they brought with them. The main problem, Hastings observed, was 'the ecclesiastical absolutization of marriage norms which had developed in the course of the centuries in the Western Church and were now being applied in such a very different social and cultural context'.[65] By the twentieth century many African Christians were bypassing ecclesiastical marriage and opting for traditional ceremonies instead. The problem of the validity of such marriages became acute. The schema of *matrimonium initiatum, ratum* and *consummatum* would have coped well with African traditional marriage which would have found room for Christian rites at appropriate places within it. But the Tridentine and Hardwicke-style insistence on church weddings, conducted by priests, and employing specific verbal forms, became a massive pastoral liability. English *civil* marriage after 1836 was accepted by the Church of England as valid marriage, but what of African

---

[64] Adrian Hastings, *Christian Marriage in Africa* (London: SPCK, 1973), p.68.
[65] Ibid., p.5.

traditional marriage? The 1920 Lambeth Conference of Anglican bishops was forced to conclude, 'The presence or absence of the Church's blessing does not affect the validity of marriage', but as Hastings notes, 'the implication of such statements was difficult to accept. They largely admitted that a customary marriage was valid for pagans and should be repeated at baptism, but to go further and admit the basic adequacy of a customary marriage for existing Christians (in the way that the Church of England admits civil marriages) seemed too much.'[66]

The issue of polygamy should not cloud Hastings' positive assessment of African traditional marriage which in his judgment 'was at the heart of social life', and 'asserted a continual range of moral responsibilities towards both your next of kin and many other people. It promoted joy as well as sound order, emotional release as well as security, the education of the young, the maintenance of the old.' There is, he insists, 'no reason to think that African traditional marriage was less effective as a forum and a stimulant for the exercise of human virtue than the traditional marriage system of any other continent'.[67] The missionaries of the modern period, probably of all denominations, exported assumptions about the entry of marriage which had been newly ecclesiasticized and were firmly Eurocentric. Cephas Lerewonu complains that Catholic marriage was 'forced' on the Kassena people of Ghana in 1908. The *ka'chari*, or betrothal, was 'the vital phase that represents the culmination of a relationship through a committed affirmation of two parties to continue in what is understood to be a marital union'.[68] But Tridentine marital theology considered betrothal as 'an unnecessary addition and thus, non-determinative of a valid marriage'. Inflexible European theology weakened a custom which was not merely socially valuable but actually replicated, at least in part, earlier European practice.

Forgetfulness of pre-Tridentine and pre-Protestant custom may have prevented fruitful parallels being drawn between traditional marriage and Christian marriage (including the practices of betrothal,[69] living together and the exchange of consent) which

---

[66] Ibid., p.19. [67] Ibid., pp.36–7.
[68] Lerewonu, 'The Betrothal Commitment', pp.1–2.
[69] For example, Maasai traditional marriage involves betrothal. See Jackson Ole Sapit, 'Maasai Traditional Marriage', in J. Bryson Arthur, *A Theology of Sexuality and Marriage*

might have avoided much theological confusion and pastoral pain. The solutions of Trent and Hardwicke did not serve the expanding churches well, but the memory of alternative marital practice was already largely lost. And these solutions do not serve the churches well any more even in their territories of origin.

Twentieth-century writing about engagement shows a remarkable puzzlement about its purpose. Collective memory loss reached such a pitch in the twentieth century that new accounts had to be given of engagement, since it had become a voluntary form of premarried behaviour whose persistence, by now wholly separated from religious sanction, liturgical celebration and theological meaning, required explanation in social-scientific terms. I call this 'engagement drift'. Four examples must suffice. In 1933 Ernest Groves thought he had written the first book, ever, on marriage.[70] Engagement is said to be a development of 'modern culture'. It is 'a relationship preliminary and preparatory to marriage'. But what precisely was the social purpose of this development? The answer lies in an increase in acquaintance. Engagement, 'by removing uncertainty in the relationship, provides favorable conditions for each person to become well acquainted with the other before making a commitment which is presumed to be a life union'.[71] Betrothal is said to be 'a contract to marry' and the new relationship of engagement is said to be in conflict with it because engagement is 'a period of final adjustment before two interested persons enter upon the status of marriage'.[72] There is no hint that betrothal was once understood as the beginning of marriage. The hope that the engaged can use engagement to remove uncertainties and make final adjustments is unconvincing, not least because commitment involves risk, and because there is no independent measure for assessing whether reservations remain or adjustments are in fact final.

(Nairobi: Uzima Press, 1998), p.43. But this involves families betrothing girls 'as early as infancy'. While a strong case exists for the moral unacceptability of this practice, how different is it from the practice assumed by Tertullian (above, p.148) and described by Swinburne (above, p.178)?

[70] 'This is a text on marriage: as far as I am able to discover, the first ever written.' See Ernest R. Groves, *Marriage* (New York: Henry Holt & Co., 1933), p.vii.

[71] For a similar explanation, that engagement offers 'extensive opportunity for companionship', see Ernest W. Burgess and Paul Wallin, *Engagement and Marriage* (Chicago: Lippincott, 1953), p.28.

[72] Groves, *Marriage*, p.145.

People who find Groves' rationalization of engagement convincing will need to explain why it performs these functions better than betrothal did.

Engagement, alternatively, is an opportunity to learn whether one is 'in love with love' or in love with one's partner. In 1942 Leslie D. Weatherhead warned against confusing 'real love with physical attraction'; engagement is the period to discover 'all the facts about each other'. Indeed, 'society ordains an engagement, during which it may be ascertained whether real love is the link between lives'.[73] The distinction between kinds of love is clearly important, but the suggestion that society has ordained the period of engagement in order to provide an opportunity to test the psychology of one's desires does not ring true. Let us assume that marriage is a relationship of committed love, and is more likely to thrive when couples have shed illusions about one another. It simply does not follow that 'society has ordained' engagement, or that engagement has this purpose. Presumably any developmental or staged approach to marriage (which would not of course culminate in the ceremony but continue on), could function in this way. Engagement signifies a loss of social purpose, and its persistence requires those who write about it to assign functional meanings to it.

In 1951 the distinguished historian of Christian sexual teaching, Derrick Sherwin Bailey, cast doubt on the value of engagement altogether, saying it 'amounts simply to a conventional way of announcing a settled intention to marry at the earliest opportunity'.[74] He admitted its former value (with Groves) as a 'get to know one another' period, and conceded that 'where the compatibility of the couple is not quite certain', it still 'affords an opportunity for them to test their relation in permitted ways, and allows an honourable way out, approved by society, should it become clear that they were mistaken'. But Bailey thought the social emphasis on the difference between engagement and marriage interrupted the continuum of deepening love in a couple's marriage, and he committed himself to a 'stages' approach to

---

[73] Leslie D. Weatherhead, *The Mastery of Sex Through Psychology and Religion* (New York: Macmillan, 1942), p.52.

[74] Derrick Sherwin Bailey, *The Mystery of Love and Marriage: A Study in the Theology of Sexual Relation* (New York: Harper & Brothers, 1952), p.38.

marriage. 'The distinction drawn between the premarital and marital stages of love tends to encourage irresponsibility and even levity where the former is concerned.'[75] Bailey, in short, recognized the justifications for engagement (as then practised) were in part specious. He maintained the sound Christian conviction that engagement and marriage were 'different modes' of a 'continuous' relationship, but failed to see how the older practice of betrothal would better express his conviction about marital continuity, and give him a reason for his misgivings about engagement.

A Lutheran report in 1959 concluded, 'Few if any of the larger Protestant bodies have any formal teaching on engagement.' 'American Protestant writers agree that engagement is not marriage but a step toward marriage ... In general, American Protestant bodies do not consider engagement a problem.'[76] But this not considering it a problem is evidence of quiescent amnesia, the silent handing over to secular thought of the process of becoming married, even for committed Protestant Christians. A typical end-of-century Protestant book on marriage continues the engagement drift. Doubtless there are dozens in this familiar milieu. 'For contemporary United States couples', wrote Andrew Eickhoff in 1996, 'engagements have come to be formal periods of testing during which the suitability of both persons for marriage and for each other is explored.' Indeed, '[a]n engagement should be long enough for the persons involved to become sure of each other'.[77] This appears to be another fairly blatant attempt to fill engagement with social meaning, predicated on the evacuation of religious meaning from the continuing practice. But baffling problems again arise. How is surety to be measured? If couples can become sure of each other, divorce statistics would seem to show that surety can be ephemeral. If engagement really is a formal period of testing, then it is surely inconceivable that sexual intercourse should be any longer excluded from it, since sexual relations at the very least provide one dimension for suitability and surety. Is that what a distant Protestantism of the future will advocate? In the meantime Protestantism in this form has allowed itself to endorse

[75] Ibid., pp.37, 39.   [76] Hansen et al., *Engagement and Marriage*, pp.131, 135.
[77] Andrew R. Eickhoff, *A Christian View of Sex and Marriage* (New York and London: The Free Press and Collier-Macmillan, 1996), pp.86–7.

extra-theological assumptions and to bring itself perilously close to the adoption of 'trial-marriage'.

It comes as no surprise, then, to discover that contemporary theologies of marriage are likely to routinize early modern Eurocentric ecclesiastical practice, assuming its normativity for the last 2,000 years. Where the past has been interrogated, there has been little attempt to investigate betrothal. Different questions have been put, generally about sacramentality, validity, or indissolubility. Entry into marriage must remain a small part of the Church's overall teaching on marriage, but when it is neglected or overlooked, it can have a distorting and reducing effect on the understanding of the whole. The disappearance of betrothal, coupled with engagement drift, leaves the churches weak in relation to marriage preparation and liturgical provision, and impedes them in their efforts to commend marriage as a sacrament which the partners administer to and for each other in a lifelong process which becomes irrevocable at the solemnization but begins well before.

Our long historical analysis of betrothal and its disappearance is now at an end. I have sought to maintain a balance between (in Monti's terms, above, p.56) the obligation of fidelity to tradition, and the obligation to contemporaneity. Tradition has, at the very least, not been neglected in this study. In the final part of the book I move to the second obligation, well served and equipped by the study of tradition. What it says about the entry into marriage, but also what it now fails to say, will enrich the theological treatment of contemporary pre-ceremonial, marital practice.

PART 3

Extending the marital norm

CHAPTER 7

Betrothal, consent and consummation

The shape of this final part of the book will be determined by the two key concepts outlined in part 1, the 'marital norm' (above, p.53) and the 'betrothal solution' (above, p.61). It is time to clinch the arguments set out earlier (above, p.71) which relied on substantiating the premiss that betrothal can be reclaimed. I take part 2 as having demonstrated the truth of several claims, e.g., that betrothal has played a major part in the history of Christian marriage; that its demise was due to historical (and not theological) circumstances; that the churches' proclamation and liturgical celebration of marriage has been weakened by a conspicuous *lack*, a forgetfulness of their marital heritage. Of course sceptics may wearily concede some or all of the historical arguments mounted in part 2, yet object that they do not indicate that betrothal can be 'reclaimed': all they show is that it was once much more pronounced than it now is, and it is neither necessary, desirable, or even possible to *reinstate* it. Part 3 addresses such sceptics, but its primary aim is to indicate the advantages of reinstatement, pastorally, theologically and liturgically.

I capitalize on parts 1 and 2 by building on them in part 3. Chapter 7 draws on a recent treatment of marriage as a path to holiness, and argues (first section) that this treatment is better articulated and commended if betrothal is incorporated into it. The pivotal role of consent in the making of marriage is broadened to include as its object the medieval idea of *consortium omnis vitae* or sharing of the whole of life (second section). Next a more adequate account of the consummation of marriage (the implausible first intercourse that ratifies it) is offered, and grounded in the *maritalis affectio* of the couple (third section). It will be shown that the pre-modern marital heritage can better describe and illuminate these

shared, personal realities than can modern Tridentine theologies
(Catholic and Protestant). Finally the Trinitarian and Christological accounts of marriage are shown to have an experiential or
anabatic basis, rooted socially in the couple's life project, as well as
katabatically[1] in the life of God. The marital norm is thus maintained and extended by means of the betrothal solution in the case
of prenuptial cohabitation.

BETROTHAL AND THE WAY OF HOLINESS

There has been an interesting discussion in recent years among
English evangelical Christians regarding appropriate theological
responses to people who request marriage while cohabiting. A
brief reference to this discussion will prepare for a more theologically grounded discussion of marriage and its beginnings. Greg
Forster bravely raised the question (in 1988) whether 'in some circumstances when a couple stand at the chancel steps, are they
in fact merely ratifying legally and hallowing spiritually a marriage which has morally already existed since they set up home
together and witnessed the same before their friends and families
(and would exist even if they did not walk down the aisle)?'[2] His cautious but affirmative answer was supported by other evangelicals.
Gary Jenkins compared marriage to Christian initiation and concluded that marriage was more like confirmation than baptism.[3]
Stephen Williams accepts there is 'a fairly strong case for saying
that cohabitation today is a form of customary betrothal', and, with
regard to biblical teaching about the matter, 'no specific guidance
is found for the couple that anticipate their marriage by sleep-
ing together'.[4] More recently Keith Warrington has concluded,

[1] For this distinction see above, ch.4, 4th section.
[2] Greg Forster, *Marriage Before Marriage? The Moral Validity of 'Common Law' Marriage* (Grove
Ethical Studies 69, Bramcote, Notts.: Grove Books, 1988), p.4. See also p.23, and his
subsequent *Cohabitation and Marriage: A Pastoral Response* (London: Marshall Pickering,
1994). Forster tells me that an article on cohabitation by John Rees (*Church Times*, 20 August
1982) had proved to be a catalyst for evangelical thinking.
[3] Gary Jenkins, *Cohabitation: a Biblical Perspective* (Grove Ethical Studies 84, Bramcote, Notts.:
Grove Books, 1992), p.3. In 1991 The *Church of England Newspaper* ran a series of articles
on living together, indicating the disagreement among evangelicals about the matter. See
Edward Pratt, et al., *Living Together: a Challenge for the Church* (London: CENBooks, 1991).
[4] Stephen S. Williams, 'I Will: the Debate about Cohabitation', *Anvil* 10.3 (1993), 211, 222.

'Cohabitation of non-Christians need not be deemed unacceptable *per se* as a form of partnership/"marriage".'[5] But responses to this question are generally still negative among evangelicals, giving rise to a further question: how was it possible for this positive approach to cohabitation to have been sustained?

The answer is twofold: these authors are aware that the Bible does not provide guidance about the time or the form of the solemnization, or recognition, of marriage; and they all appeal to 'biblical principles' to support their position. While the arguments in this book (despite possible initial disbelief) are highly congruent with these evangelicals, I think their pioneering moves in an area controversial for them lack a grounding in 'the betrothal solution' (which Williams nonetheless hints at). The uncovering of the extent of the emphasis on betrothal in the history of Christian marriage would assist these writers, but much more important, their examination of scripture does not lead them even to consider the place of betrothal in the Bible. The connection between ancient betrothal and modern living together is not generally made. Warrington's six 'biblical marital principles', for instance, make no mention of betrothal, because the prior connection between betrothal and marriage has not been secured from the start. But this lack of connection excludes the very help that an appeal to the scriptures might be able to provide. Another evangelical writer, Philippa Taylor, makes much play of her appeal to the Bible in establishing what marriage is, and then comparing it unfavourably with cohabitation.[6] Yet her 'biblical understanding of marriage'[7] both bypasses the biblical practice of betrothal, and begs the question how biblical marriage is entered into; while the comparison between cohabitation and marriage fails to allow the possibility of prenuptial cohabitation, or that cohabitation may be a beginning of marriage. The assumption that like is being compared with like is simply misleading.

I conclude that the 'betrothal solution' would be a helpful contribution to evangelical discussion of beginning marriage, in several ways. But evangelicals are no worse than other groups in the

---

[5] Keith Warrington, 'Cohabitation and the Church', *Churchman* 111.2 (1997), 139.

[6] Philippa Taylor, *For Better or For Worse: Marriage and Cohabitation Compared* (London: CARE (Christian Action Research and Education), 1998), p.3.

[7] Ibid., pp.11–18.

churches: indeed they are to be commended for recognizing a
pastoral problem and attempting to deal with it. Eugene Rogers
offers a 'provisional definition' of Christian marriage in his bri-
lliant and controversial work, *Sexuality and the Christian Body*. It is,
he says, 'an ascetic practice of and for the community by which
God takes sexuality up into God's own triune life, graciously transforming it so as to allow the couple partially to model the love between Christ and the Church'.[8] The definition deliberately plants
the Christian understanding of marriage within an experiential
and linguistic framework that includes the practice of holiness and
the maintenance of spiritual discipline within the Christian community. This community holds certain theologically derived beliefs
about persons (sexuality) and core theological doctrines about God
(Trinity, divine love, sacramentality and much else). Rogers' marital theology borrows from the best scholarship that the Roman
Catholic, Orthodox and Anglican traditions can presently provide.
The treatment of it in this chapter must be confined to the further
contribution that the 'betrothal solution' might be able to make to
this agreeable definition of the marital norm.

Rogers accuses heterosexual Christians of having been 'such
poor stewards of their almost unbelievably rich theology of marriage that they leave almost all of it to recover'.[9] This is undoubtedly
true. I merely add to his charge the detail that betrothal is also part
of this 'unbelievably rich heritage' (which even Rogers does not
seek to recover). Let us concentrate on the claim that marriage is
'an ascetic practice of and for the community'. Interestingly the
claim derives neither from traditional treatments of the 'goods' of
marriage, nor from liturgical summaries of its purpose. It comes
from insights into the practice of *celibacy*, together with the later
elevation of marriage to the level of a sacrament, thereby admitting
both vowed institutions to equal status as parallel ways of holiness.
So prior to any discussion about what marriage is or how marriage

---

[8] Eugene F. Rogers, Jr., *Sexuality and the Christian Body* (Oxford and Malden, Mass.: Blackwell,
1999), pp.72–3. Paul Evdokimov is an acknowledged influence. See his *The Sacrament of
Love: the Nuptial Mystery in the Light of the Orthodox Tradition* (Crestwood, N.Y.: St Vladimir's
Seminary Press, 1985). Clearly this cannot be a sufficient description. I should want to
include in any account of marriage reference to 'communal partnership' and 'mutually
administered sacrament'. See my *Marriage after Modernity: Christian Marriage in Postmodern
Times* (Sheffield and New York: Sheffield Academic Press and New York University Press,
1999), ch.7.
[9] Rogers, *Sexuality and the Christian Body*, p.69.

is entered is the commitment shared by all Christians everywhere to Jesus Christ. This commitment may be variously expressed, e.g., as a realization of Christian identity, conferred at baptism, within the community of the church; or, more simply, as the pursuit of holiness or sanctification. Where celibacy is received as a genuine 'gift' of God and practised, the renunciation of intimate union with a partner enables the celibate person to grow in his or her love for God and for God's people, whether in the monastic community or in the wider world. Renunciation, then, leads to freedom and empowerment.

But marriage also requires renunciation. Marriage, like celibacy, is an *ascesis*, 'a kind of ascetic practice, a communal structure that frees the body to become as a means of sanctification'.[10] There is renunciation of sexual experience with anyone else that frees one for devotion to one's beloved. Marriage as the communal practice of the church offers entrants into it a way of holiness that frees them for love for each other, and frees both of them together to share jointly in their practice of the love of God and neighbour. In this sense marriage is a 'discipline' which requires training and, of course, outcomes. Discipline is integral to the practice of marriage, as with celibacy, and it enables marriage to be a means of holiness for each partner. Eucharistic, nuptial and eschatological imagery converge in the picture of the banquet, whether the eucharistic meal, the nuptial banquet or the great feast at the end of time which celebrates the final achievement of God's reign. All such feasts are occasions of delight and thanksgiving: indeed

... in the Eastern view all the sacraments, from baptism, which makes believers, to ordination, which makes priests, to the eucharist, which confers redemption and anticipates the eschatological supper of the lamb, participate in the never-ending giving and receiving of gifts and thanks that constitute the trinitarian way in which God is love. Marriage is not different from but of a piece with this sacramental life.[11]

Our question is whether betrothal is able to enrich this striking *apologia* for marriage,[12] or, in the language of this study, whether the marital norm may be extended retrospectively to prenuptial

---

[10] Ibid., p.71. [11] Ibid., pp.76–7.

[12] Comment on Rogers' overall project to establish the legitimacy of homosexual marriages is postponed to chapter 9. I have qualms about the limited place children receive in this fascinating work.

couples by way of the betrothal solution. The answer is that it can, and in at least six different ways. First, we might recall the *processive* or *processual* nature of marriage marked by spousals and by nuptials. The relevant contrast here lies between event and process. Bankers, lawyers and tax officers may need to know exactly when a couple is legally married. But the elevation of an event within a process to become the all-determining factor within the process is not required by theology or faith. Catholic sacramental theory has connived with this static, essentially momentary, conception of the constitution of marriage: the exchange of consent immediately followed by priestly blessing became the defining moment at which sacramental grace was conferred and received. But marriage does not begin with the nuptial ceremony. The nuptial ceremony is the point within the process of marriage when the promises made become irrevocable (*matrimonium ratum*), when a new phase in the still-growing relationship is liturgically and performatively initiated. Inattention to the prenuptial phase of the marriage is perhaps the greatest mistake of pastoral theology in the modern period. A fitting analogy might be that of a professional person, say, a teacher or a doctor, certified and approved as a competent practitioner without the opportunity or apparent need for trainee or internship status.

Second, the need for thorough preparation and training for this unique mode of discipleship becomes glaringly obvious, and the period between the spousals and the nuptials in a couple's life, whether or not the spousals are liturgically observed, provides the appropriate place for it. A neutral description of marriage, such as the union of a man and a woman for life, lacks any theological weight. However, once the specifically Christian vision of marriage is depicted as a unique way of holiness, and its substance depicted as a sharing in the Trinitarian life, or an anticipation of the reign of God, or an analogue of Christ's love for the Church, then both the responsibility and the attractiveness of this institution come into view. There could hardly be weightier themes to which marriage becomes attached in the Christian life. It is all the more important, then, that prior to making unconditional and irrevocable promises to each other before God, the state, the church, the local community and one's kin, to remain in this 'discipline of denial' for the rest of one's life or one's partner's life, a period of *provisional* commitment should first be encouraged. We have seen that betrothal commitments straddled a fine line between intention and obligation. Learning *whether* to marry may take a profound effort of self-knowledge; discovering *who* to marry may take a decade or more of cautious and painful experiment; and for people of faith, learning the full potential of the marital sacrament for the pursuit of holiness, and, learning this with one's prospective partner, deserves the equivalent of a catechumenate or school for marriage (below, p.237) where personal, relational and spiritual discovery can be safely made, within a supporting community which itself seeks to grow into the fullness of life which it knows in Jesus Christ.

Third, the prenuptial phase of a marriage emphasizes the role of building a foundation for the forthcoming irrevocable consent, and this foundation is more an *immanent* matter, internal to the couple's life (including their social life), than external, relying on transcendent sources. Indeed, alongside the contrast between event and process lies the contrast between transcendence and immanence. The hypothesis, widely accepted among Christians, that the initiation of marriage is a single event (the exchange of consent in the present tense before witnesses), tacitly sanctions a vertical, external and mechanical version of grace – sacramental automatism (below, p.228) – which descends on the couple once the formulae of consent and blessing have been heard. A processive understanding of marriage allows for the possibility that grace is made available to the couple internal to their relationship as they work at it, and (in Rogers' account at least), prepare themselves for their joint calling of *ascesis*. As the late Theodore Mackin explained, every sacrament requires a matrix, i.e., 'a situation or surrounding substance within which something else originates, develops or is contained'.[13]

The matrix of a sacrament is the human conduct, conduct perhaps formed into a ritual, that is taken and made into the sacrament, or into which the sacrament is grafted and whence it draws its substance and its meaning ... Thus not water alone is the matrix of baptism, nor is it alone the bathing with water prescinding from the cultural meaning of bathing. For

---

[13] Thatcher, *Marriage after Modernity*, p.236.

baptism the matrix is water the source of life, the environment of new life, used in cleansing away the old and beginning the new.[14]

The conduct that nurtures the grace of the marital sacrament is not the conduct of the ceremony or any hallowed form of words within it. It is the loving conduct of the couple, their current achievement in their surrender to one another, that is the matrix for grace. The achievement is able to prompt the couple to undertake the irrevocable stage in their process of marrying – solemnization. Within this attractive schema for the sacrament of marriage, betrothal is the experimental stage, perhaps lengthy, in the marital laboratory, leading, if successful, to the final, nuptial step.

Fourth, the biblical understanding of marriage assumes the practice of betrothal (above, pp.119–30). There is no obligation on the contemporary churches to imitate biblical practice (as far as it is capable of reconstruction). However, many attempts have been made to construct church order and eucharistic practice on the basis of alleged ancient precedent, so one is entitled to wonder why no similar arguments are offered in favour of ancient marriage practice. The argument here is that there is a biblical theology of marriage, and much of it is discounted in today's Western churches. In particular we noted Schillebeeckx' observation that the meanings of marriage in the New Testament are principally to be found in the *expectation* of consummation rather than in the consummation itself. This anticipation of consummation, together with the nuptial feast as the anticipation of the final consummation of all things 'at the wedding day of the Lamb', prompts two further observations.

Fifth, the experience of preparing for marriage in a milieu where betrothal is practised is bound to be different from preparing for marriage when only the nuptials are observed. The situation of being in-between two states, no longer single but not yet finally and irreversibly married, itself conveys meanings that engagement is unable to convey. The experience of waiting, of love begun, of anticipation, of further joy yet to be shared; these are able to become the materials for the fashioning of deeper faith. This is because

[14] Theodore Mackin, SJ, *The Marital Sacrament* (Mahwah, N.J.: Paulist Press, 1989), p.11. And see Thatcher, *Marriage after Modernity*, pp.236–9.

a betrothed person is able to make connections between events within his or her life-cycle and the vast drama of salvation that God in Christ has initiated and not yet completed. The experience of being loved by another, and beginning to give oneself over to that other, can be valued not simply for the profound personal meanings found within it, but because it stands for God's own self-gift and the promise of future salvation where divine love finally dissolves all resistance to itself. Betrothal is able to encapsulate and articulate these theological meanings, whereas engagement is not. That is because betrothal incorporates into marriage the prenuptial experience of the couple and already values it as something begun. It is able to give structure and recognition to a temporary state of life and invest it with a signification that links it experientially to the cosmic drama of salvation. Engagement does none of these things. It is not marked by a formula or religious ritual; it is not marriage and so it cannot be the beginning of marriage either. Indeed 'engagement' provides few linguistic clues that suggest the promise of an initiated marriage. Its meanings include commencing a battle, starting a job, arranging a meeting, putting an engine into gear, and finding that the space one wants to occupy (e.g., a toilet) is already claimed by someone else. Even in its explicit premarital sense, it conveys (to intending suitors) that the possible object of one's affections is unavailable, i.e., is engaged by someone else. The linguistic suggestiveness of engagement is very impoverished, like the pale institution it stands for.

Sixth, the whole experience of the Christian life lends itself to being understood as a betrothal. If this large claim is true it follows that the lack of betrothal as a symbol within the churches impedes Christian communication and self-understanding. The Church is the bride of Christ (Eph. 5:25) but she is in the process of being made ready to meet her bridegroom for a consummation which belongs to the future as much as it belongs to the present. Betrothal is a key to the Church's self-identity. 'She' understands herself to have entered a wholly provisional state. She is the recipient of the bridegroom's promise: indeed his promise or pledge to her is his sacrificial death (Eph. 5:25). She too, through the community of the entire people of God, has declared her love for her bridegroom. The experience of her bridegroom now guarantees the heavenly consummation, the final union of Christ with the Church, the 'great mystery' (Eph. 5:32). There can be no hope if what is hoped for has already arrived, and no hope without grounds which distinguish hope from mere wishing or ungrounded optimism. The grounds for hope in the Ephesian marriage theology lie in Christ's life and death, understood as the self-gift of God in a pledge of redemptive love which is efficacious but is not yet complete (i.e., fully consummated). The Church thus finds herself in an 'in-between' state. There is no better symbol for this in-between state than the one the Bible uses – betrothal. Yet the Church has allowed this symbol to wither and die.

CONSENT AND THE *CONSORTIUM TOTIUS VITAE*

Most writers on Christian marriage, including Rogers, say nothing about how it is entered. The reason may not solely be the demise of betrothal. Another reason may be the overwhelming fondness of theologians for abstract concepts, preferring them to concrete realities. So it is easier to consider marriage in the abstract, beginning with its essence or definition, and requiring individual marriages to fit into it. Alongside abstract definitions of marriage are equally abstract assumptions about what makes people validly married (consent) and after valid marriage, what ratifies it (consummation). There is, however, a recognizable strand of Catholic theology which understands the essence of marriage, concretely and 'from below', as a *consortium totius* (or *omnis*) *vitae*, and this strand is able to contribute inestimably to the re-commending of marriage at the present time. Indeed the phrase was incorporated into canon law in 1983.[15] The entry into marriage understood this way also requires a re-think of the meaning of *consent* as the making of marriage, and first sexual intercourse as its ratification. The aim of this section is not to demolish or discard, but rather to re-affirm, further lost elements of tradition and indicate the value of premodern insights in the search for postmodern solutions.

[15] 'The matrimonial covenant, by which a man and a woman establish between themselves a consortium of the whole life (*totius vitae consortium*) ... has been raised by Christ the Lord to the dignity of a sacrament between baptized persons.' Canon 1055, para.1. See Ladislas Örsy, SJ, *Marriage in Canon Law* (Dublin and Leominster: Dominican Publications and Fowler Wright, 1986), pp.49–50.

The groundwork for this section was laid earlier (above, pp.161–4). Pope Nicholas I ruled in 866 that consent was necessary for a valid marriage.[16] Consent was intended as a universal criterion for establishing a valid marriage. It did much to establish the free decision of the parties as a necessary condition of recognition, but other factors were at work. One of these was the influence of the marriage of Mary and Joseph on canonical thought. The consent theory allowed the Church to maintain its ambivalence about sexual intercourse. If the essence of marriage is consent, then it was possible to maintain that the marriage of Mary and Joseph was both perfect yet uncompromised by carnal intercourse. A further advantage of the theory was its obvious appeal to the canonists. It was, in principle, simple to verify. Another apparent advantage was the support it provided for a contractual theory of marriage. But the rise of the consent theory brought with it considerable disadvantages. Consent eclipsed other, potentially richer, theories of the essence of marriage. It also exercised a negative influence on the development of marriage liturgies. It was too easy for the exchange of vows to become the principal focus of the nuptial ceremony, thereby relegating the other elements, including the blessing, to the status of prelude or postscript. A further disadvantage lay in the development of the meaning of consent. Consent came to mean primarily the exercise of individual freedom, a voluntary intentional act: but to what was consent given? This was a pressing question at the end of the first millennium and it needs urgently to be reopened at the beginning of the third. These disadvantages are responsible for the active dislike in the Orthodox Church of the consent theory.

One inadequate answer to the question of the object of consent is the right of access to one another's bodies (*ius in corpus*) for the purpose of avoiding fornication, paying the marital debt or having children.[17] All these were, of course, standard answers to the question down into the twentieth century. What might today be regarded as fundamental to marriage is omitted from this answer,

---

[16] William W. Bassett, 'The Marriage of Christians – Valid Contract, Valid Sacrament?', in William W. Bassett, *The Bond of Marriage: An Ecumenical and Interdisciplinary Guide* (Notre Dame: University of Notre Dame Press, 1968), p.134.

[17] See Pierre J. Payer, *The Bridling of Desire: Views of Sex in the Later Middle Ages* (Toronto: University of Toronto Press, 1993), p.142.

namely, the quality of relationship between the partners which makes the exercise of what used to be called 'conjugal rights' desirable, or even bearable. However, the emphasis on quality of life, while it has a modern ring to it, is an ancient emphasis, and one which the medieval church borrowed from Roman law. Bassett asks whether it is not

more correct to say that two persons enter a total life relationship in which the *ius in corpus* is a part? The union of bodies supposes a union of mind and heart in marriage. Those acts which are *per se* apt for the procreation of children hardly constitute marriage where the common life and the union of mind and heart are absent. The intimate life and love of two persons lead to their natural expression in sexual union, not the converse.[18]

The 'total life relationship' (*consortium omnis vitae*) or 'union of mind and heart' was once regarded as the object of matrimonial consent, and this answer is needed to invest the consent theory with new credibility. In 1979 an entire, extended edition of *Studia Canonica* was devoted to the *consortium omnis vitae* as a juridical element in Catholic marriage and explained how, when the canon lawyers came to codify the Church's law on marriage, they found Augustine's three 'goods of marriage' more conducive to the creation of legal form than the more creative and more recent (eleventh- and twelfth-century) understandings of marriage as a total life relationship.[19] The Latin *consortium* conveyed the sense of 'sharing a common lot', while *omnis vitae* conveyed either a sense of duration, a sharing to the end of life, or a sense of a 'total community of life', a sharing of everything, or what David Pellhauer calls the 'ensemble of marital togetherness'.[20] The 'goods' of children, fidelity and sacrament 'do not, of themselves, encourage a consideration of marriage as a *consortium omnis vitae*. They impede, in fact, such an understanding by reason of their restrictive character. Their very nature, simplifying and schematic as it is (and thus useful, of course), necessarily limits the scope of the institution they describe.'[21] Their explicit reductionism, however, did not prevent

[18] Bassett, 'The Marriage of Christians', pp.142–3.
[19] David E. Fellhauer, 'The *Consortium omnis vitae* as a Juridical Element of Marriage', *Studia Canonica* 13.1 (1979), 19.
[20] Ibid., 15.   [21] Ibid., 32.

them becoming indicators of the essence and validity of marriage
in Catholic thought by the sixteenth century.

There are good grounds for supplementing the bare juridical understanding of marriage with a broader personal and theological
understanding, and for this purpose the twin ideas of *consortio omnis*
(or *totius*) *vitae* and 'marital affection', *maritalis affectio*, are highly
appropriate and enjoy sound precedent. Hugh of St Victor defined the object of consent as the common life of husband and
wife. Gratian regarded 'both sexual relations and the common life
as the object of marital consent'.[22] Twelfth-century writers added
to the ends of marriage *mutuum adiutorium* ('mutual assistance') and
humanum solatium ('human solace'), and this further end presupposed marital affection between the couple.[23] For Peter Lombard,
the object of consent was the 'conjugal society'. Thomas Sanchez
(1550–1610) believed *mutua habitatio* ('mutual living together') was an
end of marriage. Living together assumed 'the obligations of love
and friendship', and so important was *habitatio* that initial failure to
live together after the wedding invalidated the marriage.[24]

While the *consortium omnis vitae* came to have little *canonical* significance it was an essential part of the theological and personal
accounts of marriage. Fellhauer speaks of 'the almost unanimous
conclusion that the heart of marriage was the "conjugal society"
or the "marital association"', which included sexual intercourse
but was not defined by it. The conjugal society included '"other
elements", some of which could be listed (such as mutual love, the
sharing of the necessities of life, living together, etc.)', but these were
difficult to quantify in legal terms. 'Only infrequently and with
hesitation did canonists and theologians assert that these "more
personal" elements of marriage – which may be called aspects of
the *consortium* – could be considered fully juridical, notwithstand-
ing their importance for a doctrinally complete understanding of
marriage.'[25]

The Second Vatican Council came close to reaffirming the
consortium omnis vitae. It is well known that the document *Gaudium
et Spes* calls marriage 'an intimate community of life and love'
(*intima communitas vitae et amoris coniugalis*). It also called marriage

[22] Bassett, 'The Marriage of Christians', p.136.
[23] Fellhauer, 'The *Consortium omnis vitae*', 49.   [24] Ibid., 53.   [25] Ibid., 71.

a 'sacred bond' (*vinculum sacrum*) and a 'marital covenant' (*foedus coniugale*).[26] The medieval *consortium omnis vitae* was not used, but as Fellhauer observes, the document 'clearly recalls the Roman and medieval expressions. It is likewise clear ... that it was the intention of the Council Fathers to attribute great importance to the personal dimension of matrimony.'[27] But while the personal dimension of marriage has enjoyed an unprecedented revival since Vatican II, there has been no relaxation of the insistence that verbal consent, understood as the 'human act by which the partners mutually give themselves to each other', is 'the indispensable element that "makes the marriage"'.[28] We have already noted that the 1980 Synod of Bishops was unsuccessful in its request for the reintroduction of a betrothal ceremony (above, p.193). The official position of the Roman Catholic Church remains that there is no marriage before an exchange of consent at the nuptial ceremony. The anticipation of nuptial relations prior to consent falls under the rubric of 'free union', when 'a man and a woman refuse to give juridical and public form to a liaison involving sexual intimacy'. The term 'trial marriage' is used to condemn 'premature sexual relations', and 'carnal knowledge is morally legitimate only when a definitive community of life between a man and a woman has been established'.[29] There is no question whether sexual relations can contribute to the formation of the community of life.

Criticism of consent is not intended to query the very foundation of marriage in Western churches. It queries the relationship between the exchange of consent and the marriage or object of consent. In standard teaching consent initiates the marriage. An alternative understanding of the link between liturgy and life need not de-emphasize the exchange of consent within the liturgy. It might rather seek a more imaginative correspondence between the consent within the liturgy, and the growing *consortium totius vitae* outside the liturgy, with the *consortium* already entered into providing the context for the consent to be meaningful. The relationship between

---

[26] *Gaudium et Spes: Pastoral Constitution on the Church in the Modern World*, section 48. Text in e.g. Austin Flannery, OP (ed.), *Vatican Council II: the conciliar and post conciliar documents* (Grand Rapids: Wm. B. Eerdmans, 1981). See Fellhauer, 'The *Consortium omnis vitae*', 109.

[27] Fellhauer, 'The *Consortium omnis vitae*', 109, and see 113.

[28] *Catechism of the Catholic Church* (London: Geoffrey Chapman, 1994), sections 1627, 1626.

[29] Ibid., section 2391, and see above, ch.2, section 1.

consent and the *consortium* need not be understood as one of initiation. Solemnization, formalization, confirmation, all come to mind as alternatives. What is initiated on this view is a new and permanent phase within the marriage. The more marriage is understood as a community or a *consortium*, the more the marital relationship is emphasized, and correspondingly less emphasis is required on consent to particular acts or the exercise of particular rights.

According to standard Catholic and Protestant teaching persons may be declared married, if they are eligible to marry and have exchanged consent in the present tense before witnesses. The consent makes the marriage, and the marriage begins when it is made. This is of course a tidy legal schema. Unfortunately when it is imposed on the less tidy unfoldings of personal lives, it often does not fit. Fortunately there remains a broader vision of marriage which is well able to accommodate prenuptial sexual experience and cohabitation. For the *consortium totius vitae* is (as we would say) a unique 'personal relationship', and the willingness to enter into *this* relationship with *this* person, is both matrimonial consent and the object of consent. The blurring of the line between prenuptial and nuptial experience, narrowly and precisely defined by the exchange of words in the ceremony, remains something of a stumbling block for the churches, much as it did for the jurists at the beginning of the last millennium. But on the view that betrothal is a beginning of marriage, these problems are removed. When the nuptials follow the spousals, what begins is not their marriage, but the new phase in the marriage which renders the commitment unconditional and the promises made, irrevocable.

Thirty years ago the problem of the fossilization of the exchange of consent was identified by the Roman Catholic scholar Eugene Hillman. Echoing Adrian Hastings' exasperation with the export of European and Tridentine assumptions to the wider world (above, p.202), he complained:

The realization of matrimonial consent, to cite just one more example, among many peoples seems hardly compatible with the Roman [Catholic] legal conception of achieving an irrevocable *consensus* at one precise moment in the course of the formal nuptial rite. Like the whole reality of marriage itself, valid *consensus* is understood by many only in terms of gradual growth. Ideals and aspirations are not realized in a moment.

In many societies authentic *consensus*, both socially and psychologically, is achieved only through a series of customary actions, involving more people than merely the two who are immediately concerned, over a long period of time, normally before the formal ceremony of marriage, and sometimes after as well. Usually it is not at all clear at what point exactly, if there is a precise point, the mutual consent is actually realized. But, without all of these customary stages, many people find it hard to accept the authenticity of the marriage union. Such misgivings, although not articulated philosophically nor even juridically, are no support for the stability of a marriage which has to be lived, after all, in that particular cultural context, not in ancient Rome.[30]

There are several telling claims in this passage. First, the reduction of the process of becoming married to a single, verbal moment is an ecclesiastical imposition on the couple's life-journey. While the liturgical moment of consent and promise is necessarily singular, the relation of that moment to the wider life-course of the couple is much more complex and deserves the church's respect. Second, consent to marry is generally understood to be acquired and expressed only gradually. Third, the couple and their relatives need to be able to articulate the different phases in becoming married. Fourth, looking for a 'point' at which consent is actually given is probably mistaken. This contention is fully consistent with exchanging consent at a nuptial ceremony – the issue is the relationship between the consent to a *consortium totius vitae* and the momentary expression of this before a priest. Fifth, the suggestion is made, thoroughly congruent with the argument of this book, that the abolition of a staged entry into marriage weakens marriage. And sixth, it is suggested (no more than that) that the cultural context should be allowed to shape the marital provision which the church provides. All these claims are justifiable.

CONSUMMATION AND THE *MARITALIS AFFECTIO*

There is a ready objection to the broader picture of consent in the previous section, viz., that if the couple have given sexual expression to their union before their trip to the altar, whether betrothed

---

[30] Eugene Hillman, 'The Development of Christian Marriage Structures', in Franz Böckle (ed.), *The Future of Marriage as Institution* (*Concilium*) (New York: Herder and Herder, 1970), pp.29–30.

or not, they have consummated their marriage prematurely. But there is a ready answer to this objection: what constitutes consummation, like what constitutes consent, also requires broadening out, and releasing from the juridical mindset that shrinks it to a fleeting postnuptial moment. The late André Guindon launched a devastating attack in the 1980s on the identification of consummation with a couple's first sexual intercourse, and several of his arguments still hold good. Guindon notes that according to the traditional doctrine, sexual intercourse renders a marriage bond indissoluble. An unconsummated marriage may be dissolved, a consummated marriage may not be, and the difference between a dissoluble and an indissoluble marriage is having sex (as seldom as only once). It follows, thinks Guindon, even from this much diminished contribution that sexual intercourse is able to bring to the relationship, that 'coition strengthens the bond of indissolubility'.[31] This is not merely a *legal* observation, but also an *existential* one, i.e., frequent, consensual sex is able to bond a couple together. Sex, then, adds something to the marriage that abstract consent cannot do. To this extent the traditional doctrine accurately reflects the dynamics of the marital bond.

However, the consent theory became dominant precisely because it could be, and was, understood to *exclude* sex from the marital bond. Here the influence is plain: the marriage of Mary and Joseph was believed to be perfect, yet to lack sexual experience, and the consent theory was thought (optimistically) to reconcile both contingencies. But leaving aside the problem of the parentage of Jesus' four brothers and an unspecified number of sisters (Mark 6:3), if the marriage of Mary and Joseph was not consummated, Catholic teaching had no alternative but to regard it as dissoluble, and so it could not have been perfect in any case.[32] Guindon rightly suspects there were other 'spiritualistic and anti-sexual biases' which influenced the adoption of the consent theory. However, if the marriage of Mary and Joseph was not consummated, there

[31] André Guindon, 'Case for a "Consummated" Sexual Bond before a "Ratified" Marriage', *Église et Théologie* 8 (1977), 137–81. This edition of the journal was devoted to the topic of 'pre-ceremonial marriage'.
[32] Ibid., 150. See my discussion of Aquinas' handling of the marriage of Mary and Joseph, above, pp.170–1.

is a further reason why it could not have been perfect. According to traditional teaching sexual experience adds something to the marriage that nothing else can (i.e., it consummates it). Unnoticed by Guindon is the further thought that a marriage only becomes sacramental after sexual intercourse. That is because without sexual intercourse a valid marriage is still dissoluble, i.e., it has not developed a permanent bond, because only sexual intercourse is able to develop this.

But other arguments further undermine the lofty role that first intercourse has come to acquire in this schema that leads (all too quickly) to indissolubility. Guindon asks, 'What kind of symbolism, what kind of sign-value does a single act of copulation actualize?'[33] The unintended message is that the consummation of a marriage is a trivial matter: a single act of sexual intercourse can bring it about. Neither does this act have to express the couple's total commitment to one another. Mechanical intra-vaginal ejaculation will do. Alternatively, it invests a single act of sexual intercourse with power to achieve a crucial transformation in the relationship in the sight of God, i.e., it becomes impossible to undo. Guindon remarks derisively, 'The sexual and sacramental automatism contained in the first-night-consummation concept recalls ... the sympathy magic found in the fertility cults which the Judeo-Christian Tradition opposed from the outset.'[34] In place of the single sex act Guindon sets the relationship of deepening love: '[N]ot only will *love* be the decisive element in both the decision to marry and the survival of this marriage, but this love must be built on a very thorough and lucid knowledge of self and of other, both as individuals and as parts of a conjugal unit.'[35] However, it will not be sacramental until its solemnization. Marriage has 'two phases'. The first phase is 'a marriage-in-the-making which should not receive full-fledged legality and sacramentalization before it does acquire the status of a *real-ized* marriage' (the second phase).[36]

When, then, is a marriage consummated, if not at first intercourse? The question probably concedes too much to the jurists and the marriage tribunals in looking for a neat temporal dividing line between these states. Guindon's answer is, when a couple

---

[33] Guindon, 'Case for a "Consummated" Sexual Bond', 156.
[34] Ibid., 157.　　[35] Ibid., 160.　　[36] Ibid., 168.

experiences 'the sort of sexual fecundity which calls forth its most privileged fruit, a child of love, they may discern that they have become a socially responsible unit. The conjugal bond has probably reached a point of consummation where legal ratifications make sense.'[37] He is prepared to countenance lengthy 'pre-ceremonial' periods in the early stages of marriage, followed by solemnization at a time when the couple desires children or sees itself as already having entered a state of indissolubility. I have taken a similar position in *Marriage after Modernity*. However, since contraception can never completely prevent pregnancy, only reduce its probability, I argue that sexual intercourse should not take place unless it signifies commitment sufficiently extensive to embrace any children that might result from it.[38] This is traditional Christian sexual ethics, of course, i.e., that sexual intercourse should take place in marriage. It differs from tradition in allowing that a couple which has made these commitments has already begun their marriage (whether or not marked or formalized by betrothal), yet if the arguments of part 2 are sound, this view has a greater claim to represent tradition than the view that marriage begins with a wedding and (descending into greater implausibility) is consummated by a single act of sexual intercourse.

Despite indebtedness to Guindon's arguments here, there are problems with them. Without the distinction between prenuptial and non-nuptial cohabitation, he is in danger of sanctifying more 'pre-ceremonial' sex than he would wish. Twenty-five years of research into non-nuptial cohabitation reveals much preventable unhappiness (above, pp.20–8). Since a couple's life together is the matrix of the sacrament of marriage, it is scarcely consistent to reserve the sacramental elements of Christian marriage for the second phase only, as Guindon does. This might seem to endorse the automatism he ridicules. Indeed, in one place he wishes to reserve the sacrament for only those Christians who intend children.[39] But a lasting accomplishment of his treatment of 'the consummated bond' lies in the linkage of consummation, not to first intercourse, but to the *consortium totius vitae* or *maritalis affectio* which constitutes

[37] Ibid., 166.   [38] Thatcher, *Marriage after Modernity*, pp.204–8.
[39] André Guindon, *The Sexual Creators: An Ethical Proposal for Concerned Christians* (Lanham, Md. and London: University Press of America, 1986), p.88.

the essence of marriage and the object of consent. This leads him
to remark 'just how impoverished is our understanding of matrimonial consent in comparison to its twelfth-century proponents'.[40]
Since the object of consent is the lifelong community of love, there
will be 'markers' along the way. The most important and obvious
of these will be the solemnization of this marital community in holy
matrimony, but where exactly in the joint pilgrimage made by the
partners this event occurs, it becomes unnecessary to stipulate.

Despite his emphasis on the two phases of marriage, and his
insistence that marriage is a process, requiring *maritalis affectio*[41] in
order to be a true marriage, Guindon does not grasp another feature of medieval marital theology: betrothal. In this respect, he is
like many other contemporary writers who assume from the current
hiatus on the matter that betrothal has no real place in the marital
tradition. Yet betrothal would give him a concrete (and liturgical)
event which inaugurates the first phase of marriage and begins the
journey out of singleness and towards the nuptiality of the next
phase. Nevertheless, his treatment of 'pre-ceremonial' marriage,
and his juxtaposition of the pastoral needs of contemporary marrying Christians (Canadians in the 1970s) alongside the medieval
matrimonium initiatum, represent a lasting achievement.

Betrothal also helps to explain the growth of the marital bond.
We have moved the emphasis on the *juridical* character of the bond
to the *existential* character of the relationship built by a couple, which
provides the matrix for their sacramental marriage. It is but a small
leap to the *theological* character of the bond. The ancient idea of
the married couple as 'one flesh' (Gen. 2:24) is confirmed by Jesus
himself (Mark 10:8). But the Letter to the Ephesians inserts the one
flesh doctrine firmly into the relationship between Christ and the
Church. It is well known that this relationship is described nuptially.
This was part of Rogers' provisional definition of marriage.

[40] Guindon, 'Case for a "Consummated" Sexual Bond', 172.
[41] Throughout this discussion it has been assumed that *maritalis affectio* in the medieval
period means a growing tender attachment or fondness of a couple for one another
as they enter into and consolidate their marriage. However, Brooke reminds us that,
while *affectio* means affection, it can also equally mean 'the intent to get married', which
need not require affection at all. However, the emotional meaning of the term came to
predominate. See Christopher Brooke, *The Medieval Idea of Marriage* (Oxford: Clarendon
Press, 1989), pp.128–9.

The Church is the bride of Christ and the metaphor of union between Christ and the Church is allowed to generate a priceless Christian theology of marriage (which can withstand the removal of its patriarchal presuppositions).[42] The Church, understood as the 'body of Christ', is incorporated into the one flesh unity that is Christ-and-the-Church. 'In loving his wife a man loves himself. For no one ever hated his own body; on the contrary, he keeps it nourished and warm, and that is how Christ treats the church, because it is his body ...' (Eph. 5:29–30). But if this analogy seems to justify incorporation, of the wife's body into her husband's, and the Church into the body of Christ, the separate identities of each continue to be emphasized. Christ could not treat the Church in any sense at all unless the Church were also other than him: neither could a relationship of love exist between husband and wife if there were not real separation between them.

So the nature of the bond between husband and wife in Christian marriage is not juridical: it is theological. Marriage, as Christian theology understands it, is able to express the devoted love that Christ expressed for the Church. Whether or not the bond between Christians is dissoluble depends on a theological point of reference. The bond is the unity of a couple who also remain separate from one another. The possibility is that this unity becomes a symbol of another unity, that between Christ and the Church. If the symbol does fragmentarily express the unity between Christ and the Church, even then there is no guarantee that the bond is durable, for the relationship will need to be continually renewed, and sacramental grace remains one of the resources for this. The criterion for the bond is the extent of the participation of the nuptial relationship in the broader nuptial relationship between Christ and the Church.

The *consortium omnis vitae*, although Roman in origin, is well suited to a sacramental theology of marriage in which the partners are the joint ministers of the sacrament to each other. There is less pressure, for this view of marriage, on defining when it is consummated, or when it becomes sacramental. Indeed the *consortium* view allows an understanding of annulment that no marriage tribunal would dare

---

[42] See Thatcher, *Marriage after Modernity*, pp.90–5.

to operate. Many marriages which are voidable on the grounds of defective consent, and from which partners wish to escape, might better be considered to have foundered on the grounds of defective consummation.[43] That is, consent was undoubtedly given, sex was had, but the relationship never reached the consummation that was its promise. This would of course revolutionize the marriage tribunals' work!

When a couple agree to marry, they enter into a *consortium omnis vitae*. Consent to enter this holy estate is realized only gradually. Consummation occurs at the end of provisional commitment and the beginning of a new and permanent phase of the marriage. Within this single process the events that were once called spousals and nuptials mark the maturing of the relationship in unmistakable ways. In the first section of this chapter, it was shown that the recovery of a phased entry into marriage was consistent with the theology that regards marriage as a way of holiness and a sharing in the relationship between Christ and the Church. The final question for this chapter is whether a phased approach to marriage is consistent with other theological rationales for marriage, specifically those which regard marriage as a sharing in the Trinitarian life of God.

The doctrine of the Trinity states that God is three 'Persons' in a single essence or substance. The Persons are co-equal, yet distinct. 'Person' in Trinitarian thought conveys better than the English word 'person' that persons are 'in-relation'. Each is what it is because of its relation to the others. 'Relationality' is a property both of the Persons and of the one God. Yet God is indivisibly one. Some theologians speak of the oneness or unity of God as the 'communion' of the Persons. God's essence, then, is communion. The relation between the Persons is covered by the Greek word *perichòrèsis*. 'God is love' (1 John 4:8, 17) and the relations between the Persons are relations of love. On the basis of Trinitarian doctrine, theologians East and West have compared the relationships between the Persons of the Trinity with the relationship of human persons within marriage, and found that the latter reflects, exemplifies or participates (and so on) in the former. That is why,

---

[43] Guindon, 'Case for a "Consummated" Sexual Bond', 174.

representing the Orthodox Church, Stavros Fotiou (among many) can say:

The married couple is first called upon to make their life an example of unity, following the example of the Holy Trinity. That is, they are called upon to experience that state of being in which, through dissimilarity, their equality of honour, and their unity, each fully encompasses the other. In this way they learn through experience that love does not erase differences; on the contrary, it brings them to the fore. Each person remains singular and unique, absolutely incapable of being compared with any other. This respect for difference is expressed through equality of honour. Within this communion of love no one is higher or lower than anyone else; all are simply different. Furthermore, while the persons in this relationship are different and equal in honour, they are simultaneously in a state of total unity.[44]

Vatican II also makes explicit the social analogy between the divine Persons of the Trinity and human persons. *Gaudium et Spes* records how 'the Lord Jesus, when praying to the Father "that they may all be one ... even as we are one" (Jn.17:21–2), had opened up new horizons closed to human reason by implying that there is a certain parallel between the union existing among the divine persons and the union of the sons of God in truth and love'.[45] Pope John Paul II, while Cardinal Wojtyla, influenced the wording of the drafts leading to the final version of *Gaudium et Spes*.[46] While *Gaudium et Spes* did not develop the analogy between divine and human persons specifically towards the relationship of marriage, Pope John Paul II frequently did so. Looking back in 1974 on the 'certain parallel' passage from *Gaudium et Spes* he felt able to say it 'captures as though the very essence of the human reality of the family'.[47] The *communio* which is the divine Trinity is able to be reflected in the *communio* which is the human family. Many

---

[44] Stavros Fotiou, 'Water into Wine, and *Eros* into *Agape* – Marriage in the Orthodox Church', in Adrian Thatcher (ed.), *Celebrating Christian Marriage* (Edinburgh: T&T Clark, 2002).

[45] *Gaudium et Spes*, section 24. Text in Walter M. Abbot (ed.), *The Documents of Vatican II* (New York: Guild Press, 1966), p.223.

[46] On the influence of Cardinal Wojtyla on the Council and the subsequent development of his personalist thought, see Mary Shivanandan, *Crossing the Threshold of Love: A New Vision of Marriage* (Edinburgh: T&T Clark, 1999), pp.70–83.

[47] Karol Wojtyla, 'The Family as a Community of Persons'. References in ibid., p.80.

theologians, East and West, now make these claims. Assuming that
Christian marriage may really be ontologically grounded in divine
love, either in the love of Christ for the Church, or in the love of the
divine Persons for each other, or in their *communio* or relationality,
and so on, I am concerned only with the question whether the
account of entry into marriage developed here is consistent with it.
Can it contribute positively to it?

The question is harder to answer than the earlier one about the
contribution of betrothal to marriage as a way of holiness. In the
present case, theological descriptions are in danger of complex-
ifying marriage and building layers of meaning into it which are
hard, even for professing Christians, to grasp. Further, the high level
of abstraction leads away from the concrete interchanges which
make up married life, while the three realities corresponding to
the Trinitarian 'Persons' seem to stretch beyond the horizon of
our imagining. Whatever the Persons are, they are eternal (i.e., beyond time), uncreated and therefore unsexed (to be created is to
be sexed), and without sin. Trinitarian persons are fully formed,
human persons are not, and that must be one of the principal differences between them, and the major difficulty for any analogy
that works katabatically downwards from divine to human communion of Persons. That said, the more an appreciation of the fullness
of marriage draws from Trinitarian sources, the more will marriage be described by means of relation, relationality, communion,
union, and so on.

There is less of a problem when marital theology begins (anaba-
tically) with developing affection between two people which leads to
deepening love and a determination to share one's body and one's
life with one's partner. Within this growing matrix, the katabatic
language of relationality and communion resonates and takes root.
Mutuality and equality (clearly properties of the divine Persons, and
clearly not properties of patriarchal marriages) are necessary to the
building of communion within the marriage, while union with a
beloved has no hope of survival without respect for individuality
and difference. These properties are also safeguarded in Trinitarian
thought. The sharing or participation which is the *consortium* or
communio of married life is already in the divine life: indeed,
being pregnant, it is suggested, is the nearest human understanding

can get to the generation of a person out of another (as the Son is 'eternally begotten' from the Father), while breast-feeding is the nearest one can get to mutual participation.[48] The remarkable 'fit' between Trinitarian language and the experience (at least potential) of the riches of married life, makes the pursuit of analogies, in both directions, worthwhile, whether or not the arguments for betrothal are sound. Betrothal, or the phased entry into marriage, fully safeguards the 'gradualist' approach to the holy mystery of marriage. Consent and consummation, embedded in the growing union of the couple or the increasing relationality between them, mark phases human persons must pass through if they are, even finitely, to resemble the *communio* that comes from, and is, God.

In the previous two sections, an attempt has been made to reclaim three important elements of medieval marital theology. Once they re-emerge they may be seen to have an important and continuing role in a postmodern period of the Church's witness. They enhance the Church's insistence on the marital norm. These elements were the *consortium omnis vitae*, the *matrimonium consummatum*, and the *maritalis affectio*. It was suggested that the *consortium omnis vitae* remains a fine summary of the object of marital consent. The technical and implausible meaning of 'consummation' (the event of first intercourse) was replaced by the shared personal desire (the process of deepening love) to proceed to an irrevocable phase of the *consortium*, consciously seeking the public solemnization of the union and the blessing of God upon it. And *maritalis affectio* was used to show that the existential quality of the marital relationship was, in fact, supremely important in medieval theologies of marriage, waning in influence only because the canon lawyers could not handle it.

These classical elements turn out to provide an excellent 'grid' or 'relational map' for contemporary couples to locate themselves. They reinforce the claims made already for the distinctions made between spousals and nuptials, between *matrimonium initiatum* and *matrimonium perfectum*. Here indeed is sound Christian wisdom for post-Christian societies. Couples who grow towards one another

---

[48] David S. Cunningham, *These Three Are One: the Practice of Trinitarian Theology* (Malden, Mass. and Oxford: Blackwell, 1998), pp.60–7, 175.

in companionship, acceptance and fondness may consider the possibility that they share the whole of their lives with one another. The decision should never be quickly made. The goal toward which the couple *may* move is the *consortium totius vitae*, and many elements of this will have been shared already. If this point is reached, betrothal is appropriate (whether or not it is available), as a public declaration of the beginnings of marital commitment which may (and may not) be taken to the stage of solemnization and permanence. This stage is *matrimonium initiatum*. The 'whole of their lives' now takes on a temporal, and not simply a personal, dimension. 'Consummation' is the completion of the betrothal phase. It is the awareness that the time has come for remaining provisionalities to be swept away. Doubtless regular love-making will already have featured prominently in the 'total sharing' of their lives to this point. Equally possible is the decision that consummation has not been achieved, and so no progression to the *matrimonium ratum* should be undertaken. Breaking-up then becomes an option, perhaps a painful one, and repetition of the option is capable of influencing a person's character in damaging ways (above, pp.25–8, propositions 17–18).

The goal of *consortium omnis vitae* and the quality of *maritalis affectio* may also serve as important 'indicators' at the point of decision to progress the relationship to solemnized lifelong marriage. It will be important for the couple to progress beyond the delights of sexual attraction and the vagaries of romantic love, to a broader level of mutual sharing and friendship which provides the basis for the enduring marriage. However, there is a further series of advantages in laying out the entry into marriage in this phased and unfolding way. This is to do with the interim nature of betrothal as part of a rite of passage, taken up in the following chapter.

CHAPTER 8

The sacramental beginning of marriage

The present chapter builds on the ground prepared in chapter 3. It advocates the betrothal solution to the pastoral problem of prenuptial cohabitation and to the theological problem of when marriage begins. The idea of a 'catechumenate for marriage' is examined. Two Roman Catholic treatments of this idea are considered, but found to have suffered from the hardening of Tridentine orthodoxy and a disowning of more imaginative medieval solutions (first and second sections). In the course of the examination, a further deficit of Tridentine insistence upon consent and consummation before a marriage becomes a sacrament looms into view: the marital history of couples prior to the solemnization of marriage is void of (marital) sacramental significance. An alternative proposal, based on betrothal as a beginning of marriage, is urged. This proposal is at least as equally congruent with tradition as its rival. It avoids the haemorrhaging of sacramental meaning found in the new complacent orthodoxy, and it avoids the mistaken hallowing of engagement (second section). Kenneth Stevenson's work on betrothal, together with a re-appropriation of the idea of liminality encountered in the first two sections, clinches the case for betrothal as the sacramental beginning of marriage (third section). In the fourth section that case is concluded.

A CATECHUMENATE FOR MARRIAGE?

Can there, should there, be a 'catechumenate' for marriage? I argue 'Yes', and begin the argument with a definition of terms. A 'catechumen' is a person who receives instruction in the Christian religion in order to be baptized. The catechumenate is the body of Christians awaiting baptism and full membership of the church. Those who advocate a catechumenate for marriage assume a parallel or analogy between preparation for baptism and preparation for marriage. One such advocate is Paul Holmes. In popular religious discussion, the Christian life and married life are often depicted as journeys, with the possibility of some structural similarities or overlap between them. Holmes treats the overlap by considering both of them as *pilgrimage*, and he draws on anthropological studies of real pilgrimages to bring the structural similarities into view. This enables him to view 'the betrothed as metaphorical pilgrims, and their betrothal as a metaphorical, catechumenal journey'.[1] Marriage is their destination. Victor Turner's studies indicate that pilgrimages are 'quite similar to rites of passage'. A pilgrimage is, for Turner, a 'liminal journey', i.e., one which involves a person crossing a threshold and thus being involved in a transitional state. A pilgrimage is liminal in that it involves a 'journey through a land of "betwixt-and-between" where one is no longer in the place one was (home), but not yet where one hopes to be (the pilgrimage center). The journey to that "center out there" affords a special kind of communion amongst the pilgrims; and this communion generates the power necessary for the transformation that is sought at the journey's end.'

An examination of the actual routes taken by pilgrims shows 'way stations' which were 'an integral part of the whole pilgrimage experience'. These build up excitement and anticipation which help to effect the psychological and spiritual preparation needed to appreciate the goal of the pilgrimage and be open to its impact.[2] It follows, thinks Holmes, that the structural similarities between pilgrimage and the sacrament of marriage require reformation of the latter. '[I]f the journey towards the celebration of a sacrament can be likened to a pilgrimage, then such a journey may *require* a ritual structure. Way stations strategically placed along the road of pre-sacramental preparation may be more than a nice idea; they may be

[1] Paul A. Holmes, 'A Catechumenate for Marriage: Presacramental Preparation as Pilgrimage', *Journal of Ritual Studies* 6 (Summer 1992), 93.

[2] Ibid., 94. Several writings of Victor Turner are cited, in particular, Victor W. Turner and Edith L.B. Turner, *Image and Pilgrimage in Christian Culture: Anthropological Perspectives* (Oxford: Blackwell, 1978).

necessary if the transformation sought at the sacramental celebration is to be effected.'[3] Betrothal is the term used for 'preparation for marriage' and other similarities are found to exist between pilgrimage and betrothal. The journeyers are 'initiands'. A liminal journey takes the initiand *to* a particular threshold, but not *through* it. Whether the journey is literal (pilgrimage) or metaphorical (betrothal), it

gets one to the door; the postliminal celebration gets one through it. Postliminal ritualizations make the candidate a full Christian, a priest, a spouse, but liminal pilgrimage rituals effect the secret, invisible initiation that empowers candidates to accept their new status with the requisite intellectual, affective, and orthodox worldview appropriate for that transformation.[4]

The structural similarities between the two catechumenates provide an evangelistic opportunity for the church to plant the faith in the fertile ground of the couple's liminal journey. The 'period of presacramental catechesis for fiancés' may be viewed as 'a kind of pilgrimage so that the "journey of faith" experienced in a catechumenate might deepen the fiancés' commitment to the truths being communicated to them'. Christian spouses 'must translate into the practical and quotidian the deepest mystery of which they are the living sacraments, namely, the paschal mystery as symbolized in the marriage of Christ and the Church. It is for this reason that viewing a catechumenate for the betrothed as a pilgrimage is much more than mere analogizing.'[5]

The spatial distinction between a journey *to* and a journey *through* the threshold carries firm implications. The couple are not married until they pass through the *limen* which is the marriage celebration. The relationship is not sacramental until after this event. The liminal analogy is allowed to demonstrate the point. Just as catechumens are not yet Christians, so the betrothed are not yet married. The view that 'catechumens are already Christians even though they have not yet been baptized', is rejected, on the grounds that it is 'counter-intuitive' and 'deprives the members of the Christian community of any real motive for treating catechumens differently ...' While catechumens are members of the 'household of

[3] Holmes, 'A Catechumenate for Marriage', 95.   [4] Ibid., 97.   [5] Ibid., 98.

Christ', they 'have not been called Christians either in ecclesial documents or in the law'.[6] The church would confuse the betrothed, and itself, if it regarded the betrothed as married. 'The goal of a marriage catechumenate would be to transform fiancés into spouses, just as the goal of the baptismal catechumenate is to transform catechumens into Christians.' The 1980 Synod of Bishops which called for a married catechumenate for 'couples who have not as yet approached the altar, but who have nonetheless begun what their own culture views as marriage' was mistaken. On the contrary, 'the marriage catechumenate suggested here is not that of a marriage in stages but rather of marriage preparation in stages'.[7] These are derived directly from *Familiaris Consortio*[8] and some suggestions are made for filling them out. There is a 'period of remote preparation' which ends with the request for marriage and 'acceptance into the order of the betrothed'. There are two further periods, 'proximate preparation', usually a year or more, 'for the deepening of the fiancés' commitment to one another and to the Christian view of marriage', followed by 'election', i.e., 'the liturgical rite by which the Christian community formally ratifies the fiancés' readiness for the sacrament of marriage and the fiancés express the will to receive the sacrament'. The period of 'immediate preparation' is 'a period of reflection, intensely centered on continuing conversion, marked by way-station rituals, for example, presentations, the formal signing of the betrothal document, and, perhaps, the blessing of marriage garments'. After the marriage a further period occurs, of 'postmarital catechesis'. This is the time, 'usually beginning a month after the celebration of the sacrament of marriage, during which the newly married are assisted by the Christian community, especially by other married couples, to appropriate the Christian mystery which is their marriage'.[9]

This proposal for a catechumenate for marriage is useful and positive. The neglect of betrothal by the Western Church is acknowledged, and the dynamic character of preparation, whether

---

[6] Ibid., 104. [7] Ibid., 106.
[8] Pope John Paul II, *Familiaris Consortio* (London: Catholic Truth Society, 1981), section 66, 'Preparation for Marriage'.
[9] Holmes, 'A Catechumenate for Marriage', 107–8.

for baptism or marriage, is acknowledged. Moreover, the proposal has been carefully set out so as to conform to the panoply of official Vatican documents about marriage. But the proposal diverges from the case that has been building in the present book in at least five fairly obvious ways. First, arguments from analogy may be successful in illustrating similarities between things, but they can never be successful in demonstrating identities between things. That is how analogies work, i.e., for things to be similar they have to be *different*, not identical. So while a fruitful series of analogies exists between the literal journey which is a pilgrimage and the metaphorical journey which is preparation for marriage, it could never quite be the case that because one of them 'requires' a ritual structure, so must the other; or because one of them requires literal sojourns at way stations in order for the pilgrimage to be finally effective, it becomes 'necessary' to 'structure in' some metaphorical way stations into the metaphorical journey of marriage preparation in order for the marriage to be effective. There needs to be a stronger basis than analogy for the proposed reforms of marital preparation, and this basis is found in the full recovery of betrothal as a real beginning of marriage.

Second, the analogy assumes the consummation of the pilgrimage is the arrival at the pilgrim site and the consummation of marriage preparation is the marriage ceremony. This seems a straightforward comparison: however, we have just had reason to query what might be meant by consummation (above, p.226). While the pilgrimage ends at the pilgrim site, the marriage journey does *not* end at the ceremony. If it did, not even sexual intercourse would be necessary to consummate it. Holmes' journey metaphor and mine differ because they are different journeys; or rather, he posits two journeys while I posit only one. The two journeys are preparation for marriage, and marriage itself. But if betrothal is a real beginning of marriage, there remains a single journey. Both the travelling and the destination are provided by the marriage itself. The ordinary language use of the term 'marriage' confirms the point well – marriage means both the wedding ceremony *and* the lifelong union of the couple.

Third, since the marriage is initiated at the wedding ceremony and not before, there can be no question of receiving the sacramental grace of marriage prior to this temporal point (below, p.245). More precisely, the sacramental grace in the couple's lives will not yet have been augmented by the grace of the sacrament of marriage. This is because only the exchange of consent in the ceremony can initiate the sacrament. Yet if the matrix of the sacrament of marriage is the deepening commitment of the couple to each other, it seems to follow that these life-changing and union-shaping processes are disconnected from the marital sacrament which still remains in the future. This is a perilous feature of now standard Roman Catholic teaching about the beginning of marriage, because the deepening human love between the couple, its expression, and the mutual joy that each finds in the other at this stage of the relationship, are not and cannot be understood as a participation in the marital sacrament. The disconnection between engagement and marriage at the theological level contributes to a parallel disconnection at the pastoral and personal level. Whatever personal changes, deepening feelings, shared plans, may be happening in this stage of couples' lives, marriage it isn't.[10]

Fourth, the analogy between the different catechumenates for baptism and for marriage yields neither the premiss that baptismal catechumens are not Christians nor the conclusion that betrothed catechumens are not married. Several authorities who support the contrary view, that catechumens are already Christians, are listed,[11] and as Holmes admits, if a candidate for baptism dies unbaptized, she or he is given a Christian burial. It is in any case unnecessary to choose between the black and white views that catechumens are or are not Christians, because there is a sensible alternative – if they are converts or beginning faith, they have begun the single journey which is the Christian life. They too are pilgrims, on the way from faith to baptism, and so are in an in-between state (just like the betrothed). The analogy can be pushed, with little force, further in this alternative direction. Faith is the personal, subjective side of discipleship: baptism the ecclesial,

---

[10] Richard Hardy laments the lost opportunity for developing the spirituality of 'pre-ceremonial couples' because of the assumption of 'a once and for all being touched by grace'. See his 'The Pre-ceremonial Couple: Reflections for a Spirituality', *Église et Théologie* 8 (1977), 184.

[11] Holmes, 'A Catechumenate for Marriage', 104.

objective side. Both together achieve the incorporation of the individual into the church. The baptismal vow, like the nuptial vow, can be thought to represent the point beyond which there is no turning back. Holmes thinks 'confusion' will be introduced if the betrothed are regarded as married. Does not greater confusion exist by regarding the betrothed as unmarried, even if this has now become the 'default' position of most of Christendom? If catechumens are members of 'the household of Christ' and deserve Christian funerals, is it not confusing to say they are *not* Christians? The analogy is more favourable to the argument developed here than to the excluding conclusion of Holmes.

Fifth, there is further confusion in the suggestion that there can be no marriage in stages, only marriage preparation in stages. Having effectively introduced the themes of betrothal and personal growth, and constructed the promising analogy of pilgrimage, marriage (like sacramentality) is now excluded from this promising picture. The reason is easy to detect: anyone who remains loyal to Roman Catholic teaching, at least since the publication of the Apostolic Exhortation, *Familiaris Consortio*, in 1980, has no alternative but to affirm that marriage begins with the wedding. That document had also compared the instruction given during the three phases of marriage preparation with 'a catechumenal process'. 'The very preparation for Christian marriage is itself a journey of faith. It is a special opportunity for the engaged to rediscover and deepen the faith received in baptism and nourished by their Christian upbringing.'[12] There is a 'journey of faith, which is similar to the catechumenate',[13] but it is a journey to marriage, and distinct from the journey which is marriage, begun at the wedding. There is no mention in this long work of betrothal. The tradition of *matrimonium initiatum* and its promise for the present time, correctly discerned by the 1980 Synod of Bishops, is spurned, and the inevitable return to it has been delayed and impeded by the reinforcement of Tridentine norms. Holmes' loyalty to papal and magisterial teaching has required him to develop his analogy in a counter-intuitive direction. This direction, specified in an official Vatican document, must now be further examined.

[12] *Familiaris Consortio*, section 52, 'The Christian family's ministry of evangelization'.
[13] Ibid., section 66.

ENGAGEMENT OR BETROTHAL?

While there is no space available to devote to the undoubted hardening of Catholic teaching on the entry into marriage since Vatican
II, we will note briefly the treatment of engagement in a more
recent Vatican document (1996), *Preparation for the Sacrament of
Marriage*. This document has a comparatively low status among
Vatican documents, and many Roman Catholic theologians may
not regard it seriously. Nonetheless it remains in the public domain,
it is noteworthy for its pastoral concern, and (my reason for examining it) it exemplifies the new conservatism of official teaching in
the area of marriage. It blames 'the process of de-Christianization'
for 'the loss of the identity of marriage and the Christian family
and hence the meaning of engagement'.[14] The period of proximate
preparation may be used 'to verify the maturation of the human
values pertaining to the relationship of friendship and dialogue that
should characterize the engagement'. The engaged couple enjoys
'the new state in life as a couple'.[15] The period of proximate preparation, the Council teaches, 'generally coincides with the period
of youth'.[16] Marriage is a vocation which can shed 'greater light
on Christian life in the context of the vocation to marriage and in
the complementarity of all the vocations'. Vocations require formation, and the period of proximate preparation should also be
'for formation during which the engaged, with the help of grace
and by avoiding all forms of sin, will prepare to give themselves as
a couple to Christ who sustains, purifies and ennobles the engagement and married life'. The formation required is mainly that of
restricting sexual contact. 'In this way, premarital chastity takes on
its full meaning and rules out any cohabitation, premarital relations, and other practices, such as *mariage coutumier*, in the process of
making love grow.' The formation required is 'in line with the sound
pedagogical principles of a gradual and comprehensive personal
growth'.[17]

Young people during this period should be made to 'understand that the commitment they take on through the exchange of

---

[14] Pontifical Council for the Family, *Preparation for the Sacrament of Marriage* (1996), section 12,
   www.cin.org/vatcong/prepmarr.html (accessed 16.03.01).
[15] Ibid., section 31.   [16] Ibid., section 33.   [17] Ibid., sections 37–8.

their consent "before the Church" makes it necessary for them to begin a path of reciprocal fidelity in the engagement period'. God helps them in 'this human commitment' because it 'will be enhanced by the specific gifts which the Holy Spirit gives to the engaged who invoke him'. The engaged should 'imitate' the 'model' of Christ's love for the Church 'and develop their awareness of self-giving which is always connected with the mutual respect and self-denial that help this love grow'.[18] 'Spousal spirituality' has its 'roots', not in the sacrament of holy matrimony, but 'in Baptism and Confirmation. Preparation of the engaged should therefore include regaining the dynamism of the sacraments, with a special role of the sacraments of Reconciliation and the Eucharist.'[19] At the end of the proximate period couples should have 'a clear awareness' of, among other things, 'the conscience of faith regarding the priority of the sacramental Grace which associates the spouses, as subjects and ministers of the sacrament, to the love of Christ, the Bridegroom of the Church'.[20] They 'should be helped beforehand to learn how to preserve and cultivate married love later', along with 'interpersonal, marital communication, the virtues and difficulties of conjugal life, and how to overcome the inevitable conjugal "crises"'.[21]

While the engaged draw their sacramental grace from the sacraments of baptism and communion, the centre of proximate preparation for marriage 'must be a reflection in the faith on the sacrament of Marriage through the Word of God and the guidance of the Magisterium'. They 'should be made aware that to become *una caro* (Matthew 19:6) in Christ, through the Spirit in Christian marriage, means imprinting a new form of baptismal life on their existence'. Through the forthcoming sacrament of marriage, 'their love will become a concrete expression of Christ's love for his Church', and through the same sacrament 'the married acts themselves, responsible procreation, educational activity, the communion of life, and the apostolic and missionary spirit connected with the life of Christian spouses are to be considered valid moments of Christian experience'. Engagement, it is stressed, is not sacramental but enjoys the presence of Christ differently.

[18] Ibid., section 40.   [19] Ibid., section 41.
[20] Ibid., section 45.   [21] Ibid., section 46.

'Although still not in a sacramental way, Christ sustains and accompanies the journey of grace and growth of the engaged toward the participation in his mystery of union with the Church.'[22]

Immediate for the sacrament of marriage 'should be the culmination of a catechesis which helps engaged Christians to retrace their sacramental journey intelligently'.[23] 'Preparation for marriage leads to married life, through the celebration of the sacrament, which is the culmination of the journey of preparation which the spouses have made and the source and origin of their married life.'[24] The writers concede that 'praiseworthy customs that belong to various peoples or ethnic groups can be brought into the celebration' but with the proviso 'that they express above all the coming together of the ecclesial assembly as a sign of the faith of the Church, which recognizes in the sacrament the presence of the Risen Lord uniting the spouses to the Love of the Trinity'. The celebration 'is to be understood not only as a legal act but also as a moment in the history of salvation of those being married'.[25] The document reemphasizes that the spouses themselves are the ministers of the sacrament. 'With the formula of the exchange of consent, the spouses will always remember the personal, ecclesial and social aspect gained from this consent for all their life, as a gift of one to the other even unto death.' The document notes that '[t]he Eastern Rite reserves the role of the minister of marriage to the assisting priest', but minimizes the importance of the difference between West and East on the point – 'In any case, according to the law of the Church, the presence of a priest or a duly authorized minister is necessary for the validity of the matrimonial union and clearly sets forth the public and social meaning of the spousal covenant, both for the Church and for all of society.'[26]

I think there are several serious anomalies in this document, all of them arising from the determination to tighten still further the Tridentine grip on the entry into marriage and to silence more liberal voices in the church who pleaded in the 1970s for further reforms in Roman Catholic sexual teaching. That said, there is

---

[22] Ibid., section 47.   [23] Ibid., section 53.   [24] Ibid., section 60.
[25] Ibid., section 62.   [26] Ibid., section 63.

much that is admirable in the document. The Vatican takes marriage preparation seriously: the same can hardly be said for most (all?) other churches. Marriage is affirmed as a 'vocation' (so not everyone is called to it), and like the other vocations, planned, structured preparation is necessary, and appropriate persons are to be trained and appointed to carry it out. The medieval doctrine that the couple are the ministers of the sacrament of marriage is reaffirmed. Especially rich for the argument of this book is the characterization of the ceremony as a 'moment in the history of salvation' of the marrying couple. There is much practical detail to accompany each of the stages of preparation which people involved in marriage ministry will find useful. The major critique of the document I wish to launch is predictable enough. It knows nothing of *matrimonium initiatum*, nothing of betrothal, nothing of *consortium totius vitae*, and it never occurs to its authors that earlier Catholic practice is better able to meet the real needs of marrying couples than its own unadventurous and deeply conservative instincts. It Christianizes engagement while allowing the remaining traces of a theology of betrothal to evaporate. It demands of all people working in marriage ministry 'unquestionable fidelity to the Magisterium of the Church'[27] with regard to the document's content, so that even raising questions of the kind raised here would attract the charge of disloyalty and result in exclusion from ministry.

The accusation that de-Christianization is responsible for (among other things), the loss of the meaning of engagement seems almost amazing, since the recent process of defining marriage and marriage preparation undertaken by the Roman Catholic Church in this and other documents itself shows a disturbing loss of Catholic tradition. The loss of meaning, not of engagement but of betrothal, lies at the root of the problem of 'the identity of marriage' and the English version of this document adds to the loss of betrothal by removing it altogether. For the loss of meaning of engagement, the churches must shoulder much of the blame. Engagement brings about a 'new state of life' but this has nothing at all to do with marriage. Indeed, since it is not marriage, the document

[27] Ibid., section 43.

labours in order to ground this new state in something else, e.g., the sacraments of baptism and confirmation, or the (unspecified and non-sacramental) presence of Christ on the journey to marriage, or the 'specific gifts' of the Holy Spirit to the engaged. If marriage begins with betrothal none of this casting around to augment the seriousness of the new state of life is necessary. It is right to say that Christ 'ennobles engagement and married life' and apposite that engagement and married life appear together in a single phrase. If engagement is the beginning of marriage, then it is easy to see how they belong together. But since engagement is not even biblical (above, p.219) and is almost entirely separated from marriage it is hard to see how Christ ennobles them both because they are different institutions.

Almost as difficult is the empirical assertion that proximate marriage preparation takes place in 'the period of youth'. People generally marry first in their (very) late twenties, well after adolescence, and having acquired (almost universally) considerable sexual experience on their 'journey' to marriage. 'Youth' must acquire additional flexibility if it is to accommodate real engagements. Engagement is helpfully described as a period of formation, but formation, like professional training, usually entails the acquisition of the requisite knowledge and skills that are professionally needed in order to practise one's vocation or training successfully. However, marital formation appears to be unlike other vocational formation since it excludes love-making from what is permitted. Indeed, couples are expected to let love grow by not making it. It has already been suggested that betrothal involves waiting (above, p.240) but the expectation that the waiting should continue until the ceremony is progressively unrealistic and theologically implausible to sustain. In any case it is almost completely ignored. While some readers may baulk at the candid admission made here, there is a logical (rather than theological) point that should not be overlooked.

Almost all learning undertaken in order to prepare for employment, for careers, etc., assumes that learning is most effective by doing; by participation in the many tasks, experiences and situations which will be encountered later. Indeed a good case can be made for saying that professional preparation has gone too far in its insistence on experiential learning. The logical point is that the marriage preparation expected here is not learning by doing, but learning by not doing, and particularly by avoiding sin, including 'cohabitation and premarital relations'. But this is unlikely to be effective: neither is it pedagogically sound, as claimed. Like *Familiaris Consortio* there are plenty of references to personal growth, but 'gradual and comprehensive personal growth' is actually considered dangerous because it undermines the vertical sacramental theology that is actualized only at the moment of liturgical consent. Personal growth belongs more to the *consortium totius vitae* understanding of marriage which admits stages but does not erect barriers. Is it uncharitable to wonder whether the rhetoric of growth has been added to a thoroughly static theology of marriage? The reasons would not be hard to find. Developmental theories are all-pervasive. They must be seen to be deployed, even at the Vatican. But their truth has not been conceded. However, if couples begin their marriage with betrothal, and the marriage grows to consummation and solemnization, a seamless process is able to be readily described, and the ceremony still able to be the grand 'moment in the history of salvation' of the couple.

There must be a strong suspicion that the assumptions attaching to consent in the document reinforce the criticisms of Hillman and others (above, pp.225–6) that consent is understood as a single event of quasi-magical significance. Mention of 'the formula' suggests this, together with the couple's relationship to their exchanged consent as one of remembrance. The criticism here is not that consent does not make marriage or is being wrongly emphasized: it is whether the centrality of consent in the Western understanding of marriage is best commended by being understood as an abstract formula, without an object, and with its relationship to the whole of life unspecified (below, p.221). On the view that consent is to the *consortium totius vitae* and that it is exchanged gradually, the quasi-magical overtones are removed. The public event involving the exchange of consent retains its symbolic and performative qualities, while the lifelong benefits for the couple derived from the giving of consent have their basis in their sacramental relationship to God and to each other, not from the efficacy of a remembered moment.

Perhaps the strangest consequence of all is the exclusion of the engaged from participation in the sacrament of marriage. (This is, of course, a different question from the troublesome debate about the role of faith in the sacrament of marriage.) The spirituality of engagement is derived from the sacraments of baptism and confirmation, and in the immediate preparatory period, reconciliation. The couple is expected to be able to give irrevocable, lifelong consent to their union, but on the basis of what experience? For many marrying couples there will be a growing devotion of each to the other, a growing together, which will already have transformed them sufficiently enough for them to wish to take the momentous step of a whole-life commitment. There could scarcely be more important changes going on in a person's life. Yet the sacramental grace given to the couple at this time of their lives is not based in, or particularized by, the sacrament of marriage. Consequently, engagement and marriage cannot be sacramentally linked. This discontinuity inevitably weakens both the church's estimate of engagement (it is sacramentally nourished in the same way as all Christians are nourished by the sacraments) and the couple's estimate of themselves. The events they are experiencing, describable by means of the vocabulary of love, devotion, commitment, self-giving, transformation, etc., are not rooted in the sacrament of marriage.

This positing of discontinuity between the two states is both harmful and unnecessary. On the alternative view, there is a single sacramental continuum which is increasingly realized and symbolized at the blessing of the couple in their ceremony. According to the official view the discontinuity between engagement and marriage is underscored by discontinuity in sacramental status. This gives rise once more to the different journeys which couples are said metaphorically to embark on. There is a 'journey of grace and growth' for the engaged. There is also a 'sacramental journey' through baptism, confirmation and reconciliation, and up to, but excluding, marriage. And then there is the journey which is marriage. So there is a journey to a journey. Is the double journey like a change of planes at an airport? No. Changing planes occurs on a single journey: what we have here are different journeys, differentiated by status. This double journey is another unfortunate consequence of the identification of marriages with weddings.

There are two remaining details which further reinforce Tridentine norms. Permission to incorporate into the ceremony 'praiseworthy customs that belong to various people or ethnic groups' is given (and has been given since the Council of Trent). But these are restricted still further, and it is unlikely that such customs would ever be regarded as signs that point to Christian faith in the resurrection and Trinity. More importantly, they have no formal contribution to make to ecclesiastical marriage, so their optional character is likely to diminish them in any case. This further 'ecclesiasticizes' marriage. The other detail is the disagreement between West and East regarding the identity of the ministers of marriage. There is considerable divergence of belief and practice at this point, yet the document is at pains to minimize it. Since Trent the presence of a priest has been required to ensure the validity of a marriage, and this highly important change is advanced as potential common ground between the two churches. But one wonders whether behind the minimizing of difference there is a different intention, i.e., to strengthen the indispensable role of the priest at marriage services. It is possible that the move towards the practice of the Orthodox may further weaken the medieval doctrine (still affirmed in the churches of the West) that the couple themselves are ministers of the sacrament. There must be a suspicion (no more than that) that the Tridentine hold on the entry to marriage is being strengthened still further.

This chapter opened with the question, should there be a catechumenate for marriage? We have found comparisons made between the literal catechumenate consisting of people receiving instruction in the faith prior to the sacrament of baptism, and the metaphorical catechumenate of engaged people receiving instruction in marriage prior to the sacrament of marriage. Much energy has been and is being expended in the effort to prepare couples more adequately for marriage. This effort of pastoral care identifies an enormous area of pastoral need and offers a structured way of meeting it. But a theological fault-line was detected right through it. The plan assumed a dubious reading of the meaning of marriage, of consent, of consummation, of the relation of liturgy to life, and of the reception of grace. Criticisms were offered out of deep commitment to Christian marriage, and not, as opponents might wish, out of hostility to it, or to Catholic teaching in general. The two Roman Catholic readings of these matters are doubly unfortunate, even if they have by now become etched upon a hardening orthodoxy. Not only do they not take into account the huge social differences between the sixteenth-century European context and the twenty-first-century global context, they refuse the rich diversity of thought actually available within the Catholic tradition. This diversity has become increasingly unavailable in Roman Catholic and Protestant practice and is eclipsed instead by a dogmatism that identifies dangerous liberal influences on the church's teaching, and, in response, removes official teaching ever further from people's lives. On the alternative view, that betrothal is a real beginning of marriage, how would a catechumenate for marriage look?

The term 'catechumenate for marriage' would signify a class of persons throughout the Christian churches – those couples who wished to get married in church, or, more precisely, who wished to have their marriages solemnized in accordance with a Christian rite. The force of 'catechumenate' is intended to emphasize the parallels between the 'in-between' state of believing Christians seeking baptism, and the 'in-between' state of persons who are no longer single and who wish to bind themselves to one another unreservedly in marriage. The catechumenate for marriage would consist of betrothed couples. The term indicates the paradigm shift required of all the churches, hinted at in *Something to Celebrate* (above, p.103), that couples who are living together and proposing to marry have already begun their marriage and know a great deal about it. The 'catechumenate for marriage' is an unambiguously inclusive term. It signals an alternative to the longstanding 'mindset', still prevalent in the churches, that identifies living together before marriage as 'living in sin'. It revolutionizes the pastoral care afforded to those beginning marriage by accepting them as already having begun the journey. But it requires a paradigm shift, from treating the ceremony as the beginning of marriage, to treating it as the confirmation, celebration and blessing of it.

The term, then, remains a metaphor, but a powerful one which may be able, along with betrothal and the other proposed revisions to marital theology, to contribute towards a much friendlier climate for the increasing number of people who live together before indicating a wish to marry formally. But the term is not without far-reaching implications for the churches' pastoral practice. It is to be hoped that churches will intensify their efforts to organize and contribute to marriage preparation in a variety of ways, including mentoring by married couples, skills training, theological and spiritual teaching, parenting, and later, marriage enrichment, and so on. But without sound theology, training and skills-acquisition are of limited value.[28]

BETROTHAL AND LIMINALITY

The quest for a catechumenate for marriage, then, cannot rest with official Vatican theology. There is, however, a further (Anglican) source for the same concept in the writings of Kenneth Stevenson. I have already drawn on Stevenson's pioneering work in several places. Stevenson's proposals are more successful because he is aware of the history of betrothal and alive to the prospects for its reintroduction. Let us begin on common ground between Holmes and Stevenson – the idea of liminality.

Arnold Van Gennep and Victor Turner both use the term. Van Gennep's work *Les Rites de Passage* posited the sequence of separation, liminality and incorporation as fundamental to rites of passage.[29] When applied to members of the catechumenate the sequence is easy to follow. 'The preliminary rites correspond to enrolling for the catechumenate; the period of preliminary [*sic*] is the final stages of catechumenate (or even the entirety?); and the incorporation finds supreme expression in the Easter Sacraments of baptism, confirmation ... and eucharist.' Stevenson makes a simple comparison between the passage into the church and the passage into marriage: 'If Van Gennep's scheme is to be applied to marriage, it must take into account betrothal (rite of separation), time of engagement (liminality), and the celebration of marriage (rite of incorporation).'[30] Elsewhere he observes: 'The first stage,

---

[28] See John Wall, 'The Marriage Education Movement: A Theological Analysis', in Adrian Thatcher (ed.), *Celebrating Christian Marriage* (Edinburgh: T&T Clark, 2002).

[29] Arnold Van Gennep, *Les Rites de Passage* (Paris: Librairie Critique, Émile Nourry, 1909), p.14. See Kenneth W. Stevenson, 'Van Gennep and Marriage – Strange Bedfellows? A Fresh Look at the Rites of Marriage', *Ephemerides Liturgicae* 100 (1986), 138.

[30] Stevenson, 'Van Gennep and Marriage', 139. And see Kenneth Stevenson, 'The Marriage Service', in Michael Perham (ed.), *Liturgy for a New Century: Further Essays in Preparation for Revision of the Alternative Service Book* (London: SPCK/Alcuin Club, 1991), p.58.

the separation, corresponds with *betrothal*. Here, the couple (and the community) accept the interim commitment to marry in the future. The way in which this has been described expresses the atmosphere of this separation, which must lead somewhere else, even if it leads to the breaking off of that commitment.'[31] Betrothal marks the separation of the couple: it identifies them as moving out of singleness and towards a different and permanent status in solemnized marriage. The marking off is public because it is acknowledged and received by the community, and like betrothal as it was understood by Aquinas and Swinburne (above, pp.169–77) the commitment is interim or provisional. It may lead to the solemnization of the marriage or back into singleness. In this respect it is again similar to enrolment in the baptismal catechumenate. Catechumens can proceed to baptism, or decide against it.

We have already described at length what happened to betrothal in the West. However, Stevenson's summary of this process adds significantly to the case for its reclamation.

Separation is expressed in different forms of ritual. In the West, it eventually came to be dominated by the notion of intentionality, so that when the Catholic Church insisted on consent as an integral part of marriage, 'Separation' at betrothal became redundant, and was a mere prelude to the nuptial mass. The Western practice, therefore, is one that draws betrothal into marriage, so that all the Church has to offer is a liturgy for the third (and final) stage, incorporation. This is what the reformers at Wittenberg, Lambeth, and Trent took over. This is also where we are left today. For the majority of Christians today, what their Church has to offer them is no more than a rite of incorporation.[32]

The theology of consent renders prior stages towards the exchange of consent superfluous. The entry into marriage becomes an event, not a process. The words of consent, exchanged liturgically, become the temporal point separating marriage from non-marriage. The rite of marriage is no longer a rite of passage with a sequence of phases. Liturgical provision remains only for the third stage of the passage rite. A rich historical legacy has been lost to view, and an

---

[31] Kenneth Stevenson, *To Join Together: The Rite of Marriage* (New York: Pueblo Publishing Company, 1987), pp.7–8.
[32] Ibid., p.8.

impoverished normativity (of marriage liturgy and theology) has established itself as beyond question.

An examination of Victor Turner's account of liminality (above, p.238) renders its application to marriage still more appropriate. 'Initiates' in the liminal phase can expect '*powerlessness*, because many things are expected of them, but they have no rights'. They can also expect a '*cultural inversion*, so that those about to be honoured are humiliated. Thirdly, the cultural *mores* are for a time *suspended*.'[33] The lives of engaged couples today are thought to show clear evidence of these elements. The humiliation of the couple through local customs surrounding marriage rites is an example. But Stevenson's treatment of the suspension phase is noteworthy:

Thirdly, many couples start living together before marriage, and may even regard this as a 'trial' experience, without any definite commitment to marry; such a phenomenon of cohabitation has a long history, and is nothing new to the so-called 'permissive society' . . . Rites of betrothal in the late Middle Ages frequently started (whether by accident or design) such relationships. In such ways, liminality is a time of confusion and adjustment.[34]

I have introduced the distinction between prenuptial and non-nuptial cohabitation (above, p.45) partly in order to distinguish, in permissive societies, between forms of living together that may arguably receive the endorsement of Christian tradition and those that may not. It may also be pointed out that once a majority of marrying couples live together before the ceremony the cultural *mores* are not merely suspended, but *altered*. However, it follows, in medieval and permissive societies alike, that the liminal period is likely to be one of 'confusion and adjustment', precisely because large transformations are being negotiated in people's lives, and in the lives of relatives and friends around them. In this respect, attempts to identify the precise moment at which couples are married have probably always imposed canonical simplicity on existential complexity. Liminality, then, is one way of describing the state of couples living together before the ceremony, and it is a pastorally helpful notion precisely because it prompts us to

---

33 Stevenson, 'Van Gennep and Marriage', 140–1 (author's emphasis).
34 Ibid., 141.

expect irregularity and confusion in negotiating massive personal change.

It follows, if Stevenson is right, that the churches must take their share of blame for failing to provide, liturgically and pastorally, for the spiritual needs of couples who are now living together prenuptially and have long come to think that the churches disapprove of or even disown them, regarding them as 'living in sin'. The failure of theology and liturgy has led to a loss of comprehension of, and provision for, couples living together in a liminal state, and this, rather than any primary unbelief or overt rejection of Christian marriage on their part, is to blame for their undoubted sense of isolation in most churches today. Stevenson thinks liminality 'is an experience Christian couples experience *after* marriage, if they take modern rites seriously'.[35] Nothing has been written, he observes (in 1986), 'about marriage, as a rite of passage through which many couples go on their own, unsupported ...' He thinks 'Van Gennep's three stages and Turner's explanation of liminality are real experiences for the majority of couples who come to the Church to ask for its blessing.' Liturgical provision is insufficient, and

[a]t a time when marriage is under severe pressure throughout Western society, it is hardly to be expected that an attenuated marriage-celebration which lasts little more than thirty minutes is really enough. Nor will it really do to regard pre-Cana week-ends as adequate preparation, because that is to succumb to the therapists and educationalists. We need to *ritualise reality*, even if it means re-thinking what we mean by marriage, and thereby asking some searching and uncomfortable questions of our respective Churches.[36]

The present volume has sought to press such questions and also to provide some answers. The charge that liminality is experienced *after* marriage is explosive, for if it is right, it follows that the marriage ceremony is not regarded by many people who go through one as a stepping into a permanent state 'till death us do part'. The chaos and confusion of the liminal period is transferred to a later phase where it is harder to deal with and is often a cause of divorce. Many couples, especially those at some distance from Christian teaching

[35] Ibid. (author's emphasis).
[36] Ibid. (author's emphasis). And see Stevenson, *To Join Together*, p.9.

on marriage, regard their ceremony in just this way, that is, as provisional. One is never inextricably committed to the marriage 'in case things don't work out'. The extrication that divorce achieves for couples might more readily and less painfully be achieved in the liminal phase before the step beyond that phase is ever made. A contemporary betrothal rite, by its very existence as a rite temporally and existentially prior to the further rite of solemnization, would initiate the liminal period and bring it into view. It would also assist couples who live together prenuptially to prepare better for their wedding. Living together lacks public status and recognition. It is also perceived by many as lacking permanence. Consequently, even prenuptial cohabitation may be experienced as separate from marriage, with the result that couples moving on to the wedding find that 'whatever work they did on the relationship while they were living together needs to be done again as a married couple'.[37] A rite of betrothal would address all these issues squarely.

The need to 'ritualise reality' arises from certain beliefs about the relation of liturgy to life, and these must very briefly be examined. For this the familiar contrast between surface structures and deep structures is required. Regarding Van Gennep's three stages, Stevenson asks whether they are

a reality that the Church is failing to identify today? To put the question in a technical liturgical way: Are these three stages the 'deep structures' of marriage? Are they so deep in the human spirit that they come to the surface willy-nilly, regardless of what the Church may or may not do in its corporate liturgies? And do they imply that recent liturgical renewal, however significant, amounts to no more than playing around with the 'surface structures,' which liturgists keep telling us are not as important to the real human need as the 'deep structures'?[38]

The question is posed whether something like a universal human experience, an essence, or a predictable process takes place, individuated in particular marriages every time a couple weds. Ritual enables the process to be identified, expressed, and enacted, and in order for this to happen ritual must first be available. I think the case

---

37 Herbert Anderson and Robert Cotton Fite, *Becoming Married* (Louisville: Westminster/John Knox Press, 1993), p.107. This work helpfully develops the experience of becoming married from the dynamic perspective of couples themselves.

38 Stevenson, *To Join Together*, p.8.

for a betrothal liturgy is unanswerable, but before it can be concluded, the problem must be admitted that the relation of liturgy to life may be unlike that proposed by Victor Turner, Van Gennep, and many others. This problem must now be briefly addressed.

Perhaps there are no deep structures to human life, discerned heroically by anthropologists, so there may be no need for liturgists and theologians to take note of them. Culture may survive perfectly well without cult. Neither is it obvious 'that rituals are thought to confer important psychological and sociological benefits upon the individuals and communities who enact them'.[39] There may be no 'remote roots' which are 'closely linked to the ontogenetic development of the human person'. Nor is it necessarily the case that 'rituals preserve and represent archaic acts, ancestral memories and provide access to the historic past' so that 'a community without rituals is a community without a memory'.[40] Nathan Mitchell has recently launched a devastating critique of this view of ritual, what he calls 'the prevailing consensus' (between anthropology, theology and social criticism). Philosophers will recognize the tone of his work as 'anti-foundational', i.e., it eschews metanarratives, ontological groundings, theoretical underpinnings, rational foundations, etc., in favour of something more modest, manageable and appropriately humble.

The removal of anthropological generalizations and metaphysical underpinnings is thought to enable a clearer view of what liturgy is about. There is much informal ritual in contemporary societies, giving the lie to accusations that modern culture is anti-ritualistic. Rituals may still confirm membership of a group or 'encourage us to interpret reality in very specific ways'. They are more likely to erupt on the margins of society.[41] Ritual may be a potent vehicle for social change. An example given is of Roman Catholic women creating their own liturgies from a position of exclusion and marginalization in their male-dominated church.[42] Rituals are 'human improvisations' which are inexact and grow out of particular needs (e.g., the needs of members of Alcoholics Anonymous).[43] They don't have to

---

[39] Nathan D. Mitchell, *Liturgy and the Social Sciences* (Collegeville, Minn.: The Liturgical Press, 1999), p.23.
[40] Ibid., p.25.   [41] Ibid., pp.38–9.   [42] Ibid., pp.41–2.   [43] Ibid., pp.42–3.

be continually validated by 'reference to the past'.[44] These features of ritual belong to a new category called 'emerging ritual'.[45] From this perspective the work of Victor Turner, including his view of the relation between anthropology and religion, is differently seen. He understood 'that society is a process punctuated by performances, that rites are not rubrics, that ritual frames must always be re-framed, that ritualising is a group's collective autobiography, that human beings invent their lives as they go along, playing games, performing their being'.[46]

There is no need to make an instant choice between 'prevailing' and 'emerging' views of liturgy, since premisses from either side of the divide can be enlisted in support of the reinstatement of betrothal and the creation of a catechumenate for marriage. It must be stressed that in seeking to retrieve and reinstate betrothal practice one pursues something that emphatically existed, not something that might not ever have existed at all. What is recovered is historical marital practice, not some mysterious essence. How-ever, let us assume that the emerging view becomes the prevailing view, and see what happens to the betrothal case. Suppose there is no grand scheme for rites of passage which can be appro-priated by or extended to Christian marriage rites. The cate-gories of separation, liminality and incorporation still remain not merely serviceable but explanatory in that they help to articulate, both to the churches and to their marrying members, the human transitions that are being negotiated, expressed, recognized and blessed. They apply to real lives. Suppose there are no deep structures, embedded in something called 'the human spirit'. Marrying couples will continue to have deep needs even if these can't be mapped on to human essences that turn out to have no being. Christians will want to ensure that deep liturgies exist corresponding to them.

Again, 'important psychological and sociological benefits' will continue to accrue to initiates whether or not the prevailing consen-sus continues to prevail. This is because the conferment of meaning on people's lives through ritual may proceed in countless ways that do not require correspondence with universal deep structures:

---

44 Ibid., p.46.   45 Ibid., pp.38–49.   46 Ibid., p.57.

the ability of a ritual to interpret to its participants themselves, to express their intentions and needs, and to raise and offer their lives to God, to experience acceptance and blessing, and so on, is independent of foundational support, whether or not it is available. The emerging consensus actually provides additional reasons for thinking betrothal to be highly appropriate. Prenuptial cohabitors are on the margins of the church. Their presence there is awkward for the church, and often for them, if they want a church wedding. This is a marginal situation that may well be resolved by an appropriate ritual. The very awkwardness of their situation may provide the catalyst for speedy liturgical innovation. Again, ritual may be proactive both in responding to and initiating social change. Prenuptial cohabitation is almost certainly here to stay (along with other forms): a betrothal rite would be a response to an obvious need. But it would also help to initiate social change and nudge it influentially towards a recognition of the difference between prenuptial and non-nuptial cohabitation, thereby sacralizing one while excluding the other.

THE SACRAMENTAL BEGINNING OF MARRIAGE

While Holmes and Stevenson may rely overmuch on a particular reading of the stages of initiation, their application of the liminality stage to beginning marriage remains a useful one. However, an informed choice between the two writers is bound to conclude that on historical, theological, psychological and pastoral grounds, the insights of Stevenson are much to be preferred. There are two further reasons why Stevenson's solution is congenial to the argument of this book. First, we have seen (above, pp.249–50) that the betrothal stage *is sacramental*. There is no confined allocation of sacramental grace to the postnuptial period only.[47] Betrothal 'has the advantage of spreading the sacrament of marriage *over a far wider terrain*

---

[47] Brennan R. Hill points out that Roman Catholic teaching currently dissociates romantic love from the sacramental theology of marriage. See his 'Reformulating the Sacramental Theology of Marriage', in Michael G. Lawler and William P. Roberts (eds.), *Christian Marriage and Family: Contemporary Theological and Pastoral Perspectives* (Collegeville, Minn.: The Liturgical Press, 1996), p.12.

than it has occupied for many centuries'.[48] This is a major claim and the justification of it is a major achievement. The growing together, the joy of loving intimacy, the planning for the future, the setting up of the matrimonial home, the re-ordering of relationships within and beyond the families of the betrothed couple, and so on, all happen within the ambience of divine grace. They do not need to be relegated to the status of awkward preliminaries, or misdescribed (by means of an unfortunate double metaphor) as a journey to a journey, when the real journey of marriage has already started. The separation of the sacramental grace of marriage from the couple's experience of the beginning of marriage has yielded a disastrous state of affairs. The very matrix of the relationship by which the grace of God is mediated to the couple is removed, ritually and theologically, from the reception of grace, because certain formalities have failed to precede it. The consequences are obvious. These marital beginnings become overlaid with guilt. The disapproval of the churches, whether overt or tight-lipped, are internalized by the marrying couples themselves, and the sense of joy and elation that accompanies these new beginnings, which is of profound spiritual significance for the couples, becomes instead closed off in ecclesial embarrassment and needless remorse.

Second, betrothal was able to cope historically with the arrival of children prior to the solemnization of marriage, and it is clearly still able to do this at a time when about a third of children in Britain and the USA are born outside marriage. On the Tridentine view the arrival of a child before the ceremony is, on all accounts, a disaster. However, Stevenson observes that the separate rites of betrothal that appeared in the later Middle Ages 'were used to start trial marriages; some rites give in to this tendency (or else to the common custom of straight cohabitation) by directing that *children born before the marriage are legitimised if they are placed under the canopy which was often used during the nuptial blessing of their parents*'.[49] We have already recorded distress at the outcomes of non-nuptial cohabitation for children (above, pp.20–3), but that is not the present issue.

[48] Stevenson, 'The Marriage Service', p.59 (emphasis added), and see above, ch. 2, 2nd section.
[49] Stevenson, 'Van Gennep and Marriage', 148.

Many thousands of pregnant couples marry. It has been entirely forgotten that for some churches in some periods this was no big problem. Neither should it be a problem for the churches of today, when approached by pregnant couples or couples with children, requesting marriage, to be unreservedly welcoming in granting their request, thankful that a Christian wedding is being sought, and mindful that liturgical minimalism and Tridentine severity have served the churches poorly and caused alienation which, even now, is not being addressed.

That marriages have a sacramental dimension in the prenuptial phase accords well with what has been claimed earlier about the need to maintain 'the marital norm' within Christian sexual ethics and the appropriateness of 'the betrothal solution' as the means by which the marital norm is able to be extended to prenuptial couples living together. The marital norm has been affirmed and strengthened, and the treatment it has received may be contrasted favourably with the treatment by those liberal church reports (above, ch.3) that inevitably weakened it by accommodating living together as a recognized *alternative* to it. In part 3, it has been further shown that if marriage is to be commended to the Church and the world as a particular pursuit of the way of holiness, the reinstatement of betrothal greatly assists its commendation. At this juncture, additional features of medieval Christian wisdom impinged themselves upon the argument.

Lack of specificity about the object of marital consent led quickly to the deployment of the ideas of *consortium omnis vitae* and *maritalis affectio*. Not only is there strong historical warrant for these ideas, their reintroduction softens the juridical, technical, quantitative approach to marriage so typical of canonical thought, and releases forgotten elements of the same tradition which stress the personal, relational and qualitative approach. However, this latter approach presupposes 'whole life' continuities and growing 'affection' within the married relationship, and is for that reason conducive to betrothal as a beginning of marriage (that is partly why it was disliked and discontinued). The juridical understanding of the consummation of a marriage was also found to be unhelpful to the point of distortion. The 'summing up' or 'completion' or 'perfection' of marriage, to which that term points, is almost bizarrely identified with the first act of sexual intercourse. While marriages may never be complete or perfect, there is a strong case for identifying 'consummation' with the completion of the preliminary phase of the marriage and the move into the next (normally) irrevocable and unconditional phase which will be marked by the wedding.

The present chapter has welcomed the metaphorical extension of the Christian catechumenate to those beginning marriage, but found that this intriguing suggestion was impeded and turned back on itself by a Tridentine orthodoxy which refuses to allow valuable elements of Christian tradition any longer to influence the development of marital theology. Further evidence was brought forward to indicate that the absence of a betrothal rite may be responsible for a psychological and spiritual hiatus within the shared experience of 'engaged' couples, and worse, may lead to the marriage ceremony being regarded as the intermediate (i.e., liminal) phase of the married relationship (thereby pervading and tainting the unconditionality of marital commitment with an unspoken provisionality). It was shown that the marital sacrament is able to cover, and account for, the prenuptial phase of marriage and the consequences of regarding prenuptiality in this way, for couples and for pastoral ministry, were pointed out. The 'marital norm' has been upheld, and the 'betrothal solution' has been tested against biblical teaching, church history, contemporary marital theology, and the pastoral and spiritual needs of marrying couples. It is now time for the churches to test this solution for themselves.

CHAPTER 9

Extending the marital norm

The argument of the book has extended marriage to couples who live together with the intention to become formally married. The 'marital norm' has been defended and re-commended at a time when the church's marital teaching is under severe pressure. The final task of the book is to suggest that the solution proffered to the problem of prenuptial cohabitation, i.e., the extension of the marital norm, may be able also to be deployed as a solution to the problem of some other sexual relationships which trouble the churches at the present time. Armed with the now familiar distinction between norms and rules in Christian teaching, a very brief description of how the marital norm might be further extended will be attempted. How might this norm illuminate a Christian understanding of the sexual behaviour of, say, the following groups of people: (i) adolescents and young unmarried adults; (ii) postmarried people; (iii) lesbian and gay partners?

ADOLESCENTS AND YOUNG UNMARRIED ADULTS

The distinction between a norm and a rule might illuminate sexual behaviour in these age groups by treating marriage as a norm to aspire to, rather than a rule that 'rules out' sexual activity in all relationships other than marriage. Since all practical learning these days proceeds experientially, some premarital sexual experience may be a welcome means towards the acquisition of both self-knowledge, and the practical knowledge needed for the maintenance of lifelong marriage. To regard adolescent sexual experience in this way is not to condone early penetrative intercourse, but to recognize that if a theology of chastity is to begin to be useful, it has to be achievable, rooted in people's lives and able to serve them during the average fifteen-year stretch between puberty and first marriage. In this regard, the Anglican bishops' commendation of 'the principle of proportion' ('the level of sexual expression should be commensurate with the level of commitment in the relationship'[1]) is wise. Sex is for marriage, but marriage may benefit from much prior preparation and experience. In this respect, it is like preparing for a professional career.

If marriage is a path to holiness (above, p.215) which embodies the values of fidelity, mutuality and reciprocal love, marriage preparation is the learning and internalizing of these values, and it begins before preparation for marriage with a particular person. Monti warns that 'the Church must accept that the entire range of sexual activity will be present in the dating relationships of single Christians', and laments 'our present functional abandonment of especially the young under the faulty morality of the peremptory "no"'.[2] I am more sanguine that within the community of faith, sexual awakening and sexual experience might one day be seen and understood more positively as an opportunity for learning and discerning the values, and acquiring the virtues, that Christian marriage requires. The long gap between puberty and marriage provides an unparalleled opportunity for marriage preparation in a broader sense, although it has yet to be properly recognized as such. In other words the marital norm may be capable of extension to the unmarried where sexual experience cultivates and affirms the values marriage presupposes. Since the territory trodden here is troublingly unfamiliar, what follows is best regarded as a series of prompts for an urgent discussion. Let us suggest two ways by which this extension might work: first, what might be called 'the enlargement of chastity' and second, the development of Christian principles whose function is to influence sexual behaviour.

The practice of chastity before marriage need entail neither celibacy nor virginity. Indeed, how could it, since celibacy is a special gift to a tiny minority, and chastity is a Christian virtue for all

---

[1] *Issues in Human Sexuality: A Statement by the House of Bishops* (London: Church House Publishing, 1991), p.19, para.3.2.

[2] Joseph Monti, *Arguing About Sex: The Rhetoric of Christian Sexual Morality* (New York: State University of New York Press, 1995), p.246.

to acquire? According to the *Catechism of the Catholic Church* chastity
is 'the successful integration of sexuality within the person ...' It
'includes an *apprenticeship in self-mastery* ...' It involves the 'practice
of an ascesis adapted to the situations that confront Christians'.[3]
People are to 'cultivate' chastity in a way that is 'suited to their
state of life'. So, while married people exercise a 'form' of chastity,
'others practise chastity in continence'.[4] Married couples exercise
chastity not by not having sex, but by having it only with each
other. The *Catechism* is clear that 'continence' is the only option
for the unmarried. Leaving aside surprise at the continued use of
this archaic term (it is generally understood to mean the ability
to prevent a discharge of bodily fluids) the claim is not justified
by the arguments. Even the *Catechism* allows that chastity *cannot be
separated* from the contexts and life-situations of Christians (it must
be 'adapted to their situations', 'suited to their state of life'). The
question to be developed is whether the only form of chastity for
the unmarried (about half of all adults) is continence. The 'state of
life' of post-pubertal but premarried people demands a more imaginative solution than an unargued insistence on continence (another
example of the 'peremptory "no"').

Is it completely daft to think one can find and appropriate from
the Christian tradition a *sexual realism* which recognizes and in the
end legitimizes the near certainty of sexual experience prior to a
wedding ceremony? We have already met this kind of realism in
the (bizarre?) custom of betrothal at seven, and in Luther's recognition that celibacy is, barring rare charisms, humanly impossible.
These elements of the tradition may provide an honest reminder to
societies which encourage citizens to marry later than ever before
that premarital sexual experience is inevitable, and to churches
still insisting on virginity before the wedding ceremony that their
gospel is likely to be heard, as Harvey Cox puts it, 'as a remnant
of cultural Christendom'.[5] The sexual realism of earlier generations may, paradoxically, help to free Christians from possible

---

[3] *Catechism of the Catholic Church* (London: Geoffrey Chapman, 1994), paras. 2337, 2339
(authors' emphasis), 2340 (pp.500–1).
[4] *Catechism of the Catholic Church*, p.503, para.2349.
[5] Harvey Cox, 'A Brothel in Noble Dimensions: Today's Sexual Mores', in John Charles
Wynn (ed.), *Sex, Family and Society in Theological Focus* (New York: Association Press, 1996),
p.50.

guilt and embarrassment about the practice and sheer extent of premarital sex. Also, the period between puberty and marriage is going to be one of 'confusion and adjustment' (Stevenson's description of the liminal period). Indeed one might say this period is itself liminal (being that broad threshold between adolescence and adulthood) and it might therefore be expected at times to display a measure of irresponsibility and provisionality. The community of faith has cause to know that Christian maturity is not acquired all at once (if ever), and so it is in a good position to offer solidarity in weakness with people who sometimes show immature conduct.

For Christians who marry, premarital sexual experience may be an opportunity to learn the values that the maintenance of married life and love requires. Since marriage is not for everyone, the opportunity may instead become the learning that one is not 'called' to marriage at all. Premarried Christians are poorly served by the supine identification of chastity with continence. At the end of the modern period they encounter further difficulties, not least that the established courtship procedures which to some extent once codified and ritualized sexual behaviour, slowed it down and oriented it towards marriage, have broken down. Amy and Leon Cass have described these procedures and lamented their passing, holding that 'going through the forms of courtship provides early practice in being married – a very different kind of practice, for a very different view of marriage, than the practice now thought to be provided by premarital cohabitation'.[6] But they do not examine the gender assumptions that undergirded these rituals and produced patriarchal marriages. Equality of the sexes does not begin only after courtship. Perhaps what is needed is Rosemary Radford Ruether's proposal for a 'new *ars erotica*' which 'would seek to help people develop their capacity for sexual pleasure and enjoyment, while integrating it into deepening friendship, so that it becomes increasingly an expression of love, commitment and a caring that seeks to be truly mutual'.[7] While it is still difficult to

---

[6] Amy A. Cass and Leon R. Cass, 'Proposing Courtship', *First Things* 96 (October 1999), 39.
[7] Rosemary Radford Ruether, 'Sex in the Catholic Tradition', in Lisa Isherwood (ed.), *The Good News of the Body: Sexual Theology and Feminism* (Sheffield: Sheffield Academic Press, 2000), p.51.

see how such an *ars erotica* could be commended, it is not difficult
to see that the values aimed at are firmly congruent with those
of marriage.

In this way it is possible to envisage more adequate forms of the
virtue of chastity which encourage the learning required for the
successful integration of sexuality into the person and for the acquisition of marital values. This is what is meant by the enlargement of
chastity, and it is an endeavour that may be assisted by the formulation and use of particular principles. Joseph Monti inserts principles
in the gap between norms and rules. 'Norms', he says, 'first *disclose*
values; principles linguistically *articulate* and cognitively *direct* the
course that such values must traverse to goods.'[8] While principles
are 'linguistic statements of ethical/moral norms', rules are 'measures and regulations for practical guidance in the actual contextu-
ally specific situations of moral decision making'.[9] Principles, then,
might connect the marital norm to the specific situations discussed
in this chapter, enabling guidance to be made in the form of rules.
'Principles', in this context, acquire a certain technicality unusual
in most ethical discussion. They have a 'dialectical interrelation'[10]
with both norms and rules. A relevant example of a mediating
principle (given by Monti) is 'sexual behaviour is a manifestation
of committed love'.[11] The rule that might result from this principle
might be 'Only make love in the context of complete commitment.'

The 'principle of proportion' just discussed invites formal consideration as a principle mediating the marital norm and resulting
in a rule. The required 'level of commitment' does not just spring
from nowhere. It springs from deeply held, 'norm-ative', Christian
convictions about marriage, in this case that it is more likely to provide the context of mutual devotion within which sexual intercourse
is best able to be meaningful as well as pleasurable. From this position the bishops would like to deduce the rule 'Only make love when
you are married', but to their credit they do not do so because they
know that Christians are aware of this rule and largely disregard it.
There is a particular principle deriving from the marital norm that
is more important than either of the two so far discussed. Christians
believe that one of the purposes of marriage is having children, and

---

[8] Monti, *Arguing About Sex*, p.134 (author's emphasis).
[9] Ibid., p.283.   [10] Ibid., p.132.   [11] Ibid., p.134.

correlatively, that children are more likely to thrive in the continual care of both biological parents. The emerging principle, endorsed by a mountain of empirical findings, might be, 'Children are more likely to thrive in the context of lifelong marriage', yielding a rule with several possible formulations – 'Only have sex if you would both be willing parents of any child you conceived'; 'Never risk conceiving a child without being committed to your partner and to the child'; 'When you make love, put children first', and so on.

There are several principles which do not derive directly from the marital norm but mediate between other fundamental Christian convictions and sexual behaviour. Beginning with, say, the doctrine that God the Word took human flesh (John 1:14), or with Paul's conviction that 'the human body is a temple of the indwelling Holy Spirit' (1 Cor. 6:19), one might forge the principle 'Your body is holy', and move fairly directly to several rules unrelated or indirectly related to sexual behaviour, such as 'Take regular exercise', 'Avoid obesity', 'Avoid alcohol and substance abuse', 'Don't smoke', and so on. These rules suffice to honour the holiness of the body. The principle also generates sexually specific rules, e.g., 'Avoid casual sex'. Another principle, 'Always honour vulnerability', has a particular sexual reference.[12] It rules out coercion and the misuse of power in sexual relations. The great Christian principle 'Love your neighbour as yourself' can also generate *sexual* rules. Sexual encounters can imprint themselves on the characters of those who have them, for good or for ill. The rule 'Never have a sexual involvement that you or your partner may regret' may commend itself because it encodes convictions deriving directly from the practice of neighbour-love. The derivation and elucidation of further principles, and their positive application in the form of rules, is an urgent task in Christian sexual ethics.

The marital norm is therefore able to reach premarital sexual behaviour and to influence it decisively. This norm is itself derived, for Christianity, not simply from the Hebrew scriptures and the teachings of Judaism at the time of Jesus, but from the covenant love of God and the self-gift of God in Christ. I suggest

---

[12] See Karen Lebacqz, 'Appropriate Vulnerability: A Sexual Ethic for Singles', *Christian Century* 104 (6 May 1988), 435–8. In my *Liberating Sex: A Christian Sexual Theology* (London: SPCK, 1993), I derive vulnerability from the wounds of the crucified Christ, calling the cross 'God's self-identification with the vulnerable' (pp.167–8).

that the marital norm can be very much richer, in its application (through principles and rules) to premarital sexual behaviour, than the peremptory and unqualified insistence on 'continence'. It is more inclusive, more welcoming in its acceptance of sexual growth and experimentation, and more pastorally serviceable and sensitive in the context of real pastoral needs. And once chastity is enlarged to encompass and encourage the acquisition of the values necessary for marriage, the pursuit and practice of it becomes both desirable and achievable.

Since, in many countries, about one in every two or three marriages fails, there are always too many men and women recovering from divorce or annulment, most of whom marry again. About 90 per cent of people who marry for a second time have already lived with their partners. Theological discussion about second marriages generally deals with the admission of such people to holy communion, or the possibility of remarriage in church. The issue to be considered here is postmarital cohabitation. The book has deliberately concentrated on prenuptial cohabitation. The sexual and spiritual needs of postmarried people deserves to be the subject of another book. But what has been learned about prenuptial cohabitation has application to postmarital cohabitation too. Most formerly married people, we may safely assume, do not have the gift of celibacy. They will also be accustomed to regular sexual intimacy. Divorce does not bring down from heaven entry into the celibate state. Do the churches teach that the experience of sexual intercourse must await a second marriage, which, in the event, they may still neither provide nor recognize? How is the gospel to be understood by postmarried people whether or not they wish to marry again? If they recommence sexual activity, does the rubric of fornication come into play once more?

The marital norm was extended to prenuptial cohabitors on the ground that they had already begun marriage. The same norm was extended to adolescents and young unmarried adults beginning sexual experience on the ground of the need (of most of them) to acquire the values necessary for entering and remaining in the sacrament of marriage. The extension of the norm in the first case occurred by extending the state of matrimony retrospectively because people begin their marriages before they have their weddings. The extension of the norm in the second case operated differently. It was argued that premarried people need to acquire those values that they will need when they marry and wish to remain married, and that these are unlikely to be acquired by remaining celibate until the wedding day. The norm of marriage was extended in this case by the enlargement of chastity and the generation of context-specific principles. In the case of formerly married people, a similar approach through chastity and principle is suggested. Principles allow for the need both to provide guidance and to allow for flexibility in treating individual cases.

In some circumstances, the norm, sexual intercourse only within marriage, might actually serve as a rule for postmarried people. Its function might be to provide vital protection and empty sexual space during a time when feelings of failure and hurt may remain to be addressed. Here is a principle that might actually function as a rule. The ground for claiming this is the need to be protected when disorientated and vulnerable. The authority of a rule, at least in the early stages of recovery from marital breakdown, might ironically provide this.

The enlargement of the virtue of chastity in relation to a person's state of life, this time the postmarried state of life, is able to generate an alternative construction to the peremptory alternatives of celibacy or remarriage. This very construction is able to be a satisfying exercise of responsible Christian freedom. What 'form' of chastity is to be hammered out in this increasingly common phase of life? Since experience is able to be a source of theology, it is important that Christians' experiences of cohabitation after marriage, including the variable support they receive from their local parishes and churches, is recorded and heard. One way of honouring marriage as a way of holiness is to review, using the experience of the marriage just ended, one's suitability for or vocation to it. Formerly married people are actually in an advantageous position when compared with premarried people because they are able (given the opportunity for reflection, and assistance from counsellors or friends) to assess the reasons for the loss of their marriage just ended. This self-assessment will be invaluable in forging a form of chastity that is appropriate to the postmarried state of life. If there is an intention to remarry, or an openness to considering it, the state of life is very like the provisional or liminal state discussed in the previous chapter. A crucial difference is the experience gained from the marriage just ended.

The principles and rules operative in premarital sexual relations are remarkably transferable to postmarital sexual contact (whether living together is involved or not). All five of the principles just discussed take on new relevance after marriage. The principle of proportion may assume a greater significance if trust has recently been betrayed, or commitments were unreciprocated or found to be superficial or conditional. To the application of the principle is now added wisdom, perhaps painfully acquired. The rule 'Never risk conceiving a child without being committed to your partner and to the child' may acquire added cogency after marriage, and would seem to exclude, i.e., 'rule out', sexual intercourse without marital intention or very reliable contraception. As we have seen, reliable contraception is generally not reliable enough. The perspective of a possible child, his or her future view of the circumstances of conception, the quality of the care received, can be considered now. Indeed, the application of another principle, that of neighbour-love, requires it.

The principle 'The body is holy' generates similar rules in a postmarried context. Postmarried people may be less inclined than premarried people to postpone the consummation of growing sexual love. The honouring of vulnerability may acquire additional force during the aftermath of a painful break-up. And the rule 'Never have a sexual involvement that you or your partner may regret' becomes a mutual obligation on either partner in a sexual encounter, since in sexual experience we are clearly responsible, not simply for our partner's pleasure (which is stressed often enough) but for his or her welfare (which is hardly stressed at all). The purpose of such principles is not to impose a particular morality on unwilling moral subjects, but rather to open the lives of formerly married people to a sense of the restoring, forgiving love of God for them, and to seek, with them, their flourishing that God also seeks. The marital norm continues to be relevant to the postmarried state, not because it readily excludes the formerly married from sexual relations, but because it continues to suggest that Christians value marriage for the values marriage embodies. These include commitment, faithfulness, and steadfast love. A relationship with these values may already approximate, to some extent, to marriage, even if the couple are unwed and maintaining separate addresses.

LESBIAN AND GAY PARTNERS

The distinction between a norm and a rule suggests the extension of the marital norm to encompass a further group of people that has good reason to feel alienated from mainstream Christianity. Elizabeth Stuart provides a comprehensive and authoritative overview of the subject of lesbian and gay attitudes to marriage from the perspectives of lesbian and gay theologians themselves.[13] She finds that the verdict of lesbian theology on marriage is very clear: where patriarchy is the theory, marriage is the practice. The feminist virtues such as mutuality and equality cannot thrive inside it. Issues of monogamy and of friendship (including the extent of its sexual nature) re-emerge in lesbian theology, but enthusiasm for marriage is pretty sparse. Gay theology, says Stuart, is not very interested in marriage either. The issue of monogamy (versus non-monogamy) has been more pressing: while monogamy for several writers has been an ideal state, marriage has been seen as a heterosexual institution. Several writers have taken up the notion of covenant or 'covenanted union' in relation to gay partnerships, but Stuart shows that, while these unions are regarded as, or equivalent to, marriages, there is considerable reluctance to admit this. Alternatively, committed gay relationships are said to sacramentalize God's reign or to be particular manifestations of friendship. But this equivalence to marriage is very significant. The reluctance to own sacramental partnerships as marriage may be due more to the use of marriage as a weapon against gays, by excluding them from it, than an antipathy towards it among gay men which leads to the problematic attempts to construct satisfactory alternatives.

[13] Elizabeth Stuart, 'Is Lesbian or Gay Marriage an Oxymoron? A Critical Review of the Contemporary Debate', in Adrian Thatcher (ed.), *Celebrating Christian Marriage* (Edinburgh: T&T Clark, 2002).

There are two ways of bringing lesbian and gay partnerships within the marital norm. First, the institution of marriage might be broadened in order to embrace and include them. That would require making explicit a covenant theology of marriage that would apply to all people who marry within Christian faith. Commitment, fidelity and steadfast love are among the values to be realized by all married people because, ultimately, these are the values which embody God's love for the world, and the love of Christ for the Church. The conception of children will belong to straight marriages only, but children are not a requirement of Christian marriages, and childless couples are sometimes better able than married parents to practise neighbour-love more widely. Second, the churches would need to adopt and authorize appropriate liturgies. Although these would be little different from the ones currently in use, authorization may never happen. Patient advocacy will be necessary for several years yet. Here the situation is similar to the advocacy of betrothal. It takes many years for a church to revise its liturgies. The absence of a betrothal rite makes the advocacy of one more urgent. If the case is strong, tomorrow's churches may think differently.

The second way is to adopt the approach that marriage is valued by the Christian community for the values marriage exemplifies. These values reveal divine love in their partial realization in actual relationships. To the extent that marital values are exemplified in long-term relationships, those relationships resemble marriages (even though they are not), and they should be honoured as such. This way, if it were to be adopted, would begin a transformation in the way the people of God are able to accept not only some lesbian and gay unions, but some informal and common-law marriages between straight couples. Again, the situation is akin to the lack of a betrothal ceremony. By urging the recovery of betrothal, one hopes to contribute to the transformation of Christian attitudes to prenuptial cohabitors, even though betrothal does not presently exist in the form advocated in this book. If the transformation happens and seizes the Christian imagination, liturgical renewal may eventually follow.

A further advantage of extending the marital norm theologically and liturgically to some lesbian and gay partners (assuming it happens) is that alternatives to marriage (e.g., acts of blessing or recognition of partnerships), or alternative sexual moralities not based on marriage (but on, e.g., justice-seeking, right-relation) are avoided. Also avoided is the search for alternative theological categories and descriptions which represent marriage in a manner appropriate to gays only. In this sense the extension of the marital norm is conservative with regard to the Christian tradition and 'hope-ful' (in the strong theological sense) that the sacrament of marriage will one day embrace some of those people who are currently marginalized by it. Marriage has undergone profound changes in every epoch, changes that Christians in previous epochs would have found unsanctionable. What is unsanctionable now may yet become tomorrow's orthodoxy.

There are many issues knowingly left untouched by these suggestions. My intention has been, not to qualify what I have already written about marriage among lesbian and gay people,[14] but to suggest that the solution adopted in earlier chapters to the problem of prenuptial cohabitation may have a wider application. Marriage has been retained as a norm generating principles and rules, but it has not been retained as a rule. But the affirmation of marriage as a norm entails the identification of marital values that make marriage normative. These values show that the norm of marriage is able to be extended beyond the limits of marriage currently observed, especially when observed only as a rule. The traditional framework is preserved. Yet the exclusivity of a rule-bound institution is consciously subverted. The more sexual practices deviate from the norm, the less will the Christian community be comfortable with them. Marriage can and must be reaffirmed as the life-giving norm for Christian sexual ethics. This is of course, very different from affirming it as a beleaguered rule that rules out sexual expression for all people except those who are formally married. Its inclusive potential, and the extension of its values, have not yet been properly explored.

---

[14] For more detailed arguments supporting the extension of marriage to lesbian and gay partners, see my *Marriage after Modernity: Christian Marriage in Postmodern Times* (Sheffield and New York: Sheffield Academic Press and New York University Press 1999), section 9.2.

A Rite of Betrothal before Marriage

This rite is in use in the parish church of St Mary Magdalene, Bolney, a small village in Sussex, England. It takes place in the parish eucharist, at the Peace. It has also been adopted by the Anglican Diocese of Koforidua-Ho in the Eastern Region of Ghana. It is reproduced here by kind permission of the Vicar of Bolney, the Revd. Canon Reg Harcus. It is based in part on *The Alternative Service Book 1980* of the Church of England. While the rite does not (and legally could not) contain several of the characteristics of betrothal described in this book (e.g., it is 'before' marriage, and there is reference to engagement ring(s)), it is a fine local response to pastoral need, expertly grounded in history and theology.[1]

BETROTHAL BEFORE MARRIAGE

The Introduction

Dear friends, we are gathered together in the presence of God to witness the betrothal of *N.* and *N.*, and to rejoice with them as they commit themselves to their forthcoming marriage.

N. and *N.*, marriage is a gift of God and a means of his grace in which a man and a woman become one flesh. It is God's purpose that, as husband and wife give themselves

---

[1] See A.R. Harcus, 'The Case for Betrothal', in Adrian Thatcher (ed.), *Celebrating Christian Marriage* (Edinburgh: T&T Clark, 2002) for the rationale (and text).

to each other in love, they shall grow together and be united in that love as Christ is united to his Church.

The union of a man and a woman is intended for their mutual comfort and help, as they live faithfully together in need and in plenty, in sorrow and in joy. It is intended that, with delight and tenderness, they may know each other in love, and through the joy of their bodily union, may strengthen the union of their hearts and lives. It is given that they may have children and be blessed in caring for them and bringing them up in accordance with God's will.

Marriage is a lifelong commitment. Husband and wife give themselves to each other, to care for each other in good times and in bad. They are linked to each other's families, and they begin a new life together in the community. It is a way of life that all should reverence, and none should lightly undertake.

In this act of betrothal, *N.* and *N.* are declaring their intention to enter this holy state, but first I am to announce the Banns of marriage between *N.* of *x* parish and *N.* of *y* parish. If any of you know any reason why these persons may not marry, you are to declare it now.

The Betrothal

The couple stand before the celebrant.

N. & N., the Church of Christ understands marriage to be, in the will of God, the union of a man and a woman, for better, for worse; for richer, for poorer; in sickness and in health; to love and to cherish each other until parted by death. Is this your intention in betrothing yourselves to one another today?

Man & Woman: **It is.**
N., have you resolved to be faithful to *N.*, forsaking all others so long as you shall live?
Man: **I have so resolved with the help of God.**

N., have you resolved to be faithful to *N.*, forsaking all others so long as you shall live?

Woman: **I have so resolved with the help of God.**

The celebrant may address the following question to the two families:

Do you, members of the families of *N.* and *N.*, give your blessing to their forthcoming marriage?

Answer: **We do.**

The celebrant addresses the congregation.

You are the witness of this betrothal now being made. Will you do all in your power to uphold *N.* and *N.* as they prepare for marriage?

Answer: **We will.**

The Sign of Betrothal

The celebrant receives the engagement ring[s] and addresses the congregation.

Dear friends in Christ, let us ask God's blessing on this ring that it may be a sign of the continuing love and care between *N.* and *N.* as they prepare for their marriage.

The congregation may pray silently, then the celebrant says:

Blessed are you, God of steadfast love, source of our joy and end of our hope.
+ Bless this ring given and received
that it may be a sign of the commitment of betrothal made today by *N.* and *N.*,
through Christ our Lord. **Amen.**

Man & Woman say together:

We wear this ring as a sign of our betrothal and of the commitment we make to each other in preparation for our marriage.

The celebrant says:

God our Father, you have taught us through your Son
that love is the fulfilling of the Law.
Grant to these your servants, that loving one another,
they may continue in your love to their lives' end,
through Jesus Christ our Lord. **Amen.**

Bibliography

Abbot, Walter M. (ed.), *The Documents of Vatican II*, New York: Guild Press, 1966.

Amjad-Ali, Charles and Pitcher, W. Alvin (eds.), *Liberation and Ethics: Essays in Religious Social Ethics in Honor of Gibson Winter*, Chicago: Center for the Scientific Study of Religion, 1985.

Anderson, Herbert and Fite, Robert Cotton, *Becoming Married*, Louisville: Westminster/John Knox Press, 1993.

An Honourable Estate: The doctrine of Marriage according to English law and the obligation of the Church to marry all parishioners who are not divorced (Report of a Working Party established by the Standing Committee of the General Synod of the Church of England (GS801)), London: Church House Publishing, 1988.

Aquinas, Thomas, *Summa Theologiae*, London: Blackfriars, 1964.
  Summa Theologica, New York: Benziger Bros, 1922.

Arthur, J. Bryson (ed.), *A Theology of Sexuality and Marriage*, Nairobi: Uzima Press, 1998.

Axinn, W.G. and Thornton, A., 'The Relationship Between Cohabitation and Divorce: Selectivity or Causal Influence?', *Demography* 29 (1992), 357–74.

Bailey, Derrick Sherwin, *The Mystery of Love and Marriage: A Study in the Theology of Sexual Relation*, New York: Harper & Brothers, 1952.

Barrett, C.K., *A Commentary on the Second Epistle to the Corinthians*, London: Adam and Charles Black, 1973.

Bassett, William W., *The Bond of Marriage: An Ecumenical and Interdisciplinary Guide*, Notre Dame: University of Notre Dame Press, 1968.
  'The Marriage of Christians – Valid Contract, Valid Sacrament?', in Bassett, pp.117–80.

Bellah, R., Madsen, R., Sullivan, W., Swidler, A. and Tipton, S.M., *Habits of the Heart: Middle America Observed*, Berkeley: University of California Press, 1985.

Bendroth, Margaret, *Fundamentalism and Gender*, New Haven: Yale University Press, 1994.

Best, Ernest, *A Critical and Exegetical Commentary on Ephesians*, Edinburgh: T&T Clark, 1998.

Biel, Pamela, 'Let the Fiancées Beware: Luther, the Lawyers and Betrothal in Sixteenth-Century Saxony', in Gordon (ed.), vol. ii, ch.7, pp.121–41.

Blanc, A.K., 'The Formation and Dissolution of Second Unions: Marriage and Cohabitation in Sweden and Norway', *Journal of Marriage and the Family* 49 (1987), 391–400.

Blankenhorn, David, *Fatherless America: Confronting Our Most Urgent Social Problem*, New York: Basic Books, 1995.

Böckle, Franz (ed.), *The Future of Marriage as Institution (Concilium)*, New York: Herder and Herder, 1970.

Bracher, M., Santow, G., Morgan, S.P. and Trussell, J., 'Marriage Dissolution in Australia: Models and Explanations', *Population Studies* 47 (1993), 403–25.

Brenner, Athalya (ed.), *A Feminist Companion to Genesis*, Sheffield: Sheffield Academic Press, 1993, repr. 1997.

Brockmann, Thomas, 'The Western Family and Individuation: Convergence with Caribbean Patterns', *Journal of Comparative Family Studies* 18.3 (Autumn 1987), 471–7.

Brooke, Christopher, *The Medieval Idea of Marriage*, Oxford: Clarendon Press, 1989.

Brown, Susan L. and Booth, Alan, 'Cohabitation Versus Marriage: A Comparison of Relationship Quality', *Journal of Marriage and the Family* 58 (August 1996), 668–78.

Browning, Don S., Miller-McLemore, Bonnie J., Couture, Pamela D., Lyon, K. Brynolf and Franklin, Robert M., *From Culture Wars to Common Ground: Religion and the American Family Debate*, Louisville: Westminster/John Knox Press, 1997.

Brundage, James A., *Law, Sex, and Christian Society in Medieval Europe*, Chicago and London: University of Chicago Press, 1987.

Bumpass, Larry and Sweet, James, 'National Estimates of Cohabitation', *Demography* 24.4 (1989), 615–25.

Bumpass, Larry L., Sweet, James A. and Cherlin, Andrew, 'The Role of Cohabitation in Declining Rates of Marriage', *Journal of Marriage and the Family* 53 (November 1991), 913–27.

Burgess, Ernest W. and Wallin, Paul, *Engagement and Marriage*, Chicago: Lippincott, 1953.

Cahill, Lisa Sowle, *Sex, Gender and Christian Ethics*, Cambridge: Cambridge University Press, 1996.

The Canons and Decrees of the Council of Trent, tr. H. J. Schroeder, Rockford, Ill.: Tan Books, 1978.

Carey, John J., 'The Theological Foundations of the Presbyterian Report', in Carey (ed.), pp.25–35.

(ed.), *The Sexuality Debate in North American Churches, 1988–1995*, Lewiston, N.Y.: Edwin Mellen Press, 1995.

Carlson, Elwood, 'Couples Without Children: Premarital Cohabitation in France', in Davis (ed.), ch.4.4, pp.113–32.

Carlson, Eric Josef, *Marriage and the English Reformation*, Oxford, UK and Cambridge, Mass.: Blackwell, 1994.

Carmichael, Gordon A., 'Consensual Partnering in the More Developed Countries', *Journal of the Australian Population Association* 12.1 (1995), 51–86.

'From Floating Brothels to Suburban Semirespectability: Two Centuries of Nonmarital Pregnancy in Australia', *Journal of Family History* 21 (July 1996), 281–316.

'Living Together in New Zealand: Data on Coresidence at Marriage and on *de facto* Unions', *New Zealand Population Review* 10.3 (1984), 41–54.

Cass, Amy A. and Cass, Leon R., 'Proposing Courtship', *First Things* 96 (October 1999), 32–41.

Catechism of the Catholic Church, London: Geoffrey Chapman, 1994.

Chemnitz, Martin, *Loci theologici*, Frankfurt and Wittenberg: Chr. Hein. Schumacher, 1690.

Cherlin, Andrew, *Marriage, Divorce and Remarriage*, Boston: Harvard University Press, 1992.

Church of Scotland Panel on Doctrine, *Report on the Theology of Marriage*, 1994.

Clarke, Lynda and Berrington, Ann, 'Socio-Demographic Predictors of Divorce', in Simons (ed.), vol.1, pp.1–38.

Cox, Harvey, 'A Brothel in Noble Dimensions: Today's Sexual Mores', in Wynn (ed.), pp.38–60.

Cressy, David, *Birth, Marriage and Death: Ritual, Religion, and the Life-Cycle in Tudor and Stuart England*, Oxford: Oxford University Press, 1997.

Critchlow, F.L., 'On the Forms of Betrothal and Wedding Ceremonies in the Old-French *Romans D'Aventure*', *Modern Philology* 2 (1904–5), 497–537.

Crook, J.A., *Law and Life of Rome*, London: Thames and Hudson, 1967.

Cunningham, David S., *These Three Are One: the Practice of Trinitarian Theology*, Malden, Mass. and Oxford: Blackwell, 1998.

Curran, Charles E. and McCormick, Richard A., SJ (eds.), *Readings in Moral Theology No.8: Dialogue About Catholic Sexual Teaching*, New York: Mahwah, 1993.

David, Miriam E. (ed.), *The Fragmenting Family: Does It Matter?*, London: IEA Health and Welfare Unit, 1998.

Davies, Jon, 'Neither Seen nor Heard nor Wanted: The Child as Problematic. Towards an Actuarial Theology of Generation', in Hayes, Porter and Tombs (eds.), pp.326-49.

Davies, Jon and Loughlin, Gerard (eds.), *Sex These Days: Essays on Theology, Sexuality and Society*, Sheffield: Sheffield Academic Press, 1997.

Davies, W.D. and Allison, Dale C., *A Critical and Exegetical Commentary on The Gospel According to Saint Matthew*, 2 vols., Edinburgh: T&T Clark, 1988.

Davis, Kingsley, 'The Future of Marriage', in Davis (ed.), ch.1, pp.25-52.

(ed.), *Contemporary Marriage: Comparative Perspectives on a Changing Institution*, New York: Russell Sage Foundation, 1985.

DeMaris, Alfred and MacDonald, William, 'Premarital Cohabitation and Marital Instability: A Test of the Unconventional Hypothesis', *Journal of Marriage and the Family* 55 (May 1993) 399-407.

DeMaris, A. and Rao, K.V., 'Premarital Co-habitation and Subsequent Marital Stability in the United States: A Re-assessment', *Journal of Marriage and the Family* 54 (1992), 178-90.

Division for Church in Society and its Writing Team, *Human Sexuality Working Draft: A Possible Social Statement of the Evangelical Lutheran Church in America, with Accompanying Documents*, October 1994.

Division for Church in Society, Department for Studies of the Evangelical Lutheran Church in America, *The Church and Human Sexuality: A Lutheran Perspective: First Draft of a Social Statement*, Chicago: 1993.

Doctrine Commission of the Church of England, *The Mystery of Salvation*, London: Church House Publishing, 1995.

Dominian, Jack, *The Capacity to Love*, London: Darton, Longman and Todd, 1985.

Christian Marriage: The Challenge of Change, London: Darton, Longman and Todd, 1967.

The Church and the Sexual Revolution, London: Darton, Longman and Todd, 1971.

Let's Make Love: the meaning of sexual intercourse, London: Darton, Longman and Todd, 2001.

'Marriage Under Threat', in Curran and McCormick (eds.), pp.444-9.

'Masturbation and Premarital Sexual Intercourse', in Dominian and Montefiore, pp.37-50.

Sexual Integrity: The Answers to AIDS, London: Darton, Longman and Todd, 1987.

Dominian, Jack and Montefiore, Hugh, *God, Sex and Love*, London and Philadelphia: SCM Press and Trinity International, 1989.

Dormor, Duncan, 'Marriage and the Second Demographic Transition in Europe – A Review', in Thatcher (ed.), *Celebrating Christian Marriage*.

Duff, J. and Truitt, G.G., *The Spousal Equivalent Handbook*, Houston: Sunny Beach Publications, 1990.

Economic and Social Research Council, *Population and Household Change, Research Results 1–13*, 1997–8.

Eichrodt, Walther, *Ezekiel: A Commentary*, London: SCM Press, 1970.

Eickhoff, Andrew R., *A Christian View of Sex and Marriage*, New York and London: The Free Press and Collier-Macmillan, 1996.

Ermisch, John, *Pre-Marital Cohabitation, Childbearing and the Creation of One Parent Families*, Colchester: Working Papers of the ESRC Research Centre on Micro-social Change, No.95–17, 1995.

Ermisch, John and Ogawa, Naohiro (eds.), *The Family, the Market and the State in Ageing Societies*, Oxford: Clarendon Press, 1994.

Evdokimov, Paul, *The Sacrament of Love: the Nuptial Mystery in the Light of the Orthodox Tradition*, Crestwood, N.Y.: St Vladimir's Seminary Press, 1985.

Fellhauer, David E., 'The *Consortium omnis vitae* as a Juridical Element of Marriage', *Studia Canonica* 13.1 (1979), 1–171.

Fiorenza, Elisabeth Schüssler and Copeland, M. Shawn, (eds.), *Concilium: Violence Against Women*, Maryknoll, N.Y.: Orbis Books, 1994.

Flannery, Austin, OP (ed.), *Vatican Council II: the conciliar and post conciliar documents, vols.1–2*, Grand Rapids: Wm. B. Eerdmans, 1981.

Ford, David, *Self and Salvation: Being Transformed*, Cambridge: Cambridge University Press, 1999.

Ford, Jeffery E., *Love, Marriage, and Sex in the Christian Tradition from Antiquity to Today*, San Francisco: International Scholars Publications, 1999.

Ford, Reuben and Millar, Jane (eds.), *Private Lives and Public Responses*, London: Policy Studies Institute, 1998.

Forster, Greg, *Cohabitation and Marriage: A Pastoral Response*, London: Marshall Pickering, 1994.

Marriage Before Marriage? The Moral Validity of 'Common Law' Marriage (Grove Ethical Studies 69), Bramcote, Notts.: Grove Books, 1988.

Fortune, Marie, *Love Does No Harm: Sexual Ethics for the Rest of Us*, London: Continuum, 1998.

Fotiou, Stavros, 'Water into Wine, and *Eros* into *Agape* – Marriage in the Orthodox Church', in Thatcher (ed.), *Celebrating Christian Marriage*.

Frost, Ginger Suzanne, 'Promises Broken: Breach of Promise of Marriage in England and Wales, 1753–1970', PhD dissertation, Rice University, 1991.

Fuchs, Esther, 'Structure, Ideology and Politics in the Biblical Betrothal Type-Scene', in Brenner (ed.), pp.273–81.

Gallagher, Maggie, *The Age of Unwed Mothers: Is Teen Pregnancy the Problem?*, New York: Institute for American Values, 1999.

Gaudium et Spes (Pastoral Constitution on the Church in the Modern World). English text in e.g. Flannery, 1, pp.903–1001.

General Assembly Special Committee on Human Sexuality, Presbyterian Church (USA), *Keeping Body and Soul Together: Sexuality, Spirituality and Social Justice*, 1991.

Gershuny, Jonathan and Berthoud, Richard, *New Partnerships? Men and Women in the 1990s*, University of Essex: Extracts from the Research Programme of the ESRC Research Centre on Micro-social Change, June 1997.

Giddens, Anthony, *The Transformation of Intimacy: Sexuality, Love and Eroticism in Modern Societies*, Cambridge: Polity Press, 1992.

Gill, Robin, *Churchgoing and Christian Ethics*, Cambridge: Cambridge University Press, 1999.

Gillis, John R., *For Better, For Worse: British Marriages, 1600 to the Present*, New York and Oxford: Oxford University Press, 1985.

Gledhill, Tom, *The Message of the Song of Songs: The Lyrics of Love*, Leicester: Inter-Varsity Press, 1994.

Glenn, Norval, *Closed Hearts, Closed Minds: The Textbook Story of Marriage*, New York: Institute for American Values, 1995.

Gold, Rabbi Michael, *Does God Belong in the Bedroom?*, Philadelphia: Jewish Publication Society, 1992.

Goldscheider, Frances K. and Kaufman, Gayle, 'Fertility and Commitment: Bringing Men Back In', *Population and Development Review* 22 (supp.) (1996), 87–99.

Gordon, Bruce (ed.), *Protestant History and Identity in Sixteenth-Century Europe*, 2 vols., Aldershot and Vermont: Ashgate Publishing and Scolar Press, 1996.

Gottlieb, Beatrice, 'The Meaning of Clandestine Marriage', in Wheaton and Hareven (eds.), pp.49–83.

Gray, A., 'Aboriginal Marriage and Survival', *Journal of the Australian Population Association* 1 (1984), 18–30.

Grootaers, Jan and Selling, Joseph A., *The 1980 Synod of Bishops 'On the Role of the Family'*, Leuven: Leuven University Press, 1983.

Gross, David C. and Gross, Esther R., *Under the Wedding Canopy: Love and Marriage in Judaism*, New York: Hippocrene Books, 1996.

Groves, Ernest R., *Marriage*, New York: Henry Holt & Co., 1933.

Grubbs, Judith Evans, '"Pagan" and "Christian" Marriage: The State of the Question', *Journal of Early Christian Studies* 2.3 (1994), 361–412.

Guindon, André, 'Case for a "Consummated" Sexual Bond before a "Ratified" Marriage', *Église et Théologie* 8 (1977), 137–81.

The Sexual Creators: An Ethical Proposal for Concerned Christians, Lanham, Md. and London: University Press of America, 1986.

Gundry, Robert H., *Matthew: A Commentary on His Literary and Theological Art*, Grand Rapids: Wm. B. Eerdmans, 1982.

Hall, David R., 'Marriage as a Pure Relationship: Exploring the Link Between Premarital Cohabitation and Divorce in Canada', *Journal of Comparative Family Studies* 27.1 (Spring 1996), 1–12.

Hall, David R. and Zhao, John Z., 'Cohabitation and Divorce in Canada: Testing the Selectivity Hypothesis', *Journal of Marriage and the Family* 57.2 (May 1995), pp.421–8.

Hansen, Paul B., Feucht, Oscar E., Kramer, Fred and Lueker, Erwin L., *Engagement and Marriage: A Sociological, Historical, and Theological Investigation of Engagement and Marriage*, St. Louis: Concordia Publishing House, 1959.

Hao, LingXin, 'Family Structure, Private Transfers, and the Economic Well-Being of Families with Children', *Social Forces* 75 (1996), 269–92.

Harcus, A.R., 'The Case for Betrothal', in Thatcher (ed.), *Celebrating Christian Marriage*.

Hardy, Richard P., 'The Pre-ceremonial Couple: Reflections for a Spirituality', *Église et Théologie* 8 (1977), 183–95.

Harrington, Joel F., *Reordering Marriage and Society in Reformation Germany*, Cambridge: Cambridge University Press, 1995.

Haskey, John, 'Families: Their Historical Context, and Recent Trends in the Factors Influencing Their Formation and Dissolution', in David (ed.), pp.9–47.

'One-Parent Families and their Dependent Children in Great Britain', in Ford and Millar (eds.), pp.22–41.

Trends in Marriage and Cohabitation: Population Trends 80, Office of Population Censuses and Surveys, 1995.

Hastings, Adrian, *Christian Marriage in Africa*, London: SPCK, 1973.

Hayes, Michael A., Porter, Wendy and Tombs, David (eds.), *Religion and Sexuality*, Sheffield: Sheffield Academic Press, 1998.

Hendry, Joy, 'Japan: Culture versus Industrialization as Determinant of Marital Patterns', in Davis (ed.), pp.197–222.

Hill, Brennan R., 'Reformulating the Sacramental Theology of Marriage', in Lawler and Roberts (eds.), pp.3–21.

Hillman, Eugene, 'The Development of Christian Marriage Structures', in Böckle (ed.), pp.25–38.

Hoffmann-Nowotny, J., 'The Future of the Family', in *European Population Conference 1987, Plenaries*, Helsinki: Central Statistical Office of Finland, 1987, pp.113–200.

Holmes, Paul A., 'A Catechumenate for Marriage: Presacramental Preparation as Pilgrimage', *Journal of Ritual Studies* 6 (Summer 1992), 93–113.

Ilan, Tal, 'Premarital Cohabitation in Ancient Judea: The Evidence of the Babatha Archive and the Mishnah (*Ketubbot* 1.4)', *Harvard Theological Review* 86.3 (1993), 247–64.

Isherwood, Lisa (ed.), *The Good News of the Body: Sexual Theology and Feminism*, Sheffield: Sheffield Academic Press, 2000.

Issues in Human Sexuality: A Statement by the House of Bishops, London: Church House Publishing, 1991.

Jeffreys, Sheila, *The Spinster and Her Enemies: Feminism and Sexuality 1880–1930*, London and New York: Pandora, 1987.

Jenkins, Gary, *Cohabitation: a Biblical Perspective* (Grove Ethical Studies 84), Bramcote, Notts.: Grove Books, 1992.

Kasper, Walter, *Theology of Christian Marriage*, New York: Seabury Press, 1980.

Kiernan, Kathleen, 'Cohabitation in Western Europe', *Population Trends* 96 (1999).

Kling, Melchior, *Matrimonialium Causarum Tractatus, Methodico ordine scriptus*, Frankfurt, 1553.

Kravdal, Øystein, 'Wanting a Child without a Firm Commitment to the Partner: Interpretations and Implications of a Common Behaviour Pattern among Norwegian Cohabitants', *European Journal of Population* 13 (1997), 269–98.

Lacey, T.A., *Marriage in Church and State*, London: Robert Scott, 1912.

Laeuchli, Samuel, *Power and Sexuality: The Emergence of Canon Law at the Synod of Elvira*, Philadelphia: Temple University Press, 1972.

Lake, Stephen, *Using Common Worship: Marriage*, London: Church House Publishing/Praxis, 2000.

Landale, N. and Hauan, S., 'The Family Life Course of Puerto Rican Children', *Journal of Marriage and the Family* 54 (1992), 912–24.

Larrivee, D. and Parent, P., 'For More and More Canadians, Common-Law Unions Make Good Sense', Census of Canada article series: 1993.

Lasch, Christopher, 'The Suppression Of Clandestine Marriage In England: The Marriage Act Of 1753', *Salmagundi* (1974), 90–109.

Laumann, E. and Michael, R. (eds.), *Studies on Sex*, Chicago: University of Chicago Press, 1999.

Lawler, Michael G., 'Marriage and the Sacrament of Marriage', in Lawler and Roberts (eds.), pp.22–37.

Lawler, Michael G. and Roberts, William P. (eds.), *Christian Marriage and Family: Contemporary Theological and Pastoral Perspectives*, Collegeville, Minn.: The Liturgical Press, 1996.

Lebacqz, Karen, 'Appropriate Vulnerability: A Sexual Ethic for Singles', *Christian Century* 104 (6 May 1988), 435–8.

Lerewonu, Cephas N., 'The Betrothal Commitment in the Making of Marriage', PhD thesis, Katholieke Universiteit Leuven, 1996.

Leridon, H., 'Cohabitation, Marriage, Separation: An Analysis of Life Histories of French Cohorts From 1968 to 1985', *Population Studies* 44 (1990), 127–44.

Lesthaeghe, Ron and Surkyn, Johan, 'Cultural Dynamics and Economic Theories of Fertility Change', *Population and Development Review* 14.1 (March 1988), 1–45.

Lewis, Jane, *Marriage, Cohabitation and the Law: Individualism and Obligation*, Lord Chancellor's Department Research Secretariat, 1999.

Lewis, Jane and Kiernan, Kathleen, 'The Boundaries Between Marriage, Nonmarriage, and Parenthood: Changes in Behavior and Policy in Postwar Britain', *Journal of Family History* 21 (July 1996), 372–88.

Luther, Martin, *Babylonian Captivity*, in *Luther's Works*.
On Marriage Matters, in *Luther's Works*.

Luther's Works, Jaroslav Pelikan and Helmut Lehman (eds.), American edition, 55 vols., Philadelphia: Fortress Press, 1955– .

Luther's Works, Robert Schultz (ed.), American edition, Philadelphia: Fortress Press, 1967.

Macfarlane, Alan, *Marriage and Love in England: Modes of Reproduction 1300–1840*, Oxford: Blackwell, 1987.

Mackin, Theodore, S J, *The Marital Sacrament*, Mahwah, N. J.: Paulist Press, 1989.

Manning, Wendy D., 'Marriage and Cohabitation Following Premarital Conception', *Journal of Marriage and the Family* 55 (November 1993), 839–50.

Manning, Wendy D. and Landale, Nancy S., 'Racial and Ethnic Differences in the Role of Cohabitation in Premarital Childbearing', *Journal of Marriage and the Family* 58 (February 1996), 63–77.

Manning, Wendy D. and Lichter, Daniel T., 'Parental Cohabitation and Children's Economic Well-Being', *Journal of Marriage and the Family* 58 (November 1996), 998–1011.

Marquardt, Elizabeth, *The Moral and Spiritual Experience of Children of Divorce*, University of Chicago Divinity School: Religion, Culture and Family Project, 1999.

Marriage: A teaching document from the House of Bishops of the Church of England, London: Church House Publishing, 1999.

Marriage and the Church's Task: The Report of the General Synod Marriage Commission (The Lichfield Report), London: CIO Publishing, 1978.

McDonnell, Albert, *When Strangers Marry: A Study of Marriage Breakdown in Ireland*, Blackrock, Co Dublin: Columba Press, 1999.

McLean, Stuart D., 'The Covenant and Pre-Marital Sex', in Amjad-Ali and Pitcher (eds.), ch.9, pp.111–22.

Melton, J. Gordon (ed.), *The Churches Speak on Family Life: Official Statements from Religious Bodies and Ecumenical Organizations*, Detroit: Gale Research Inc., 1991.

Metzger, Bruce M. and Coogan, Michael D. (eds.), *The Oxford Companion to the Bible*, New York: Oxford University Press, 1993.

Mezger, Georg, *Entwürfe zu Katechesen über Luthers Kleinen Katechismus*, St. Louis: Concordia Publishing House, 1907.

Mitchell, Nathan D., *Liturgy and the Social Sciences*, Collegeville, Minn.: The Liturgical Press, 1999.

Monti, Joseph, *Arguing About Sex: The Rhetoric of Christian Sexual Morality*, New York: State University of New York Press, 1995.

Moore, Carey A., 'The Book of Tobit', in Metzger and Coogan (eds.), pp.745–7.

Morehouse Research Institute and Institute for American Values, *Turning the Corner on Father Absence in Black America*, Atlanta and New York, 1999.

Morgan, Patricia, *Marriage-Lite: The Rise of Cohabitation and its Consequences*, London: Institute for the Study of Civil Society, 2000.

The National Marriage Project, *The State of our Unions, 1999*, New Brunswick, N.J.: Rutgers, The State University of New Jersey, 1999.

Nefedov, Gennady, 'The Sacrament of Matrimony: The Betrothal Service', *Journal of the Moscow Patriarchate* 9–10 (1989), 75–7.

Örsy, Ladislas, SJ, *Marriage in Canon Law*, Dublin and Leominster: Dominican Publications and Fowler Wright, 1986.

Outhwaite, R.B. (ed.), *Marriage and Society: Studies in the Social History of Marriage*, London: Europa, 1981.

Parker, Stephen, *Informal Marriage, Cohabitation and the Law*, New York: St. Martin's Press, 1990.

Parrado, Emilio A. and Tienda, Martin, 'Women's Roles and Family Formation in Venezuela: New Forms of Consensual Unions?', *Social Biology* 44.1–2 (September 1997), 1–24.

Parsons, Greg W., 'Guidelines for Understanding and Utilizing the Song of Songs', *Bibliotheca Sacra* 156, no.624 (October–December 1999), 399–422.

Payer, Pierre J., *The Bridling of Desire: Views of Sex in the Later Middle Ages*, Toronto: University of Toronto Press, 1993.

Perham, Michael (ed.), *Liturgy for a New Century: Further Essays in Preparation for Revision of the Alternative Service Book*, London: SPCK/Alcuin Club, 1991.

Petras, David M., 'The Liturgical Theology of Marriage', *Diakonia* 16.3 (1981), 225–37.

Pontifical Council for the Family, *Preparation for the Sacrament of Marriage*, 1996, (www.cin.org/vatcong/prepmarr.html (accessed 16.03.01)).

Pope John Paul II, *Familiaris Consortio* (Apostolic Exhortation On the Family), London: Catholic Truth Society, 1981.

Popenoe, David, *Disturbing the Nest*, New York: Walter de Gruyter, 1988.

Popenoe, David and Whitehead, Barbara Dafoe, *Should We Live Together? What Young Adults Need to Know about Cohabitation before Marriage: A Comprehensive Review of Recent Research* (The National Marriage Project), New Jersey: Rutgers, The State University of New Jersey, 1999.

Porter, Muriel, *Sex, Marriage and the Church: Patterns of Change*, North Blackburn, Victoria: Dove, 1996.

Porter, R., *English Society in the Eighteenth Century*, Harmondsworth: Penguin, 1982.

Poska, Allyson M., 'When Love Goes Wrong: Getting Out of Marriage in Seventeenth-Century Spain', *Journal of Social History* 29.3–4 (1996), 871–82.

Pratt, Edward, et al., *Living Together: a Challenge for the Church*, London: CENBooks, 1991.

Rawson, Beryl, 'The Roman Family', in Rawson (ed.), ch.1, pp.1–57.

(ed.), *The Family in Ancient Rome: New Perspectives*, London and Sydney: Croom Helm, 1986.

Reynolds, Jenny and Mansfield, Penny, 'The Effect of Changing Attitudes to Marriage on its Stability', in Simons (ed.), pp.1–37.

Reynolds, Philip Lyndon, *Marriage in the Western Church: The Christianization of Marriage During the Patristic and Early Medieval Periods*, Leiden: E.J. Brill, 1994.

Rindfuss, Ronald R. and VandenHeuvel, Audrey, 'Cohabitation: A Precursor to Marriage or an Alternative to Being Single?', *Population and Development Review* 16.4 (December 1990), 703–726.

Roberts, A. and Donaldson, J. (eds.), *The Ante-Nicene Fathers*, 10 vols., Grand Rapids: Eerdmans, 1951.

Rogers, Eugene F., Jr., *Sexuality and the Christian Body*, Oxford and Malden, Mass.: Blackwell, 1999.

The Roman Catechism, or *The Catechism of the Council of Trent*, tr. John A. McHugh and Charles J. Callan, Rockford, Ill.: Tan Books, 1982.

Rouner, Arthur A., Jr., *Struggling With Sex: A Serious Call to Marriage-Centered Sexual Life*, Minneapolis: Augsburg, 1987.

Rowland, C. and Vincent, J., *Liberation Theology UK (British Liberation Theology 1)*, Sheffield: The Urban Theology Unit, 1995.

Ruether, Rosemary Radford, 'Sex in the Catholic Tradition', in Isherwood (ed.), pp.35–53.

Sacraments and Services, Book One, Northridge, Calif.: Narthex Press, 1995.

Santow, Gigi and Bracher, Michael, 'Change and Continuity in the Formation of First Marital Unions in Australia', *Population Studies* 48 (1994), 475–96.

Sapit, Jackson Ole, 'Maasai Traditional Marriage', in Arthur (ed.), pp.43–6.

Schillebeeckx, Edward, *Marriage: Secular Reality and Saving Mystery*, 2 vols., London: Sheed and Ward, 1965.

Schoen, R. and Owens, D., 'A Further Look at First Unions and First Marriages', in South and Tolnay (eds.), pp.109–17.

Schoen, Robert and Weinick, Robin M., 'Partner Choice in Marriages and Cohabitations', *Journal of Marriage and the Family* 55 (May 1993), 408–14.

Scott, David A., 'Living Together: Education for Marriage?', *Journal of Pastoral Counselling* 18 (1983), 47–55.

Scott, Kieran and Warren, Michael (eds.), *Perspectives on Marriage: A Reader*, New York: Oxford University Press, 1993.

Seff, Monica A., 'Cohabitation and the Law', *Marriage and Family Review* 21.3–4 (June 1995), 141–68.

Sheehan, Michael M., CSB, 'Marriage Theory and Practice in the Conciliar Legislation and Diocesan Statutes of Medieval England', *Medieval Studies* 40 (1978), 408–60.

Shivanandan, Mary, *Crossing the Threshold of Love: A New Vision of Marriage*, Edinburgh: T&T Clark, 1999.

Simons, John (ed.), *High Divorce Rates: The State of the Evidence on Reasons and Remedies, Vols. 1–2*, I, Lord Chancellor's Department Research Secretariat, 1999.

Smout, T.C., 'Scottish Marriage, Regular and Irregular, 1500–1940', in Outhwaite (ed.), ch.9, pp.204–36.

Something to Celebrate: Valuing Families in Church and Society (Report of a Working Party of the Board for Social Responsibility), London: Church House Publishing, 1995.

South African Anglican Theological Commission, *The Church and Human Sexuality*, Marshalltown, South Africa, 1995.

South, S.J. and Tolnay, S.E. (eds.), *The Changing American Family: Sociological and Demographic Perspectives*, Boulder and Oxford: Westview Press, 1992.

Spanier, Graham B., 'Cohabitation in the 1980s: Recent Changes in the United States', in Davis (ed.), ch.3, pp.91–112.

Spong, John Shelby, *Living in Sin? A Bishop Rethinks Human Sexuality*, San Francisco: Harper and Row, 1988.

Stevenson, Kenneth, 'The Marriage Service', in Perham (ed.), ch.6, pp.51–62.

To Join Together: The Rite of Marriage, New York: Pueblo Publishing Company, 1987.

'Van Gennep and Marriage – Strange Bedfellows? A Fresh Look at the Rites of Marriage', *Ephemerides Liturgicae* 100 (1986), 138–51.

Stone, Lawrence, *The Family, Sex and Marriage in England 1500–1800*, London: Weidenfeld and Nicolson, 1979.

Uncertain Unions: Marriage in England 1660–1753, Oxford: Oxford University Press, 1992.

Stuart, Elizabeth, 'Is Lesbian or Gay Marriage an Oxymoron? A Critical Review of the Contemporary Debate', in Thatcher (ed.), *Celebrating Christian Marriage*.

Sturma, M., 'Eye of the Beholder: The Stereotype of Women Convicts, 1788–1852', *Labour History* 34 (1978), 3–10.

Sudharkasa, N., 'African and Afro-American Family Structure: A Comparison', *Black Scholar* 11 (1980), 37–60.

Sweet, James A. and Bumpass, Larry L., 'Religious Differentials in Marriage Behavior and Attitudes' (National Survey of Families and Households Working Paper 15), Madison: Center for Demography and Ecology, 1990.

Swinburne, Henry, *A Treatise of Spousals or Matrimonial Contracts*, London, 1711.

Taylor, Charles, *Sources of the Self: The Making of the Modern Identity*, Cambridge: Cambridge University Press, 1989.

Taylor, Philippa, *For Better or For Worse: Marriage and Cohabitation Compared*, London: CARE (Christian Action Research and Education), 1998.

Teachman, J.D. and Polonko, K.A., 'Cohabitation and Marital Stability in the United States', *Social Forces* 69 (1990), 207–20.

Thatcher, Adrian, 'A Strange Convergence? Popes and Feminists on Contraception', in Isherwood (ed.), pp.136–48.

Liberating Sex: A Christian Sexual Theology, London: SPCK, 1993.

Marriage after Modernity: Christian Marriage in Postmodern Times, Sheffield and New York: Sheffield Academic Press and New York University Press, 1999.

'Postmodernity and Chastity', in Davies and Loughlin (eds.), pp.122–40.

(ed.), *Celebrating Christian Marriage*, Edinburgh: T&T Clark, 2002.

Thomson, E. and Colella, U., 'Cohabitation and Marital Stability: Quality or Commitment', *Journal of Marriage and the Family* 54 (1992), 259–67.

Thornton, Arland, 'Cohabitation and Marriage in the 1980s', *Demography* 25.4 (November 1988), 497–508.

Thornton, Arland, Axinn, William G. and Hill, Daniel H., 'Reciprocal Effects of Religiosity, Cohabitation, and Marriage', *American Journal of Sociology* 98.3 (November 1992), 628–51.

Trevett, R.F., *The Church and Sex*, New York: Hawthorn Publishers, 1960.

Trost, J., 'A Renewed Social Institution: Non-Marital Cohabitation', *Acta Sociologica* 21 (1978), 303–15.

Trussell, James and Vaughan, Barbara, 'Contraceptive Failure, Method-Related Discontinuation and Resumption of Use: Results from the 1995 National Survey of Family Growth', *Family Planning Perspectives* 31.2 (March/April, 1999), 64–72.

Turner, Victor W. and Turner, Edith L.B., *Image and Pilgrimage in Christian Culture: Anthropological Perspectives*, Oxford: Blackwell, 1978.

United Nations, *Patterns of First Marriage: Timing and Prevalence*, New York: United Nations, 1990.

Van Gennep, Arnold, *Les Rites de Passage*, Paris: Librairie Critique, Émile Nourry, 1909.

VanGoethem, Jeffery J., 'Pastoral Options With Cohabiting Couples', PhD thesis, Dallas Theological Seminary, 1998.

Villeneuve-Gokalp, Catherine, 'From Marriage to Informal Union: Recent Changes in the Behaviour of French Couples', *Population: An English Selection* 3 (1991), 81–111.

'Vivre en Couple Chacun Chez Soi', *Population* 5 (September–October 1997), 1058–82.

Vincent, John, 'Liberation Theology in Britain, 1970–1995', in Rowland and Vincent, pp.15–40.

Waite, Linda J., 'Cohabitation: A Communitarian Perspective', unpublished paper, University of Chicago, January 1999.

Waite, Linda J. and Joyner, Kara, 'Emotional and Physical Satisfaction in Married, Cohabiting and Dating Sexual Unions: Do Men and Women Differ?', in Laumann and Michael (eds.).

Wall, John, 'The Marriage Education Movement: A Theological Analysis', in Thatcher (ed.), *Celebrating Christian Marriage*.

Warrington, Keith, 'Cohabitation and the Church', *Churchman* 111.2 (1997), 127–42.

Watkins, Oscar D., *Holy Matrimony: A Treatise on the Divine Laws of Marriage*, New York: Macmillan, 1895.

Watt, Jeffrey R., *The Making of Modern Marriage: Matrimonial Control and The Rise of Sentiment in Neuchâtel, 1550–1800*, Ithaca and London: Cornell University Press, 1992.

Weatherhead, Leslie D., *The Mastery of Sex Through Psychology and Religion*, New York: Macmillan, 1942.

Wheaton, Robert and Hareven, Tamara K. (eds.), *Family and Sexuality in French History*, Philadelphia: University of Pennsylvania Press, 1980.

Whelan, Robert, *Broken Homes and Battered Children: A Study of the Relationship Between Child Abuse and Family Type*, London: Family Educational Trust, 1993.

White, Keith, 'The Case for Marriage', *Third Way* 19.1 (February 1996), 11–14.

Whitehead, Evelyn Eaton, and Whitehead, James D., *Marrying Well: Possibilities in Christian Marriage Today*, New York: Doubleday, 1981.

Williams, James G., 'The Beautiful and the Barren: Conventions in Biblical Type-Scenes', *Journal for the Study of the Old Testament* 17 (June 1980), 107–19.

Williams, Stephen S., 'I Will: the Debate about Cohabitation', *Anvil* 10.3 (1993), 209–24.

Willis, Robert J. and Michael, Robert T., 'Innovation in Family Formation: Evidence on Cohabitation in the United States', in Ermisch and Ogawa (eds.), ch.1, pp.9–45.

Witte, John, Jr., *From Sacrament to Contract: Marriage, Religion and Law in the Western Tradition*, Louisville: Westminster/John Knox Press, 1997.

Wojtyla, Karol, 'The Family as a Community of Persons', in Wojtyla, pp.315–27.

Person and Community: Selected Essays (Catholic Thought from Lublin, Vol.4), Peter Lang: 1994.

Wu, Zheng, 'Premarital Cohabitation and Postmarital Cohabiting Union Formation', *Journal of Family Issues* 16 (March 1995), 212–33.

Wu, Zheng and Balakrishnan, T.R., 'Cohabitation After Marital Disruption in Canada', *Journal of Marriage and the Family* 56 (August 1994), 723–35.

'Dissolution of Premarital Cohabitation in Canada', *Demography* 32.4 (November 1995), 521–32.

Wynn, John Charles (ed.), *Sex, Family and Society in Theological Focus*, New York: Association Press, 1996.

Index

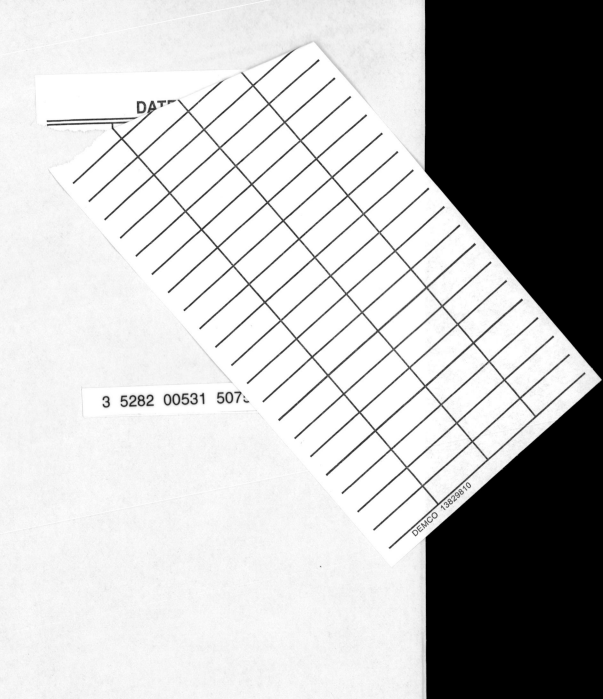

DATE

DEMCO 13829810